DEFENDING THE CORPORATION IN CRIMINAL PROSECUTIONS:

A Legal and Practical Guide To The Responsible Corporate Officer And Collective Knowledge Doctrines

By Alan Zarky

Copyright © 1990
The Bureau of National Affairs, Inc.
1231 25th St., N.W.
Washington, D.C. 20037

International Standard Book Number 1-55871-180-5

Extra copies of this special report (BSP-185) are $95.00 each and may be obtained from BNA's Customer Service Center, 9435 Key West Ave., Rockville, Md. 20850, or by telephone from BNA's Response Center, toll-free (800) 372-1033. The following discounts are available: 6-10 copies, 10%; 11-25, 15%; 26-50, 20%; 51-500, 25%; 501-1,000, 30%; and more than 1,000 copies, 35%.

For customized research and copies of documents or court decisions related to this report, call BNA PLUS toll-free (800) 452-7773 nationwide; (202) 452-4323 in Washington, D.C. Cost estimates and additional information about BNA PLUS services provided upon request.

This publication is designed to provide accurate and authoritative information regarding the subject matter covered. It is sold with the understanding that the publisher is not engaged in rendering legal, accounting, or other professional service. If legal advice or other expert assistance is required, the services of a competent professional person should be sought.

TABLE OF CONTENTS

I. INTRODUCTION 1
    ABOUT THE AUTHOR 5
    ACKNOWLEDGMENTS 5

II. THE RESPONSIBLE CORPORATE OFFICER DOCTRINE 7
    LIABILITY OF CORPORATE OFFICERS UNDER TRADITIONAL DOCTRINES 9
    ORIGINS OF THE RESPONSIBLE CORPORATE OFFICER DOCTRINE 10
    THE ENVIRONMENTAL STATUTES 13
        Legislative History 14
    GOVERNMENT THEORY OF THE DOCTRINE ... 16
        United States v. Frezzo Bros. 21
        United States v. Cattle King 23
        United States v. Schwitters 26
        United States v. Dee 27
    CONCLUSION 30
        Endnotes 33

III. THE COLLECTIVE KNOWLEDGE DOCTRINE 35
    CORPORATE CRIMINAL LIABILITY DOCTRINES . 36
    IMPLICATIONS OF COLLECTIVE KNOWLEDGE DOCTRINE 37
    CRIMINAL CASE LAW 39
    CIVIL CASE LAW 44
    CONCLUSION 50
        Endnotes 56

IV. LITIGATION STRATEGIES 57
    NEGOTIATING FOR THE OFFICER 58
    NEGOTIATING FOR THE CORPORATION 60
    TRIAL STRATEGY UNDER THE RESPONSIBLE CORPORATE OFFICER DOCTRINE 60
        Joint Defendants 65
        Aggressive Briefing 68
        Litigation Strategies for Sentencing 70

REPRESENTING THE CORPORATE OFFICER
  AT THE CORPORATION'S GUILTY PLEA 77
    Endnotes 79

V. PREVENTIVE MEASURES 83
  PROTECTING THE CORPORATION WITH
    CORPORATE POLICY 86
    Hiring of Independent Contractors 89
  PROTECTING CORPORATE OFFICERS WITH
    CORPORATE POLICY 92
    Indemnifying Corporate Officers 94
    Endnotes 95

VI. CASE STUDIES 99
  SEA GLEANER MARINE, INC. 99
    Endnotes 101
  MARINE POWER, INC. 103
    Endnotes 106
  PENNWALT CORP. 107
    Endnotes 110
  PROTEX INDUSTRIES 111
    Endnotes 114
  BANK OF NEW ENGLAND 115
    Endnotes 116

VII. CONCLUSION 117

APPENDICES 119

  APPENDIX A – SAMPLE APPENDIX TO SENTENCING
    MEMORANDUM DISCUSSING COMPARABLE
    SENTENCES IN ENVIRONMENTAL CASES . . . A-1

  APPENDIX B – MATERIALS FROM
    UNITED STATES v. SCHWITTERS B-1
    Opening Brief of Appellants B-3
    Brief of Appellee B-79
    Reply Brief of Appellants B-152
    Order on Appeal B-196

I. INTRODUCTION

During the past decade, a dramatic trend by prosecutors has brought together two normally divergent legal specialties: criminal defense and corporate law. That trend, evident to practitioners and corporate executives alike, is a greatly intensified emphasis on prosecuting corporations and their officers. Now, a second trend is developing, which could significantly heighten the first. Prosecutors are seeking significant extensions of the law, which would allow them to expand their power to prosecute corporate crime.

These legal shifts would make corporations and corporate officers criminally liable under circumstances that many people would find lacking in culpability. Some court cases in the 1980s illustrate this developing trend, which would alter the substantive law and facilitate many prosecutions of corporate officers and corporations.

The heightened concentration on corporate prosecution has led to more convictions of corporate officers and stiffer penalties for corporations. For example, the Justice Department office responsible for investigating government, corporate, and other types of fraud reported 102 convictions in fiscal 1989, twice as many as in fiscal 1988. The office collected $6.4 million in criminal fines and special assessments in fiscal 1989, compared to $851,800 in 1988.

Heading into the 1990s, developments in two cases involving large corporations showed that such companies could be subject to enormous penalties. In 1989, Drexel Burnham Lambert Inc. agreed to pay a $650 million fine in a securities fraud case. In 1990, Exxon faced an even larger penalty for its role in an Alaskan oil spill. A grand jury returned a five-count indictment that could result in fines of up to $700 million.

Copyright © 1990
The Bureau of National Affairs, Inc.

In the environmental realm, nearly 70 percent of the indictments filed in 1986 included corporate officials. Of the 143 environmental indictments filed against individuals between 1982 and 1986, 118 involved management level employees. Directors, presidents, vice presidents or owner-operators represented 88 of the indicted individuals.

Legitimate concerns motivate the focus on corporate prosecutions. Corporate entities increasingly are being accused of hiding or commiting criminal activities—the use of banks for laundering of illegal drug profits is an obvious example. Also, the social harms addressed by the regulatory laws, such as environmental statutes, are problems that call for strong measures.

At the same time, appearing tough on corporate crime can lead to political benefits for prosecutors. These political realities, combined with prosecutors' goals of addressing the social problems mentioned above, make the increased prosecution of corporations for a broad range of crimes one of the clearest trends in criminal law today.

In one case attracting nationwide attention, a federal judge refused to allow counsel for Pennwalt Corp. to enter a guilty plea on the corporation's behalf. Instead, the judge required Pennwalt's chief executive officer to come to court to enter the corporation's guilty plea for various environmental offenses, even though the CEO had no involvement with these violations. While this maneuver garnered nationwide publicity because of the apparently unprecedented action by the judge, the case itself presents other threats to corporate officers.

Three high-level officials of Pennwalt had been charged with Clean Water Act violations under a novel legal theory, pursuant to which they could have been convicted even if they had no personal involvement in the offense. That theory, the "responsible corporate officer doctrine," threatens to increase substantially the criminal exposure faced by corporate officers. The doctrine could render corporate officers guilty of felonies if they bore a "responsible relationship" to the violation, even if they had no knowledge of the problem and acted reasonably in attempting to keep the corporation in compliance with the law. The responsible corporate officer doctrine is a major focus of this work. The details of the Pennwalt case itself are set forth in Chapter VI.

In another case, *United States v. Bank of New England, N.A.*, 821 F.2d 844 (1st Cir. 1987), the Second Circuit Court of Appeals greatly broadened the ability to convict a corporation. Corporations traditionally have been guilty if any one employee commits a crime in the course of his employment. But the *Bank of New England* decision renders the corporation guilty even though no individual employee is guilty, as long as the combined knowledge of all the employees would yield the guilty state of mind necessary for conviction. This work concentrates on this theory, the "collective knowledge doctrine," as well. The specifics of the *Bank of New England* case are discussed in Chapter III.

The increase in corporate prosecutions is coming at a time when the ante has been upped significantly: The potential punishment for those convicted has radically increased. The days when one found guilty of a white collar crime could count on a probationary sentence are gone. Under the Sentencing Reform Act of 1984 (18 U.S.C. § 3551 et seq.), judicial discretion is greatly limited, and judges must sentence in conformance with the Federal Sentencing Guidelines.

Two examples, taken from the types of cases analyzed in this report, give sobering evidence of how white collar sentencing has changed. An individual convicted of an environmental crime, involving a repetitive discharge, without a permit or in violation of one, would have a sentencing range of 15 to 21 months, assuming the defendant had no prior offenses. If the pollutant were a hazardous or toxic substance, the range would be 21 to 27 months. Add another year if cleanup required a substantial expenditure. Even a one-time discharge in violation of a permit yields a six- to 12-month sentence. Anyone experienced with virtually any plant in almost any industry will know that a single permit violation is likely.

A bank employee convicted of failing to report a cash transaction of more than $10,000 will face a sentencing range of 12 to 18 months if the court concludes that the defendant reasonably should have believed the funds were criminally derived. The defendant's actual belief that the funds were legitimate will not help reduce his guidelines. Again, this sentence is for a first-time offender.

While the U.S. Sentencing Commission has yet to establish guidelines for corporations, the various draft guidelines provide for fines that most in the business community regard as onerous. The commission's draft recommendations include the relatively novel proposal of active probation for corporations, where the court or its referee could assume control of various corporate activities. *Proposed Federal Guidelines for Sentencing of Organizations*, 46 Cr.L.Rptr 2001, 2019 (November 15, 1989).

In the following chapters, the author closely examines the responsible corporate officer doctrine and the collective knowledge doctrine. Flaws in both theories are discussed as the author seeks to establish that the great weight of legal authority falls against them.

The author then discusses some of the strategic considerations facing corporate counsel and criminal defense counsel. These include steps counsel can take to reduce the chances of criminal charges and the tactics counsel might follow in defense of any charges. While the emphasis is on prosecution under the collective knowledge and responsible corporate officer doctrines, this report touches on defensive measures applicable to white collar prosecutions generally.

The report emphasizes substantive areas of law in which corporations and their officers risk violations. Most of the examples come from environmental prosecutions only because much of the thrust of white collar prosecutions have been in the environmental realm. But if attempts to make corporate prosecutions ever easier succeed, it will radically affect corporate officers and their companies doing any kind of business.

The appendix focuses on pleadings from one responsible officer case—*United States v. Schwitters*. Although the decision in that case is not reported, it is the first, and to date, the only decision ruling on proper use of the responsible corporate officer doctrine in environmental statutes. The opinion also covers a range of issues arising under the Clean Water Act. Finally, the briefs from both sides provide comprehensive coverage of several important issues likely to arise in many regulated industries, issues beyond the scope of this work but important for both attorneys and corporate officials facing the broadening reach of the criminal law.

ABOUT THE AUTHOR

Alan Zarky is an associate with Dan R. Dubitzky, P.S., a Seattle firm specializing in white-collar criminal defense. After graduating summa cum laude from UCLA Law School, Mr. Zarky spent three years with the federal Public Defender's Office in Los Angeles. He then taught criminal law at the University of Puget Sound Law School. Zarky and Dubitzky together have defended most major federal environmental prosecutions in the state of Washington. They also have handled several RICO and other white collar cases with multi-state reach, ranging from the largest bribery case in Alaskan history to the prosecution of a Long Island, N.Y., aerospace parts distributor.

ACKNOWLEDGMENTS

This special report was prepared by the BNA PLUS Research and Special Projects Unit of The Bureau of National Affairs, Inc. Drew Douglas is managing editor of the unit and Susan Korn is assistant managing editor. Mark Williams, staff editor, served as project coordinator and edited the report. Julie Steinberg, legal editor for BNA's *Toxics Law Reporter* and *Product Safety & Liabilty Reporter*, served as technical editor. Karen Ott-Worrow, staff editor, served as production editor.

Copyright © 1990
The Bureau of National Affairs, Inc.

II. THE RESPONSIBLE CORPORATE OFFICER DOCTRINE

Current legal doctrines impose nearly strict liability on corporations for the acts of their employees. As this report discusses in more detail in Chapter III, a corporation is vicariously liable whenever any one employee, while acting in the scope of his employment, commits a crime. The corporation has virtually no defenses; the employee's crime, by itself, renders the corporation guilty.

To prosecutors in environmental cases, however, this easy route to convicting corporations seems insufficient. While such vicarious liability doctrines create a ready ability to impose criminal fines on corporations, prosecutors assert that there must be personal accountability. Frequently, however, proof of guilt on the part of individuals is limited to lower-level employees. These are not the people the government generally wishes to prosecute. Deterrence — a goal of criminal law — arguably is more effective at the management level. It also may be seen as unfair to prosecute those who had no power to prevent the violations, whose only choice was to obey or to lose their jobs.

Proof may be lacking against higher-level employees for one of several reasons. Because these employees often are not physically involved in the violation, convincing evidence against them may not be available. Also, executives have a greater ability than lower-level personnel to hide complicity behind a wall of those directly involved.

Finally, proof may be lacking because upper-level employees lack complicity, at least under traditional criminal law doctrines. Typically, an individual is only guilty of a crime if the prosecution proves he committed some forbidden act while possessing a particular state of mind specified by the law.

Under various doctrines of vicarious liability, he can be guilty even if he did not personally perform the act, as long as he caused its performance (e.g. by inciting another to act), again with the requisite mens rea, or prohibited state of mind.

The problem, as prosecutors see it, is that corporate officers may have caused a violation, in the broader, common-sense meaning of "cause," without satisfying the essential elements of the particular crime. Failure to commit sufficient resources, creating a general atmosphere of non-compliance, or over-emphasis on generating profits all may result in a violation, without the officers ever being aware of the specific problem.

It is these people whose behavior must be changed if environmental and other problems are ever to be corrected, prosecutors contend. But if these officers are not aware of the particular problem, they lack the state of mind necessary to conviction under normal criminal law doctrines.

Viewed less charitably, the prosecution is engaged in a dangerous attempt to revamp the criminal justice system. Corporate officers can make easy targets, and their prosecutions can generate big headlines and launch political careers. Rather than undertake the task of seeking out evidence of complicity, the traditional but non-glamorous role of prosecutors, the government now seeks to bypass the need even to prove guilt as it has traditionally been understood.

Whether for lofty motives of protecting the public, or in pursuit of glory, prosecutors are seeking to change long-standing doctrines of criminal liability. Having been largely successful in weakening the procedural protections afforded criminal defendants by the Warren Court, the prosecution now is trying to forge significant changes in the substantive law. This section reviews the expansion of the responsible corporate officer doctrine and attempts to ask, and perhaps answer, some of the broader questions posed by what may at first seem to be minor differences in jury instructions. Since the precise wording of the instructions tells the jury how to apply the facts to the law, that language can make all the difference between a guilty verdict and an acquittal.

LIABILITY OF CORPORATE OFFICERS UNDER TRADITIONAL DOCTRINES

Before examining the government's efforts to alter corporate officer liability, it is worth reviewing the traditional doctrines of liability that would apply to corporate officers. Obviously, corporate officers and managers can be guilty of crimes, even without a special corporate officer doctrine. The corporate officer cannot defend a crime on the grounds that his act was at the corporation's direction. *United States v. Wise*, 370 U.S. 405, 410 (1962).

The liability of an officer or manager is clearest when the officer or manager personally commits the act, such as filling out a false report or turning a valve that releases an unlawful discharge. Presumably, all other situations beyond direct involvement by the officer must satisfy normal vicarious liability principles, namely aiding and abetting a crime or conspiracy to commit a crime.

Under general aider and abettor principles, one is liable if he knowingly associates himself with a criminal venture, wishes to bring it about, and seeks by his actions to make it succeed. *United States v. Broadwell*, 870 F.2d 594 (11th Cir. 1989). He must act with the knowledge and intention of facilitating the commission of a crime. *United States v. Raper*, 676 F.2d 841, 849 (D.C. Cir 1981).[1]

Similar elements are required to impose liability under a conspiracy theory. Although liability as a conspirator does not require that one help commit the offense, a joint plan to commit the offense must exist, and the defendant must have joined the conspiracy knowing of the plan and intending to carry it out. *United States v. Davis*, 810 F.2d 474 (5th Cir. 1987).

Applying these principles, the result under certain scenarios is as clear as with a direct act. Where the officer or manager instructs an employee to fill out the false report or turn the valve, he is as liable as the actual actor. More difficult fact patterns can readily be imagined. A manager may never explicitly direct an employee to commit a certain act; it may be long-standing plant practice and no direction may be necessary. If the manager is well aware of the illegal actions, is he vicariously liable?

Copyright © 1989
The Bureau of National Affairs, Inc.

This issue has garnered little discussion by the courts. Presumably a jury could find the necessary element of help by looking at indirect assistance. By engaging in all the various managerial actions that keep a plant running, the manager arguably helps the violation occur. Similarly, the violation may not be an explicit goal of the manager as he undertakes his normal duties, but he may be found to have intended the violation if it made plant operations possible or less expensive.

If a jury were given a normal aiding and abetting instruction, an appellate court would almost always find sufficient evidence to justify conviction under such facts.

The more difficult question is whether the government could get an aiding and abetting instruction more carefully tailored to the manager-officer fact pattern. In some sense, this is the problem the government has tried to address with the responsible corporate officer instructions it has tendered so far. As this report will suggest, those instructions are not well-tailored to address that issue.

ORIGINS OF THE RESPONSIBLE CORPORATE OFFICER DOCTRINE

The current focus of the prosecution's efforts to broaden the responsible corporate officer doctrine has been one enigmatic statement by Congress. The Clean Water Act, a major piece of environmental legislation, contains a single-sentence admonition that the act's criminal provisions shall apply to "responsible corporate officers." 33 U.S.C. § 1319(c)(6).

The responsible corporate officer doctrine derives from cases dealing with the federal Food, Drug and Cosmetic Act, 21 U.S.C. § 31, a regulatory statute with no specific reference to corporate officers. FDA, as a strict liability statute, is a relative rarity in criminal statutes. Violators are strictly liable for shipments of adulterated foods. Shipments are "punished by the statute if the article is misbranded [or adulterated], and the article may be misbranded [or adulterated] without any conscious fraud at all." *United States v. Dotterweich*, 320 U.S. 277, 281 (1943).

FDA is in sharp contrast to most criminal statutes, which require far more than the occurrence of a prohibited result (here, adulterated foods). Generally, a person is not guilty of a crime unless he personally commits (or helps others commit) a prohibited act, and does so with a specified state of mind. Under the strict liability in FDA, however, the defendant is guilty even if he did nothing to cause the adulteration, and even if he had no awareness that the adulteration existed.

Dotterweich made clear that the persons who may be prosecuted under the act include any corporate officer or employee "standing in responsible relation" to an event forbidden by the act. *Id.* In *United States v. Park*, 421 U.S. 658 (1975), the Supreme Court set forth the standards to be applied in determining if such a "responsible" person in fact has violated the act. Under *Park*, a person is guilty if he had, "by reason of his position in the corporation, responsibility and authority either to prevent in the first instance, or promptly to correct, the violation complained of, and ... he failed to do so." 421 U.S. at 673-74.[2]

The *Park* standard establishes a doctrine of criminal complicity quite different from that of most statutes, as to both the mental element and the physical act. The defendant is strictly liable for any FDA violations that occur, as long as he had the ability to prevent or undo them. No mental element is involved: He need not have any awareness that the prohibited result exists, or even that it is possible. Also, no physical act is required, only the ability to have prevented the violation.

Two points from *Park* are critical to understanding the discussion of the responsible corporate officer doctrine as applied under other statutes. The first is that, while the elements of the crime under FDA are quite different from those in many other statutes, this difference exists for all defendants. The elements are the same for corporate officers as for other employees. In particular, FDA does not make the prohibited mental state for corporate officers any different from that for other employees. Actual awareness of the violation is no more necessary for the employee who physically causes the violation than for the corporate officer.

Given the strict liability under FDA, the physical act required for conviction is, at most, minimally different for employees and officers. The employee who ships adulterated food need not have performed any acts to cause the adulteration. The employee's attenuated connection to the crime is little different from that of the corporate officer, who does not physically ship the food but bears a "responsible relation" to the adulterated shipment.

The second critical point is that the *Park* doctrine of making liable all who stand in "responsible relation" to a violation belongs only to strict liability offenses. This is the case for two separate, although related, reasons. First, as discussed earlier, the responsible relation doctrine—when applied to a strict liability offense—treats all persons equally whether or not they are corporate officers.

But when dealing with a crime such as knowing discharges of a pollutant, which normally includes some element of fault, reaching officers who stand in "responsible relation" to the violation creates two quite different methods of prosecution. The first requires direct involvement and wrongful intent, while the second allows conviction based only on the possibility of preventing the violation, regardless of intent. Applying the "responsible relation" doctrine to non-strict liability offenses actually transforms them into strict liability offenses, but just for corporate officers. Because the officer can be convicted based only on his relation to the violation, as opposed to his actual acts and actual mental state, he is, in effect, being made strictly liable. The *Park* decision was never intended to create two brands of criminal justice, one for most people and a stricter standard for corporate officers.

The second reason *Park* does not apply to fault-based offenses relates to the act requirement. As noted, *Park* applies an attenuated requirement of involvement with the violation, moving from the normal requirement of direct involvement to a mandate that one simply stand in a "responsible relation" to the event. The idea of holding people responsible for acts with which they had no involvement normally would offend traditional notions of personal accountability. But given the lack of a fault requirement in normal strict liability, the *Park* doctrine, with no requirement of involvement, is only a small step away.

Because the crime has no element of blameworthiness, the level of involvement essentially is irrelevant.

In fact, *Park* itself confirms this essential link between the "responsible relation" doctrine and strict liability.

> [W]here the statute under which they were prosecuted dispenses with "consciousness of wrongdoing," an omission or failure to act was deemed a sufficient basis for a responsible corporate agent's liability. It was enough in such cases that, by virtue of the relationship he bore to the corporation, the agent had the power to prevent the act complained of.

421 U.S. at 671. When dealing with fault-based offenses, however, elimination of the act requirement, and substitution of a "responsible relation" test, significantly alters the basis for liability.

THE ENVIRONMENTAL STATUTES

Prosecutors have begun using the *Park* and *Doterweich* responsible officer notion to convict officers under the various environmental statutes. The Clean Water Act, 33 U.S.C. § 1251 et seq., is a broad-ranging statute designed to address the problems of water pollution. In addition to a whole host of civil provisions, the act makes criminal a number of activities. *See* 33 U.S.C. § 1319 (c)(1).

The most frequently used prohibition is that banning the discharge of any "pollutant" (broadly defined at 33 U.S.C. § 1362(6)) into the "navigable waters of the United States," (likewise defined expansively, 33 U.S.C. § 1362(7)) without an National Pollutant Discharge Elimination System (NPDES) permit, (33 U.S.C. § 1342). Like almost all criminal statutes (and unlike FDA), the Clean Water Act only criminalizes a combination of act and state of mind. Because the act prohibits certain discharges, it requires that the defendant have committed some act or else that he be vicariously liable for some other person's act. Discharges (or any other violation) are only rendered criminal if the defendant acted "negligently" or "knowingly." (§ 1319 (c)(1)).

The Clean Water Act defines "persons" to include individuals, corporations, and such other entities as partnerships and municipalities. 33 U.S.C. § 1362(5). In establishing criminal penalties, the act provides that "any person who knowingly or negligently" commits various acts shall be guilty of a crime (felonies for knowing violations, misdemeanors for negligent violations). 33 U.S.C. § 1319(c). The act then explains that "for the purposes of this subsection, the term 'person' means, in addition to the definition contained in § 1362(5) of this title, any responsible corporate officer." 33 U.S.C. § 1319(c)(6). The Clean Air Act has the same language. 42 U.S.C. § 7413(c)(3).

The government has, through its application of the "responsible corporate officer" language in the statute, sought to eliminate or minimize any act or mental state requirements of the statute. This effort aims to make possible the conviction of corporate officers, regardless of whether they committed any act (or were vicariously responsible for another's act under traditional doctrines), and regardless of whether they acted knowingly or negligently.

The "responsible corporate officer" language in the Clean Water Act is the source of much current litigation, as the government tries to convict high corporate officers for acts with which they have minimal, if any, direct involvement. For example, *United States v. Pennwalt* (see Case Studies, Chapter VI). involved the rupture of a chemical storage tank in Tacoma, Wash. The government indicted not only the Tacoma plant manager, but three corporate managers from the Pennsylvania headquarters who had no day-to-day responsibility for the plant. While the government and defense counsel differed greatly in their views of just what role these individuals had in relation to the spill, the government fully conceded that it was stretching the perimeters of traditional theories of criminal liability.

Legislative History

Just what did Congress mean by its admonition to include "responsible corporate officers" within the definition of the term "person"? Literally applying Congress's instruction means substituting the phrase "responsible corporate officer" where the word "person" appears and concluding that "any responsible corporate officer who knowingly" (or negligently) commits certain acts shall be guilty of a crime. In other words, corporate officers are to be treated just as other persons are.

Because the conclusion appears to be so unremarkable, it suggests that Congress must have had some other intent in including the "responsible corporate officer" language. But the language may have been viewed as necessary, or at least helpful, to ensure that corporate officers were treated the same as other individuals.

In *United States v. Wise*, 370 U.S. 405 (1962), the defendant contended that, because the Sherman Act lists corporations, but not corporate officers, as potential violators, the antitrust law does not govern an officer who acts solely for the corporation. The Supreme Court rejected that contention in *Wise*. Congress, when inserting the "corporate officer" language in the Clean Water Act, may have simply wanted to ensure the same result under the Clean Water Act as the court did under the Sherman Act. Alternatively, Congress may simply have been admonishing prosecutors that they should not omit corporate officers when naming defendants, assuming that the officers (like anyone else) committed a prohibited act with the requisite guilty state of mind.

The language seems clear in the Clean Air Act and Clean Water Act. Corporate officers are guilty only if they knowingly or negligently commit certain acts, under traditional doctrines of personal and vicarious liability. Under the plain meaning rule, "courts in applying criminal laws generally must follow the plain and unambiguous meaning of the statutory language. Only the most extraordinary showing of contrary intentions in legislative history will justify a departure from that language." *United States v. Albertini*, 472 U.S. 675, 680 (1985) (citations omitted).

In fact, no legislative history exists regarding § 1319(c)(3) of the Clean Water Act. A provision identical to that section was added to the Clean Air Act in 1977, five years after its inclusion in the Clean Water Act. The sole comment regarding the Clean Air Act amendment states:

> The Committee intends that criminal penalties be sought against those corporate officers under whose responsibility a violation has taken place and not just those employees directly involved in the operation of the violating source.

Report of the Committee on Environment and Public Works, United States Senate, Report No. 95-127, 51, *reprinted at 6, A Legislative History of the Clean Air Act Amendments of 1977,* 1371, 1425.

This comment is susceptible to several interpretations. The most obvious is that it is an admonition to prosecutors to charge corporate officers (when they are guilty), rather than an expression of intent to enlarge criminal responsibility. But even if intended as a comment on the scope of the statute, the phrase "under whose responsibility a violation has taken place" is subject to a whole range of possible meanings.

The word "responsible" has widely varying connotations. The passage could refer to responsibility in the sense of having actually caused a violation. Or it could pertain to an individual with general responsibility for the operation that led to the violation. This vague language hardly can constitute the "most extraordinary showing," *Albertini, supra,* necessary to overcome the plain meaning of the Clean Air Act. It is no expression of congressional intent regarding the plain language of the Clean Water Act, adopted years before this single comment was made.

GOVERNMENT THEORY OF THE DOCTRINE

The government has tried to use the responsible corporate officer doctrine — established under a strict liability statute — to prosecute defendants under fault-based statutes.

If corporate officers were to be subject to some special liability, and therefore to a special jury instruction beyond that applied to other individuals, a whole range of possibilities would arise. At one extreme, a corporate officer could be found guilty simply because of his position in the corporation. Whenever a violation occurs, for example, in a division for which he bears responsibility, he could be convicted. No act or state of mind considerations would be relevant. However, this is the result reached by importing the *Park* standard — implicating one who had the ability to prevent a violation — from the strict liability of the FDA to crimes requiring some wrongful state of mind.

At nearly the other extreme, the special corporate officer instruction could impose the mental elements normally required under the particular statute, but simply make clear that failure to act renders the officer just as culpable as acting. Thus, the officer who knows an illegal discharge is to occur, but fails to exercise his power to act, would be just as culpable as one who actively authorizes the discharge. The same would be true for negligence: The lack of response, despite awareness of an unreasonable risk of a violation, would be as criminal as taking some action while aware of its unreasonable risk.

It is not always clear when a failure to act can render the non-actor criminally liable. Normally, an omission is criminal only if the statute imposes a specific duty to act, such as filing tax returns or filing reports of pollutant discharges. However, the law may impose a duty to act, even absent a statute. This duty for example, could be based on a special relationship between individuals (parent and child) or on a contract. See, generally, LaFave, Wayne and Austin Scott, *Substantive Criminal Law* §3.3 (1986). LaFave points to a few cases holding that a duty to act can arise based on one's employment status.

Standing in a bank, knowing that a friend is committing a robbery, does not make someone an aider and abettor if he lacks the intent to help commit the robbery. Similarly, the person in the bank is not a conspirator unless he has agreed with the robber to help him. Also, the bystander is not guilty as a principal simply because he fails to take action to prevent the robbery. But if the bank teller is filing a false statement with the Internal Revenue Service, and the bank manager knows this and fails to take action, what then? If the manager has no intent to help, and has made no agreement to help, he is not vicariously liable. The question then becomes his liability as a principal based upon his failure to prevent the crime, on the grounds that his status creates a duty for him to act.

An instruction that unequivocally establishes such a duty would address the problem discussed earlier, the manager who knows a violation is occurring but takes no action. While this manager may lack vicarious liability as aider and abettor or conspirator, he still could be convicted as a principal. His omission, combined with his knowing state of mind, would render him guilty regardless of whether he intended to help the actual violator.

Because of the scarcity of case law, it is hard to say whether an instruction based on the action-inaction issue would create any significant change in the law. But eliminating a requirement of action would comport with most people's concept of a fair rule and would still be consistent with traditional notions of personal accountability. Can anyone doubt that the low-level employee, the one who actually operates a valve, is guilty of knowingly causing a discharge, regardless of whether the discharge results from turning the valve or from not turning the valve? It would seem that the rule should be no different for managers and officers, so long as the requisite intent still is clearly an element of the crime. The same analysis would seem to apply to other states of mind besides "knowingly" — particularly negligence.

If the government seeks through the responsible corporate officer instruction to impose liability for inaction as well as action, the goal can be achieved through an instruction imposing no special standards for officers, but simply expounding on the implications of commission versus omission. Talk about a defendant standing in a "responsible relation" to the violation risks injecting other issues far beyond the action-inaction question.

Certainly, potential instructions can fall between the two extremes that we have discussed — imposing strict liability versus making no alteration in the law. One could, for example, impose a lowered (but not strict) mental element for corporate officers. Perhaps that which is a felony for low-level employees when done knowingly, and a misdemeanor when done negligently, could be a felony for corporate officers when done with gross negligence. Arguably, the greater power to control events may require that corporate officers assume a greater standard of care. A host of other variations could be envisioned. The point is that, regardless of whether any variations might be supported by policy considerations, none of them is supported by the statutory language of the Clean Water Act.

Previously, this chapter discussed why the traditional responsible corporate officer doctrine belongs only to strict liability offenses. In fact, until recently, the doctrine had never been applied outside the strict liability arena. Comment, *Limits on Individual Accountability for Corporate Crimes*, 67 Marquette L. Rev. 604, 618 n. 85 (1985). The recent exceptions include *United States v. Cattle King Packing Corp., Inc.*, 793 F.2d 232 (10th Cir.), cert. denied, 107 S.Ct. 573 (1986) and *United States v. Dee*, Cr. HAR-88-0211, District of Maryland, both discussed in more detail later in this chapter.

Faced with the doctrine's inapplicability to crimes with a mental element, the government never has settled on a consistent theory of how the corporate officer language should be applied. In one Clean Water Act case, *United States v. Schwitters,* No. CR 86-129S, Western District of Washington (see Case Studies, Chapter VI), the government initially proposed an instruction allowing conviction if the individual negligently allowed violations to occur or if he had the power to prevent violations by a guilty corporation. The latter alternative would impose strict liability.

The government's supplemental proposed instruction contained language allowing conviction for failure to exercise the power to prevent violations. But in summarizing that theory, the instruction required that the defendant be a responsible corporate officer "who was negligent and thereby allowed" violations. This latter instruction addressed the action-inaction issue and steps back from a strict liability position.

On appeal, the government defended the court's instruction, which, like the government's original instruction, allowed conviction solely on the basis of a finding that the defendant had the power to correct violations but failed to do so.

In another Clean Water Act case, *United States v. Sea Port Bark Supply,* CR 88-56 TB, Western District of Washington, the government proposed yet another standard: The defendant had the authority to prevent the violations and 1) he was aware of the violation and knowingly failed to prevent it or 2) he negligently failed to exercise the power to detect and prevent the violations. Like the supplemental instruction in *Schwitters,* this instruction approaches an issue discussed earlier, establishing the same liability for failure to act as for action.

All of these proposed versions of the responsible corporate officer doctrine came from the U.S. Attorney for the Western District of Washington. Yet other variations have been submitted in other districts. For example, in *United States v. Dee,* Crim. No. HAR-88-0211, District of Maryland, in dealing with a "knowing" violation, the court instructed the jury that it could convict those in responsible relation to the violation if they "acted knowingly in failing to prevent, detect or correct the violation."

In *United States v. Protex Industries, Inc.*, 874 F.2d 740 (10th Cir. 1989) (see Case Studies, Chapter VI), the government submitted an instruction similar to that in *Dee*, covering one who "willfully failed to exercise [his] authority of power to prevent, detect, or correct [a] violation." Unlike the *Sea Port Bark* instruction, the *Dee* and *Protex* instructions deal with a curious concept, knowingly or willfully failing to detect an unknown condition. The problems with these instructions are discussed later in this chapter.

The former director of the Environmental Crimes Section, U.S. Department of Justice, described yet another view of the doctrine, a much more limited one. "This doctrine is available to prosecutors when the evidence indicates some willfulness by the executive who seeks to 'blind' himself from the occurrence of illegal acts performed within his bailiwick." Starr, *Countering Environmental Crimes*, 13 Environmental Affairs 379, 391 n. 47 (1986). But none of the instructions cited above have anything to do with willful blindness. In addition, current legal doctrines already can deal with an individual who seeks to protect himself from the knowledge element of a statute by deliberately avoiding the facts. Special instructions allow the jury to find knowledge where such willful blindness occurs. *See, e.g.*, Ninth Circuit Pattern Instruction 5.07; Eleventh Circuit Pattern Jury Instructions, Special Instruction 15.

In short, the government at times has tried to import the responsible corporate officer doctrine intact from the strict liability FDA to statutes with a fault element. But perhaps recognizing how blatantly such a posture revamps the congressionally established elements of the crime, the government also has submitted hybrid responsible corporate officer doctrine instructions. The meaning of these instructions is not always clear, but in most cases they still alter the elements of the crime without statutory authority. Sometimes, the instruction has not, when read literally, changed the elements of the crime, but in those circumstances, a special instruction is at best unnecessary, and at worst risks giving the jury freedom to apply some vague standard of "responsibility" beyond the proper elements of the crime.

Finally, the Clean Water and Clean Air Acts use the phrase "responsible corporate officer," although *Park* and *Dotterweich* focused their discussions on "corporate agents." If Congress did intend "corporate officers" to be held to a different standard of criminal liability than other persons, several additional questions arise. Is the different standard, whatever it may be, to be applied only to corporate agents who officially are designated as officers, or to anyone with a "responsible relation" to the violation? Can Congress constitutionally impose different criminal standards on different classes of individuals, or does that violate guarantees of equal protection? These and other issues will have to be addressed as the government continues its pursuit of this doctrine.

United States v. Frezzo Bros.

The government frequently has cited one case, *United States v. Frezzo Bros. Inc.*, 602 F.2d 1123, 1130 n. 11 ((3d. Cir. 1979) as endorsing its interpretation of the responsible corporate officer language. In fact, *Frezzo Bros.* does not address the elements of the crime for corporate officers. The U.S. Court of Appeals for the Third Circuit stated:

> The Government argued the case on the "responsible corporate officer doctrine" recognized by the United States Supreme Court in *United States v. Park*, 421 U.S. 658 (1975) and *United States v. Dotterweich*, 320 U.S. 277 (1943). We have examined the judge's charge and we perceive no error in the instruction to the jury on this theory.

At first reading, this might seem to be just what the government has claimed. But the defendants in *Frezzo Bros.* were not objecting to how liability for corporate officers had been defined. Instead, they complained that, although they had been charged in the indictment solely on a corporate officer theory, the jury was told that the defendants could be found guilty under normal individual liability doctrines. On appeal, the defendants challenged this disparity between the theory in the indictment and the theory as expressed in the jury instructions. They did not contest, and the appellate court was not even considering, the propriety of, or the appropriate language for, a responsible corporate officer charge.

The defendants' objections to the jury charge are discussed in more detail in the ruling on their motion for a new trial, *United States v. Frezzo Bros. Inc.*, 461 F. Supp. 266, 272-273 (E.D. Pa. 1978). The sole issue was the claimed discrepancy between the indictment and the instruction. The defendants never challenged the language of the corporate officer instruction. The opening brief on appeal and the objection to the charge in the trial transcript are available to help rebut any government claim that the appellate court was addressing the proper scope of a responsible corporate officer instruction.

The meaning of the *Frezzo Bros.* decision was addressed in *United States v. Schwitters*, discussed in detail later in this chapter. The *Schwitters* court looked beyond the reported appellate decision in *Frezzo Bros.* and relied also on the district court opinion, the appellate brief, and the trial transcript. The court concluded that "the issue of 'strict liability' or the necessary mens rea of the corporate officer was not argued to the Third Circuit." The court's opinion in *Schwitters* is included in Appendix B.

The government is not alone in misinterpreting the state of the law. We find in legal literature unsupportable statements that blithely ignore the complicated nature of the responsible corporate officer doctrine. For example, one law review article incorrectly treated the matter as settled, and in doing so, relied on a case that did not even address the issue:

> Moreover, courts seeking to define the standard of liability in this area [environmental statutes] have held that under the "responsible corporate officer" theory, corporate officials may be responsible for wrongdoings affecting public health and welfare if the government can prove that official was in a position to seek out, discover and stop the illegal act and failed to do so. Actual knowledge of the act is not required.

McMurry and Ramsey, *Environmental Crime: The Use of Criminal Sanctions in Enforcing Environmental Laws*, 19 Loyola L.A.L.R. 1133, 1153 (1986).

McMurry and Ramsey cite to *United States v. Johnson & Towers, Inc.*, 741 F.2d 662 (3d. Cir. 1984) as endorsing the responsible corporate officer doctrine. However, they mischaracterize the Third Circuit's holding. As in *Dotterweich*, the issue in *Johnson & Towers* was who can be prosecuted under the statute, in this case, RCRA, 42 U.S.C. § 6901 et seq. RCRA, the Resource Conservation and Recovery Act, is another broad environmental statute, which, like the Clean Water Act, is primarily civil in focus. The statute regulates hazardous waste storage, transportation, treatment and disposal through a so-called "cradle to grave" system of permits and monitoring. Criminal penalties are set out at 42 U.S.C. § 6928(d). Guilt under RCRA demands a knowing violation.

The defendants in *Johnson & Towers* contended that, because only owners and operators of waste-generating facilities could obtain a permit, only owners and operators could be prosecuted for disposing of waste without a permit. The court held instead that any person, including employees of the facilities, could be prosecuted.

The court did not hold that any person, officer or not, could be convicted without the requisite knowledge. In fact, the court held that the necessary state of mind included not only awareness of the act but knowledge of the permit requirement. Thus, *Johnson & Towers* has nothing to do with the responsible corporate officer doctrine. Its sole observation on the doctrine, contrasting the "responsible officer" language in the Clean Air and Clean Water Acts to the lack of such language in RCRA, was that the language "seems to expand rather than limit the class of potential defendants." This comment is clearly dicta, involving a statute not even before the court. Even if the corporate officer language did expand the class of potential defendants, that does not mean that the elements of the crime depend on the defendants' status.

Yet, that is the holding McMurray and Ramsey attribute to *Johnson and Towers*. Thus, even when well-respected authorities make firm pronouncements, there is no substitute for counsel's own careful research.

United States v. Cattle King

Besides *Frezzo Bros.*, the only circuit court decision involving a non-FDA responsible corporate officer charge is *United States v. Cattle King Packing Corp., Inc.*, 793 F.2d 232 (10th Cir.), cert. denied, 107 S.Ct. 573 (1986). Unlike *Frezzo Bros.*, *Cattle King* actually does address the propriety of a responsible corporate officer jury instruction.

The case involved violations of the Federal Meat Inspection Act. This act, like FDA, creates a strict liability misdemeanor offense for any violations but makes it a felony if the violation involved intent to defraud. 21 U.S.C. § 676

The trial court gave a responsible corporate officer instruction, Instruction 42. (Unfortunately, the text of the instruction is not quoted in the opinion.). The Tenth Circuit first held that the teachings of *Park*, allowing conviction of those in a "responsible relation" to a violation, are not limited to misdemeanors. Next, the court agreed that a responsible corporate officer theory could not be the basis for conviction where the statute requires an intent to defraud. The court stated:

> The statute at issue in *Park* permits a felony sentence if the violation charged is committed with an "intent to defraud." In *Park*, however, the defendant was not charged with a felony, but rather with a misdemeanor. The issue of whether the defendant in *Park* could be convicted under the felony provision of that statute, therefore, was not before the Court. Instruction No. 42, therefore, without more, would not be sufficient to find Stanko [the defendant] guilty of a felony.

793 F.2d at 240-241.

The court stated that a responsible corporate officer instruction cannot suffice when the statute requires proof of intent to defraud. The court did not explicitly broaden its holding to situations where the statute requires proof of some mental element, but not intent to defraud. However, it is hard to see anything unique about intent to defraud, as opposed to other state-of-mind requirements. It therefore seems that the *Cattle King* court would accept the position that a *Park* instruction cannot be a substitute for the appropriate-state-of-mind instructions. *Cattle King* would appear to be a case defense counsel can cite when the government relies on a responsible corporate officer theory.

Unfortunately, the *Cattle King* court muddied the waters when it considered the instructions as a whole. The instructions for each substantive count had stated the intent-to-defraud requirement and another instruction required proof of specific intent for conviction.[3] The court held that the specific intent instruction "complements Instruction 42 rather than contradicts it" and that "Instruction No. 42 [the corporate officer instruction] gave the jury the opportunity to decide whether [defendant] Butch Stanko was responsible for Cattle King's violations of federal meat inspection law."

The holding makes no sense, in this author's view. What does it mean to give the jury the opportunity to decide whether the defendant was responsible? As noted earlier, criminal liability basically revolves around two issues: act and intent. The typical instructions, defining what mental state and acts are required, give the jury the opportunity to decide responsibility, as defined by the elements of the crime.

How then, can the corporate officer instruction help the jury decide responsibility? The *Cattle King* decision makes clear that status as a corporate officer does not eliminate the requirement of personally harboring the requisite intent. But if the mental element is not altered for corporate officers, the only thing left is the requirement of an act.

Is the *Cattle King* decision saying that somehow the responsible corporate officer instruction gives the jury a particular method of deciding whether the corporate officer is responsible for the physical act? As discussed earlier in this chapter, well-established doctrines, unrelated to corporate officer status, govern responsibility for acts a person does not commit himself. Under these doctrines, a person can be vicariously liable if he counsels another to commit the act (aiding and abetting), or if he enters into an agreement to commit a crime (conspiracy). Using a *Park* instruction in this context alters the principles of vicarious liability, allowing a jury to find a corporate officer "responsible" for the act of another, even if he did nothing, and intended nothing, which would render him liable under long-standing principles of aider and abettor liability.

The *Cattle King* court evidently was swayed by the strong evidence that defendant Stanko was vicariously liable, under traditional principles, for the acts in question:

> [T]his is not an instance where Stanko was in Scottsbluff, Nebraska, *not* knowing what his employees were doing in Adams County, Colorado. Rather, the evidence is that Stanko set in motion the very acts which were carried out, pursuant to direction, by his employees, clearly a form of aiding, abetting, ordering, commanding, or inducing. 18 U.S.C. § 2. Scottsbluff is not a shield for Stanko. (Emphasis in original.)

The *Cattle King* court thus made an error frequently made by appellate courts. Recognizing that the defendant probably would be convicted under proper instructions, the court approved an improper instruction. While the result in *Cattle King* might be appropriate, the decision risks unjust results, with unjust instructions, in future cases.

In another case, for example, the defendant (to paraphrase the facts from *Cattle King*) might have been off in Scottsbluff, Neb., not knowing what his employees in another state were doing. He might not have set in motion the criminal acts, so he would not be guilty under an aiding and abetting theory. Yet if a future court allows a responsible corporate officer instruction, in reliance on *Cattle King*, a jury could find the defendant guilty, simply because his position put him in "a responsible relation" to the violation. Such an instruction gives the jury the power to apply their own standards of "responsibility," completely apart from the well-established statutory and case law standards for assessing criminal accountability.

While the right result may have occurred in *Cattle King*, despite the corporate officer instruction, the wrong result may develop in another case, because of that instruction. It is not surprising that where the facts reveal a particularly egregious crime, the prosecution emphasizes the facts, while the defense tries to point out the broader implications of the legal ruling beyond the particular facts. Only careful parsing of the *Cattle King* opinion, revealing its gaps in logic, will prevent future error.

United States v. Schwitters

Another court refused to follow *Cattle King's* error when ruling in *United States v. Schwitters*. In that case, the trial court gave a responsible corporate officer instruction that clearly allowed conviction if the corporation was guilty and if Schwitters "had the power to prevent or correct such a violation" and failed to do so. In addition, the prosecution strongly argued its case to the jury on this vicarious liability theory.

On appeal, the prosecution backed away from any argument that a special vicarious liability doctrine exists for corporate officers. Instead, it contended that the court's other instructions, which required proof of willfulness or negligence, satisfied the statutory elements.

The appellate court rejected this position. Under the trial court's instructions "a reasonable juror could have found [Schwitters] guilty of the three separate counts on the basis of strict liability. This is contrary to the provisions of the Clean Water Act, requiring a finding that he 'willfully or negligently' violated the Act." The court thus reversed Schwitters' conviction.

Although the opinion in Schwitters has not been published, it is the first clear pronouncement on the Clean Water Act's elements. It should be brought to the attention of any other court facing these issues.[4]

The court applied a liberal standard in striking down the instructions: Could a reasonable juror have understood the instruction to apply the wrong elements? This standard was enunciated in *Sandstrom v. Montana*, 442 U.S. 510, 514 (1979) and has been used in several other cases; see, e.g., *Francis v. Franklin*, 471 U.S. 307 (1985); *California v. Brown*, 107 S.Ct. 837, 839 (1987) (quoting *Francis*). See also *Dick v. Kemp*, 833 F.2d 1448, 1451 (11th Cir. 1987) (quoting *Francis*). Accord, *United States v. Walker*, 575 F.2d 209, 214 (9th Cir.), cert. denied, 439 U.S. 931 (1978) (jury instruction requires reversal because it is "subject to an interpretation that is prejudicial to the accused.")

In general, a strong trend exists in criminal cases to apply a lax harmless error standard, so that even where trial errors are detected, the appellate court declines to reverse the conviction. The cases cited here establish a standard so strict that an error when instructing the jury on the elements of the crime is quite likely to result in reversal. Because the harmless error standard for instructions on the elements of the crime is so different from normal harmless error standards, counsel should be aware of these cases when predicating an appeal on error in the elements instructions.

United States v. Dee

The responsible corporate officer doctrine does serious damage to traditional doctrines of culpability, unless it is limited to its origins in strict liability offenses. In one case, the doctrine has been removed even from its tenuous place in the Clean Water Act.

In *United States v. Dee*, Crim. No. HAR-88-0211, District of Maryland, the court gave a responsible corporate officer instruction when the defendants were charged with RCRA violations, for storing, treating, and disposing of hazardous wastes without a permit. Two striking elements of this case make it potentially far-reaching.

First, unlike the Clean Water Act, RCRA contains no responsible corporate officer language. The court apparently accepted the government's position that the doctrine could be applied independent of any specific congressional authorization. If that approach is followed in other cases, the doctrine would not be limited to the Clean Water Act and RCRA, and it would not even be limited to environmental statutes. It would become a court-made doctrine that applies special rules of criminal liability to corporate officers charged with any type of offense.

Secondly, RCRA only criminalizes actions done with a "knowing" state of mind. The court instructed the jury that, to convict the defendants under the responsible corporate officer doctrine, it must find as follows:

> First, that each defendant has a responsible relationship to the violation. That is, that it occurred under his area of authority and supervisory responsibility.
>
> That each defendant had the power or the capacity to prevent the violation.
>
> That each defendant acted knowingly in failing to prevent, detect or correct the violation.

The last sentence lists three different types of "action," presenting two quite different situations. The "knowingly fail to correct" language addresses the commission-omission issue discussed previously. This language imposes a duty to act upon those with the power or capacity to act regarding violations. As noted, imposing a duty to act, when one has the requisite state of mind, is effecting a relatively small change in the law, if a change at all. Nevertheless, it is a step that should be taken only explicitly, with careful deliberation, and preferably legislatively.

"To knowingly fail to prevent" means that one knows the violation is impending, and fails to take action. The analysis is the same as that for failing to correct.

But consider the concept "knowingly failed to detect" a violation. What does this mean, to knowingly fail to know (detect) something? If one is to make any sense of this phrase, it means to be aware of the likelihood that there is a violation, but to fail to take additional steps to determine if in fact there is a violation.

In fact, the *Dee* standard is two steps less stringent than even simple negligence. First of all, negligence requires that one's action be unreasonable, while a corporate officer is liable under *Dee* as long as he knew of some facts that render "knowing" his failure to detect the violation. The jury was given no guidance in determining how aware the defendant must be that a violation was likely before his failure to detect was rendered "knowing." Second, under negligence, one still must have caused the prohibited result (the discharge, for example, or an accident while speeding). The *Dee* instruction, however, would convict the officer for mere failure to detect the result.

Even putting aside these distinctions from negligence, the *Dee* jury charge is striking. Where Congress has explicitly required proof of a knowing action, the *Dee* court allowed conviction for what is essentially negligence, an extremely different level of culpability. The convictions in *Dee* were on appeal as this report was being published, so it was not yet known whether these significant judge-made revisions in criminal law would be upheld under scrutiny.

The Rivers and Harbors Act, 33 U.S.C. § 401 et seq., provides another example of how the responsible corporate officer doctrine could negate explicit congressional intent. Title 33 U.S.C. § 411 provides that "Every person and every corporation that shall violate, or that shall knowingly aid, abet, authorize, or instigate a violation of the provisions of §§ 407, 408, and 409 of this title shall be guilty of a misdemeanor."

The Rivers and Harbors Act has been held to be a strict liability offense, requiring no intent or even negligence on the part of the actor. *United States v. Ashland Oil*, 705 F. Supp. 270 (W.D. Penn. 1989). However, the statute clearly states that one is guilty of vicariously causing a violation only if one acts "knowingly." If the responsible corporate officer doctrine were applied to render officers vicariously liable, simply because of their corporate position, this would allow the prosecution to circumvent a specific statutory mandate. No court has yet adopted this extreme position, although it seems to flow logically from the instruction given in *Dee*.

CONCLUSION

In undertaking a review of the responsible corporate officer doctrine, its antecedents and the case law, it is easy to lose sight of the full implications of this doctrine. When applied to a non-strict liability offense, it may establish an extremely radical revision of American doctrines of criminal liability.

In *United States v. United States Gypsum Co.*, 438 U.S. 422, 436, (1978), the Supreme Court reiterated "the familiar proposition that '[t]he existence of a mens rea is the rule of, rather than the exception to, the principles of Anglo-American criminal jurisprudence.'" 438 U.S. at 436 (quoting *Dennis v. United States*, 341 U.S. 494, 500, (1951)). Strict liability offenses have a "generally disfavored status," and "intent generally remains an indispensable element of a criminal offense," 438 U.S. at 437.

Even in highly regulated and dangerous activities, true strict liability rarely is applied. For example, possession of a firearm that must be registered can be criminalized, even if the possessor did not know that unregistered possession was prohibited. But the mental element is not completely eliminated: He must at least know that he is in possession of the weapon. The nature of the item gives him notice of the potential for regulation. *United States v. Freed*, 401 U.S. 601 (1971). Yet some of the government's interpretations of the corporate officer doctrine, including the instruction given in *Schwitters*, would require no mental element for the officer, and would convict based only on his corporate status and the occurrence of an act done by others.

The problem goes beyond the elimination of this fundamental of criminal law. The doctrine would remove the mental element for some defendants, but not others, solely because of their job descriptions. Regardless of whether this distinction would withstand an equal protection challenge, it poses significant questions about the fairness of this approach.

The problems the government seeks to address with this doctrine are significant. The risks posed by corporate criminal activity are troubling, be it in environmental violations or money-laundering. And traditional doctrines of criminal culpability may well be inadequate to remedy these problems. As was discussed in the introduction, these limitations are two-fold. First, management may need to be deterred from actions that pose risks to society but do not render them criminal under traditional liability standards. Second, frequently difficulties exist in establishing the culpability of upper management, even when the individuals are in fact guilty under those traditional doctrines.

The existence of these limitations may well call for remedial actions. But this author would argue that the approach adopted by the prosecution in these cases, while an arguably well-intentioned one, is clearly a poor one.

First, if current criminal doctrines are ill-suited to resolving these societal problems, it does not follow that changes in those doctrines are the solution. While using the criminal justice system may be the easiest, most personally satisfying, and most politically astute approach, it is not necessarily the most appropriate. The proposed doctrine could send a person to prison for several years because of events over which he had no practical control.

Even versions of the doctrine that impose some unreasonableness requirement work a radical change. Negligence standards in the criminal law are few and are almost exclusively limited to misdemeanors. The thought of branding someone a felon, and imprisoning him for years, simply because, in restrospect, his actions are later deemed unreasonable should cause serious hesitation.

It is true that civil enforcement often is more costly and cumbersome than criminal prosecution. But sizable costs also can accompany a drastic reworking of the fundamentals of criminal justice.

This author's policy objections to the corporate officer doctrine go beyond concerns about tinkering with fundamental principles of law, and even beyond issues of fairness. Imposing strict criminal liability would have significant policy implications, many of them negative. What does the corporate officer do, knowing that he faces prosecution, no matter how reasonably and responsibly he acts? For one, the officer may refuse to serve as a corporate officer. People who could contribute to correcting some of the environmental and other problems discussed earlier may be deterred from accepting corporate positions, out of fear that some prosecutor will seize upon them to set an example. The responsible corporate officer doctrine alone will not cause people to leave the business world in droves, but along with the various civil hazards to which corporate officers now are subject, the incremental effect could be significant.

If the officer decides to stay, how will the law motivate him to behave? Ideally, he should authorize $100 in costs to prevent a one-tenth chance of $1,000 in potential harm. This is the traditional measure of reasonableness in civil tort law, the famous formula of Judge Learned Hand, *United States v. Carrol Towing Co.*, 159 F.2d 169, 173 (2d Cir. 1947).

If the officer's negligence is not just criminalized but he is rendered a felon despite reasonableness, he will be inclined to spend far more of the corporation's money, just to protect himself. This will, of course, be costly to the corporation. But it also will result in a net societal loss, because the excess funds should be going to create other benefits, such as increased productivity, rather than to overprotect against the occurrence of some violation.

If changes are needed to address the shortcomings of the criminal system, those changes need not be in the criminal system. For example, assume the government is right and penalties against corporations often are inadequate to motivate behavioral changes by management. One possibility for motivation is creating personal penalties, but civil ones, against those in management who meet some level of culpability, such as unreasonableness.

Civil fines against corporate officers would provide the incentives the government seeks, especially if a ban exists on indemnification by the corporation. Yet such penalties would lack the extreme stigma (and under the federal Sentencing Guidelines, significantly increased jail terms) of criminal sanctions. Given the lesser burden of proof in civil actions, such an approach would lead to shorter, and probably less frequent, trials. As a result, the government's cost of imposing a penalty would be greatly reduced.

Even if changes in substantive criminal law are warranted, the prosecution's means to that end is fraught with danger. The maxim that "hard cases make bad law" is well-founded. Faced with a corporate officer under whose command terrible environmental damage occurred, a court will be likely to uphold a conviction. But that court may give far too little thought to the implications of its holding for future fact patterns. The criminal law, like most, is full of examples of an evolution in doctrine that never was intended by the judges of the individual cases.

The substantive principles of criminal complicity have stood this country well. They should not be over-hauled by piecemeal, ad hoc, responses of courts and prosecutors to the egregious facts of individual cases. Instead, they should be modified through careful consideration by legislative bodies. Approaching the problem legislatively, rather than judicially, creates at least the potential for a serious public debate before dramatic changes are wrought in the criminal justice system.

Endnotes

[1] Whether this last requirement simply means the defendant must have the intention of helping the principal commit an act that in fact violates the law, or instead means he must actually know that the act was criminal, is unclear. The language used in most cases is ambiguous on this point. Traditionally, aiding and abetting instructions have included a requirement of willfulness and have explicitly defined that to mean "the specific intent to do something the law forbids." The Ninth Circuit Model Instructions have eliminated reference to specific intent (5.05), as have the Seventh Circuit's Instructions (5.07). However, the Fifth and Eleventh Circuit Pattern Instructions include a requirement of willfulness in their aiding and abetting instructions. Eleventh Circuit Pattern Jury Instructions, Basic Instruction 9.1, Special Instruction 6; Fifth Circuit Pattern Jury Instructions, Basic Instruction 9A, Special Instruction 1. For the most explicit presentation of the requirement that the defendant actually know a crime is to be committed, see *United States v. Barnett*, 507 F. Supp. 670 (E.D. Cal. 1981), rev'd on other grounds, 667 F.2d 835 (9th Cir. 1982) (accused "must intend that an activity succeed which the accused knows is of a criminal nature"); 1 Wharton Criminal Law, § 29 at 158 (1978) ("[a]n 'abettor' by definition knows that a crime is about to be committed.")

[2] *Dotterweich* and *Park* have been the subject of numerous law review articles, including O'Keefe & Shapiro, Personal Criminal Liability Under the Federal Food, Drug and Cosmetic Act—The Dotterweich Doctrine, 30 Food Drug Cosm. L.J. 5 (1975); Abrams, Criminal Liability of Corporate Officers for Strict Liability Offenses—A Comment on

Dotterweich and Park, 28 U.C.L.A.Rev. 463 (1981); Brickey, Criminal Liability of Corporate Officers for Strict Liability Offenses—Another View, 35 Vand.L.Rev. 1337 (1982) (reprinted in 1983-84 Corp. Prac. Comm., 443); O'Keefe & Isley, Dotterweich Revisited—Criminal Liability Under the Federal Food, Drug, and Cosmetic Act, 31 Food Drug Cosm. L.J. 69 (1976); Rodwin, A Violation of the Federal Food, Drug and Cosmetic Act—A Crime In Search of a Criminal, 31 Food Drug Cosm. L.J. 616 (1976); Sethi & Katz, The Expanding Scope of Personal Criminal Liability of Corporate Executives—Some Implications of *United States v. Park*, 32 Food Drug Cosm. L.J. 544 (1977); Recent Developments, the Standard for Criminal Responsibility under the Federal Food, Drug and Cosmetic Act—*United States v. Park*, 13 Am. Crim. L. Rev. 299 (1975); Case Note, Prosecution of Corporate Officials Under the Federal Food, Drug and Cosmetic Act—*United States v. Park*, 37 Ohio State L.J. 431 (1976).

[3] The term "specific intent" is the source of much controversy in the law. It frequently is used to refer to an intent to violate the law. Other times, it refers to an intent that a specific result occur, such as an assault with intent to commit grievous bodily harm. Leading commentators and many in the federal judiciary object to the term as confusing at best, and requiring proof of non-existent mental elements at worst. They urge instead instructions tailored to the specific elements of the crime, elements that may or may not involve an intent to violate the law or cause a specific result.

[4] The court ruled against the defense on several other issues, holding that "willfully" does not require proof that the defendant was aware of the need for a permit, and that simple negligence, rather than gross negligence, is the proper standard. (Since Feb. 1, 1987, the "willfully" element has been replaced by "knowingly.") The court declined to resolve other issues, holding that any error was harmless under the facts of the case. These included a challenge to the negligence instruction, which looked to "all the surrounding circumstances," rather than just those known to the defendants, and the instruction on corporate liability, which did not define what are the "authorized representatives" who could render the corporation liable (see Chapter V).

□□□

III. THE COLLECTIVE KNOWLEDGE DOCTRINE

In its attempt to make convictions easier, the government is seeking another extension of the law, this one aimed at corporations rather than at their officers. This doctrine, the collective knowledge doctrine, is illustrated in *United States v. Bank of New England, N.A.*, 821 F.2d 844 (1st Cir. 1987). In *Bank of New England*, the U.S. District Court for the District of Massachusetts instructed the jury that it could find the bank guilty of violating a reporting statute even if no individual employee possessed "guilty knowledge," as long as the knowledge possessed by all the employees added up to the knowledge required under the statute. The instruction seriously undermines a century of criminal law as applied to corporations, this author believes.

Under the Currency Transaction Reporting Act, 31 U.S.C. § 5313, a bank is required to file a report to the IRS when a customer deposits more than $10,000 in cash. The obligation applies also when a customer makes multiple transactions, each less than $10,000, but totalling more than $10,000. The Bank of New England was charged with failure to report such multiple, or "structured," transactions.

The failure to report, however, only is criminal if it is "willful." Willfulness in this context requires knowledge of the obligation to report. The trial court properly instructed the jury that if any one employee knew of the requirement, the bank knew it, also. But the court further instructed:

> In addition, however, you have to look at the bank as an institution. As such, its knowledge is the sum of the knowledge of all the employees. That is, the bank's knowledge is the totality of what all the employees know within the scope of their employment. So, if Em-

ployee A knows one facet of the currency reporting requirement, B knows another facet of it, and C a third facet of it, the bank knows them all.

821 F.2d at 855. The Court of Appeals upheld this instruction, finding that "a collective knowledge instruction is entirely appropriate in the context of corporate criminal liability." 821 F.2d at 856.

CORPORATE CRIMINAL LIABILITY DOCTRINES

A brief review of the federal black letter law of corporate criminal liability is useful in explaining how the *Bank of New England* decision radically re-works traditional corporate liability. A corporation generally is liable for the acts of its agents. The doctrine is one of respondeat superior by explicit analogy to civil tort law. *New York Central and Hudson River Railroad v. United States*, 212 U.S. 481 (1909). The principle applies both to strict liability offenses and to those requiring proof of wrongful intent. *Boise Dodge, Inc. v. United States*, 406 F.2d 771 (9th Cir. 1969).

The corporation is not vicariously liable unless the agent is acting within the scope of his employment. But this concept is applied quite broadly, just as it is in civil law. An agent's acts are within the scope of employment if they are related to, or ordinarily performed in the course of, the employment. *United States v. American Radiator & Standard Sanitary Corp.*, 433 F.2d 174, 204 (3d Cir.), cert. denied, 401 U.S. 948 (1970). Scope of employment also includes those acts that outsiders could reasonably assume the agent to have authority to do. *United States v. Hilton Hotels Corp.*, 467 F.2d 1000, 1004 (9th Cir. 1972), cert. denied, 409 U.S. 1125 (1973). It is no defense that the specific criminal act was not authorized, because this would render null the entire vicarious liability doctrine.

The agent's act must be performed with the intent to benefit the corporation. No actual benefit need accrue to the corporation, however. *United States v. Beusch*, 596 F.2d 871, 877 (9th Cir. 1979). Where the employee acts totally for his own benefit, this element has served as a defense, *See, e.g., Standard Oil Corporation of Texas v. United States*, 307 F.2d 120 (5th Cir. 1962) (conviction reversed where employees, in course of their illegal acts, stole from the corporation). *Accord, United States v. Ridglea State Bank*, 357 F.2d 495 (5th Cir. 1966) (bank's civil liability for fraud reversed where agent's acts were in furtherance of his own personal embezzlement scheme). However, where the agent's acts are primarily for his benefit, but he has some intent to benefit the corporation, the defense has not succeeded. *Hilton Hotels*, 467 F.2d at 1004 (employee's extortion and treatment of hotel supplier motivated by personal dislike, but resulted in kickback to trade association).

IMPLICATIONS OF COLLECTIVE KNOWLEDGE DOCTRINE

As the preceding section demonstrates, a corporation generally is liable whenever an employee commits a crime while acting in the scope of his employment. But under the case law, a corporation has been guilty only if some employee committed the crime. The *Bank of New England* holding allows a corporation to be convicted, regardless of whether any individual is guilty, as long as the aggregated knowledge of all the employees yields a guilty state of mind. This result has important implications.

The *Bank of New England* case involved knowledge of a reporting requirement, but its logic and broad language would apply equally to knowledge of other facts. For example, an employee allows a tank to empty into a river, believing it to contain simply clean water. Another employee knows the tank contains pollutants but has no knowledge that the discharge will occur.

The corporation perhaps is guilty of negligence, for failure to maintain an adequate flow of information between employees. But under any logic or policy, can it be said the corporation is guilty of acting knowingly? The difference between acting knowingly and negligently can be crucial: Negligence is a misdemeanor under the Clean Water Act, knowing discharges are a felony. Under many statutes, the difference would be between guilt and innocence.

The examples need not be limited to banking or environmental law. A defense contractor employee, in justifying the price of a contract, represents that the price of a given item is $1, a belief reasonably held after diligent inquiry. Another employee in a different division has determined that the item can be acquired for 50 cents but has no knowledge that the item is currently being used to price a new government contract. If one combines the knowledge of the two employees, the corporation knows that the item can be obtained for 50 cents and that it is telling the government the item will cost $1.

An individual who possessed both those items of knowledge would be guilty of fraud, but under no reasonable concept of fraud would anyone say the corporation has criminally defrauded the government. Yet such a scenario follows directly from the instruction in *Bank of New England*.

The issue basically is a policy one, not a logical one. Corporate liability is a legal fiction, as are all attributes of a corporation. It is neither logical nor illogical to base corporate liability on collective knowledge, just as it is neither logical nor illogical to base it on the crimes of an employee who acts contrary to corporate directive.

As discussed in Chapter II, the problem of accountability of corporate officers may warrant changes in the doctrines of individual culpability. So too, the problem of compartmentalized information may call for new doctrines of corporate criminal liability. Perhaps corporations should be punished when they unreasonably fail to channel information within their structure. (However, under existing law, if a corporation's employee deliberately limits information flow, so as to create a defense to the knowledge element of a crime, the "willful blindness" doctrine allows the conviction of the employee and thus of the corporation. *United States v. Jewell*, 532 F.2d 697 (9th Cir.) (en banc), cert. denied, 426 U.S. 951 (1976)).

The *Bank of New England* trial court got close to this concept in another part of its charge, when it allowed the jury to find willfulness if the corporation was "flagrantly indifferent to [the law's] obligations." However, the "collective knowledge" doctrine, as enunciated by the First Circuit, is not limited to flagrant indifference or even negligence. It penalizes the corporation whenever separate items of knowledge within the corporation combine to satisfy the elements of a crime.

In terms of deterrence, the collective knowledge doctrine thus is overinclusive as to which corporations it punishes. No way exists for a large corporation to ensure that all information held by employees is shared with all other employees. Yet this is the only way a corporation could prevent "crimes" that are only deemed crimes by collecting each employee's knowledge. It might be argued that applying this doctrine will deter corporations from being reckless or negligent in their channeling of information. But it also would deter corporations from engaging in beneficial activities, because they would risk criminal charges despite their best efforts at channeling information.

Traditional corporate criminal liability is far less likely to deter the pursuit of beneficial activities: If a corporation adequately seeks to prevent criminal activity by its employees, it may be able to defend on the ground that the employees' acts were not intended to benefit the corporation. See Chapter V. Even where that defense is not allowed, traditional corporate criminal liability limits the corporation's criminal exposure to occasions on which an actual crime has been committed by some employee. It is thus at least possible for the corporation to identify the acts it must prevent and to focus its employee-education activities accordingly. By creating a hybrid sort of crime where no individual need be guilty, the collective knowledge doctrine spreads a much wider net, making corporate compliance far more difficult.

CRIMINAL CASE LAW

How did the *Bank of New England* court come to its result? The court talks as if the collective knowledge doctrine is a well-established one, citing to six other cases, *Steere Tank Lines, Inc. v. United States*, 330 F.2d 719 (5th Cir. 1964); *Riss & Co., Inc. v. United States*, 262 F.2d 245 (8th Cir. 1958); *Inland Freight Lines v. United States*, 191 F.2d 313 (10th Cir. 1951); *Camacho v. Bolling*, 562 F. Supp. 1012 (N.D. Ill. 1983); *United States v. T.I.M.E.-D.C., Inc.*, 381 F. Supp. 730 (W.D.W.Va. 1974); *United States v. Sawyer Transport Inc.*, 337 F. Supp. 29 (D. Minn. 1971), aff'd, 463 F.2d 175 (8th Cir. 1972). However, few of the cited cases even arguably support the "collective knowledge" doctrine. Those few cases that could be construed to support the doctrine arise out of a narrow theory applicable only to a fairly unusual act, the Motor Carriers section of the Interstate Commerce Act, 49 U.S.C. § 32, and are properly limited to that context.

The collective knowledge doctrine is sufficiently new and without acceptance in other circuits. An extensive analysis of the supposed precedents on which the *Bank of New England* court relied is necessary to persuade other courts not to follow the First Circuit.

The earliest of these cases, *Inland Freight*, involved the Commerce Act's prohibition against maintaining false time logs for the drivers. The court's description of the facts was as follows:

> [I]nconsistencies existed between the log and the report ... . The logs and the reports did not find their way into the hands of a single agent or representative of the company after they were filed. No single agent or representative in the offices of the company had actual knowledge of their conflicts and falsities. But one agent or representative had knowledge of the material contents of the logs and another had knowledge of the material contents of the reports. And the knowledge of both agents or representatives was attributed to the company.

(citing *New York Central*) 191 F.2d at 315. But this observation was not a holding that the two items of knowledge, in disparate parts of the company, must be summed to equal knowledge of the inconsistencies. The court went on to explain that willfulness is a question of fact, proof of which is inferable from the circumstances, and that the evidence and inferences were sufficient to take the case to the jury. Had the court been applying a collective knowledge doctrine, it would have said this evidence indisputably established guilt.

Another indication that *Inland Freight* does not support the collective knowledge doctrine was its resolution of a challenge to the instructions. The court reversed the conviction because, while one instruction properly allowed conviction for knowingly accepting false logs, another improperly allowed conviction if the falsity merely would have been discovered had the company performed its duty of inspecting the logs. If the court had been applying a collective knowledge doctrine, this latter instruction would have been more than adequate, and not grounds for reversal. The existence of the inconsistent logs and reports, albeit in the hands of different company agents, would have combined to create knowledge, regardless of whether inspection would have revealed the falsity.

The next Motor Carrier case, *Riss & Co., Inc.*, also fails to support a collective knowledge doctrine. The company had a procedure for a log clerk to inspect the drivers' logs, checking for violation of on-duty hours. Apparently the clerk failed to detect some of these hours. The company contended that it was innocent because none of the employees who handled these logs acquired actual notice of the violations. The court rejected this position but not because of a collective knowledge doctrine. Instead, it held that under a malum prohibitum statute such as the Motor Carrier Act, the elements of knowingly and willfully are satisfied by one who "either intentionally disregards the statute or is plainly indifferent to its requirements." The log clerk's failure to detect the excess hours, which were discoverable by "a mere 'glance' at the logs," 262 F.2d at 250, constituted an indifference to the performance of the duty imposed on the corporation. The case therefore has nothing to do with aggregating different pieces of information held by different employees.[1]

Steere, too, is not a collective knowledge case. It repeats the general proposition that knowledge of employees and agents is attributable to the corporation. But the case was not decided in the context of compartmentalized knowledge. The undisputed evidence was that a trucking terminal manager knew of false records being maintained by the truck drivers.

Sawyer has intimations of being a collective knowledge case but again rests its result on the peculiar scienter requirement of the Interstate Commerce Act, which imposes an affirmative duty on companies to monitor their records. The drivers' logs falsely showed them to be off-duty or in some certain locale at the same time that they were in fact receiving citations at other locations. The evidence also showed that safety inspectors had warned the company several times that the logs were false. The court held:

> It is true that different corporate employees of defendant handled the logs than those to whose attention came the various citations and fines and who authorized the posting of bail or the payment of the fines. ... [However] both were corporate employees and knowledge of each is to be imputed to the corporation which thus had knowledge.

337 F. Supp. at 30. Despite this language, the court was not relying on collective knowledge. Instead, the court concluded that the Commerce Act made criminal the failure to exercise an affirmative duty.

> Congress did not deem it an undue burden to require all drivers to file [logs], nor to impose on the motor carrier the burden of policing such to determine their truth or falsity.

337 F. Supp. at 30.

T.I.M.E.-D.C. involves the most explicit pronouncement of the collective knowledge doctrine. On several occasions, the company's dispatcher received notice that a driver was sick and would not be working. The dispatcher advised the driver that this would be considered an unexcused absence, and the driver later reported for work.

In what this author views as a misreading of *Steere, Riss & Company, Inland Freight* and *Sawyer,* the U.S. District Court for the District of West Virginia said:

> A corporation cannot plead innocence by asserting that the information obtained by several employees was not acquired by any one individual employee who would then have comprehended its full import. Rather, the corporation is considered to have acquired the collective knowledge of its employees and is held responsible for their failure to act accordingly.

381 F. Supp. at 738. But the court also was relying on the special lowered scienter requirements under the act, namely, that a violator "is deemed to have had knowledge of a regulatory violation if the means were present by which the company could have detected the infractions." 381 F. Supp. at 739. This language shows the court is applying the same affirmative duty of detection that *Sawyer* imposes.

In short, the act requires companies to take affirmative steps to detect all violations. Failure to take such steps is a crime. It is not the case, as supporters of the collective knowledge doctrine would probably contend, that the act requires knowledge, with a substitute for knowledge to be found through the legal fiction of summing different employees' knowledge.

Camacho, the most recent case cited in *Bank of New England,* has nothing to do with the collective knowledge doctrine. It involves the Department of Labor's denial of unemployment benefits because of a claimant's failure to present detailed evidence of his job searches to an appeal tribunal. The claimant had provided this information earlier on a form to the department. The department did not advise the claimant that the form would be unavailable at the tribunal hearing (or even that his job searches would be at issue at the hearing).

Under these facts, the court held that the tribunal referee had constructive knowledge of the information already given to the agency. This decision, explicitly grounded on concerns of fairness, clearly gives no guidance for criminalizing on a collective knowledge basis.

In sum, the cases relied upon by the First Circuit do not support the broad collective knowledge doctrine that the court pronounced. They relate instead to a narrow doctrine of affirmative duty to detect violations, imposed upon corporations by Congress in one statute.

Kathleen Brickey, a major author in the field, cites one additional criminal case. Brickey states that the Ninth Circuit applied a "variant of the collective knowledge doctrine in holding that the criminal intent of one corporate agent and the conduct of another innocent agent could be collectively imputed to the corporate entity." Brickey *Corporate Criminal Liability, 1989 supp., at 30.* To the contrary, the case, *United States v. Shortt Accountancy Corp.*, 785 F.2d 1448 (9th Cir.), cert denied, 106 S.Ct. 3301 (1986) involves a straightforward application of aider and abettor and corporate liability principles. A certified public accounting firm was involved in filing fraudulent tax returns, using backdated documents. The accountant who organized the scheme, Ashida, did not actually sign or prepare the return; the individual doing so had no knowledge that the returns were false. The company said it could not be convicted under 26 U.S.C. § 7206(1), making a false return, but only under § 7206(2), assisting in the preparation of a false return.

The court rejected this approach, stating: "A corporation will be liable under § 7206(1) when its agent deliberately causes it to make and subscribe to a false income tax return." 785 F.2d at 1454. While its discussion is under the heading "Collective Intent," the decision does not rely on any new doctrines. Ashida, by creating false information with the intent that it be used in a false return, caused the innocent preparer to file a false return. He was thus guilty under standard aiding and abetting principles, which therefore rendered the corporation guilty. Imposing vicarious liability for causing an innocent other to commit a crime does involve collecting one's guilty state of mind with the other's physical act, but it does not entail collecting several innocent states of mind to create a hybrid guilty state of mind.

CIVIL CASE LAW

As mentioned earlier, the traditional doctrines of corporate criminal liability are grounded in an analogy to tort law. In analyzing the propriety of the collective knowledge doctrine, then, it is appropriate to look to the civil cases for guidance.

Brickey cites several cases in civil law as supporting this collective knowledge doctrine. Brickey, *Corporate Criminal Liability*, § 4.05 at 94, n. 39 (1984): *Browning v. Fidelity Trust Co.*, 250 F. 321 (3d Cir. 1918); *Sarna v. American Bosch Magneto Corp.*, 195 N.E. 328 (Mass. 1935), *Paloeian v. Day*, 13 N.E.2d 398 (Mass. 1938); *Gem City Motors, Inc. v. Minton*, 137 S.E.2d 522 (Ga. 1964); *Alabama Power Co. v. McIntosh*, 122 So. 677 (Ala. 1929); *Slater v. Missouri Edison Co.*, 245 S.W.2d 457 (Mo. 1952). However, most of these cases do not appear to support Brickey's contention that the collective knowledge doctrine is well-grounded in civil case law. Additionally, other recent cases directly reject the doctrine.

Browning, in fact, directly supports the position that one cannot aggregate the knowledge of different employees to determine a corporation's liability. In that case, a mortgage trustee was sued after it released several tracts of a mortgaged property. The plaintiff was the holder of a bond secured by the mortgaged property. The terms of the bond provided that the trustee could release portions of the property as long as it had no knowledge of existing default by the mortgagor. The suit alleged that the paying teller of the banking department had knowledge that the mortgagor had defaulted. The release was executed by the trust department, which had no knowledge of the default.

In language that at first seems to support a collective knowledge doctrine, the court said:

> On the bare question of knowledge, we agree ... that the trustee cannot thus divide itself into units or parts and cannot escape liability, when based upon knowledge, because one of its parts was without it while another possessed it.

250 F. at 324. However, the bondholder's contract provided that the trustee was immune from suit except for acts per-

THE COLLECTIVE KNOWLEDGE DOCTRINE 45

formed in bad faith. The court found that the trust officers lacked actual knowledge of the default. The court said:

> While the knowledge of the existing default imputed to the corporation extended to its officers, their lack of actual knowledge has a bearing on the intent or motive that entered into the gross negligence and bad faith with which the corporate trustee is charged ... .

250 F. at 326. The court concluded that because the trust officers, who performed the act, did not act in bad faith, the corporation was not guilty of gross negligence or bad faith. Thus, at least for torts requiring a state of mind, the court refused to cumulate the knowledge of different employees. In short, *Browning* actually provides authority against the use of the collective knowledge doctrine.

One case, not cited by Brickey, rejects a collective knowledge approach in a manner similar to *Browning*. In *Woodmont, Inc. v. Daniels*, 274 F.2d 132 (10th Cir. 1959), suit was brought for compensation beyond the contract amount on the grounds of fraudulent representations. The defendant's employees made representations in good faith regarding the nature of the work to be performed. The board of directors knew that the work actually would be more onerous, and they had reason to know that the plaintiff was unaware of this condition. The board lacked actual knowledge, however, of the employees' representations.

While upholding the fraud claim on other grounds, the Tenth Circuit refused to predicate fraud on these facts.

> [W]hile in some cases, a corporation may be held constructively responsible for the composite knowledge of all of its agents, whether acting in unison or not, [citing to *Inland Freight Line* and *Sawyer*] we are unwilling to apply the rule to fix liability where, as here, intent is an essential ingredient of tort liability as for deceit. See Restatement, Agency 2d, § 275, Comment B.

274 F.2d at 137. Because tort doctrines are the underlying source of corporate liability in criminal law, it is useful to look to the Restatement of Agency. Comment B states,

> If knowledge, as distinguished from reason to know, is the important element in a transaction, and the agent who has the knowledge is not one acting for the principal in the transaction, the principal is

not affected by the fact that the agent has the knowledge. In many situations, in order for one to be responsible, it is necessary that the act should be done with knowledge in a subjective sense, and it is not sufficient that one has means of information.

The comment gives the following illustration:

> P, in the business of buying and selling horses, employs A as a manager, part of A's duties being to report to P the quality of horses which P has to sell. A fails to report that one of the horses is vicious. In a sale to T, P innocently represents that the horse is gentle. P is liable in an action for fraud if, but only if, A had intended P to make the misrepresentation.

The commentary explains that if A were authorized to sell the horse and does so, making the misrepresentation, P is liable in an action for deceit.

The commentary and its example suggest a result favorable to the corporation in the examples discussed at the beginning of this chapter. The employee with the knowledge that an item cost only 50 cents is not involved in the transaction of making a statement to the government that the item cost $1. The commentary might not be applicable in other cases, such as the *Bank of New England* fact pattern, where the transaction presumably includes each of the employees involved in the financial dealings. On the other hand, it is not those employees, but someone at a higher level, who is involved in the "transaction" of not filing a Currency Transaction Report (CTR) (the forms required of banks when handling cash transactions of more than $10,000), so arguably the corporation is protected by the Restatement's position.

Gem City Motors, another case cited by Brickey, deals not with collective knowledge but with the particularities of pleading. A salesman represented a car as being new and its odometer correct when in fact the car had a previous owner and the odometer had been rolled back by the dealer from 5,000 to 900 miles. The defendant demurred, arguing that the complaint must allege that the particular agent who made the misrepresentations must actually know of their falsity. The court rejected the demurrer, simply holding, after quoting *Walker v. State*, 78 S.E.2d 545 (Ga. 1953), that the plaintiff had sufficiently alleged knowledge on the part of the corporation through its agents.

To the extent that this portion of *Gem City* suggests that a corporation is guilty of fraud when no individual agent is, it is inconsistent with the Restatement. The facts of the case make such a suggestion unnecessary, because the court explicitly held that there were sufficient facts for the jury to find that the salesman's misrepresentation was made willfully with the intent to deceive.

Slater is a difficult case to analogize to criminal law. There, the defendants' employee, in cutting a power line, trespassed onto the plaintiff's land and cut down some trees. The employee reasonably believed he was on other land but another utility employee was at fault for not advising him specifically where to cut. There was no question that the corporation was liable in trespass, a strict liability offense. In question was the applicability of a statute that barred punitive damages if the defendant had probable cause to believe he was not trespassing.

The court made the general statement that a corporation is to be charged with the composite knowledge of its officers. In the context of this case, the principle makes good sense. The corporation cannot claim the benefit of an exemption for innocent actors when it is at fault for not providing that actor with the proper knowledge. However, this result cannot fairly be transformed into a principle that a corporation is criminally liable when none of its actors are at fault.

Walker, to which *Gem City* looks, contains a broad statement supporting collective knowledge:

> [T]he trend of authority ... is that ... [a corporation] cannot escape liability on the ground that the agent who actually performed the forbidden act on behalf of the corporation was entirely innocent, in that such agent lacked knowledge which was possessed by other agents of the corporation ... . A company is chargeable with the composite knowledge acquired by its officers and agents acting within the scope of their duties.

78 S.E. 2d at 549. *Walker* cites *Sarna*, *Inland Freight* and *Slater* for this proposition, which goes far beyond the meaning of these cases. *Walker* deals with an unusual situation. A company extended credit to a customer and then revoked that credit. The customer was charged with criminal fraud after she presented her credit card and claimed it was valid. The court held

that the company could not have been defrauded because the credit department knew that the credit had been revoked, even though the salesperson did not.

Whether *Walker* would be good law today is questionable. The idea that one can attempt to defraud a company, but be exonerated because someone in the company happened to know the truth, would be anathema to most courts. In any event, *Walker* deals only with whether an entity can be a victim of fraud, because of knowledge held by one of its units. The case presents a completely different question from whether a company should be punished for a crime by aggregating different employees' knowledge.

Paloeian is another case containing the general statement that a corporation is charged with the combined knowledge of all of its agents, but again is a poor basis for establishing a broad collective knowledge doctrine in criminal law. At issue was whether an insurance company was estopped from defending on the grounds that an insurance policy had been canceled. The acceptance of a premium by a receipt clerk was found to be grounds for such estoppel. This simply is an application of normal principles of agency, under which the insured properly relied on the apparent authority of the insurance company's agent. It does not depend upon the collective knowledge doctrine.

Two other cases cited by Brickey directly apply the collective knowledge doctrine but do so in the context of negligence. In both *Alabama Power* and *Sarna*, the defendant's employee engaged in activities that, unknown to them, were dangerous. As stated in *Sarna*:

> It was not necessary for the plaintiff to show that some one agent or employee of the defendant was cognizant of all the facts necessary to establish that he was as an individual was negligent. The defendant is chargeable with the combined knowledge which all its agents acquired within the scope of their authority together with legitimate inferences from all the evidence.

196 N.E.2d at 330. *Accord, Alabama Power*, 122 So. at 681. Vicarious liability is misapplied here, in this author's view. Vicarious liability means the corporation is liable when one of its agents is. *Sarna* and *Alabama Power,* however, make the corporation liable when none of its agents is. The corporation could

be directly liable for negligence, as opposed to being vicariously liable, based on negligent failure to properly supervise its employees and ensure that they are properly informed. Harper, James and Gray, 5 *Law of Torts*, § 26.1 at 4 (1986). Research for this report suggests that these holdings are isolated ones and do not reflect a genuine trend in tort law on which the criminal cases may rely.

Additionally, two recent cases, one before and one after *Bank of New England*, are especially important to show that civil case law does not support the collective knowledge doctrine. In *Kern Oil and Refining Co. v. Tenneco Oil Co.*, 792 F.2d 1380 (9th Cir. 1986), cert. denied, 480 U.S. 906 (1987), one contention was that Kern Oil had made overpayments voluntarily, with full knowledge of the facts. Under Texas law, this would have been a defense to a suit for restitution. The trial court found that no single Kern employee had full knowledge of the facts, but Tenneco asserted that the knowledge of the various employees should be imputed to Kern. In doing so, Tenneco relied on *T.I.M.E.-D.C., Inc.*

The court rejected this approach, holding that the voluntariness required by Texas law could not be established by pooling knowledge. It distinguished *T.I.M.E.-D.C., Inc.* because there, the statute imposed a legal duty on the corporation to ensure its employees complied with the regulation.

Another civil opinion has directly rejected the doctrine enunciated in *Bank of New England*. The passage is worth quoting in full:

> Plaintiffs' theory of liability is premised on the principle that knowledge of a corporate employee is imputed to the corporation. See, e.g., United States v. Bank of New England, 821 F.2d 844 (1st Cir.), cert. denied, — — — U.S. — — —, 108 S.Ct. 328, 98 L.Ed. 2d 356 (1987). Arguing from this principle, plaintiffs seek to attribute to Standard & Poor's the combined knowledge of several of its employees in order to hold the corporation liable for fraud. But plaintiffs' theory is flawed. While it is not disputed that a corporation may be charged with the collective knowledge of its employees, it does not follow that the corporation may be deemed to have a culpable state of mind when that state of mind is possessed by no single employee. A corporation can be held to have a particular state of mind only when that state of mind is possessed by a single individual.

First Equity Corp. v. Standard & Poor's Corp., 690 F. Supp. 256, 257-258 (S.D.N.Y. 1988), affirmed 869 F.2d 175 (2d Cir. 1989). Judge Michael Mukasey's opinion in *First Equity* goes a long way to clearing up the confusion engendered by *Bank of New England.* But he has not gone quite far enough. He attempts to make the distinction between charging the corporation with the collective knowledge of its employees (acceptable) and imputing a state of mind possessed by no individual employees (unacceptable). Instead, he should distinguish between charging a corporation with the knowledge held by any given employee (acceptable) and charging it with the collective knowledge of its employees (unacceptable).

It appears that the court actually meant to make the distinction suggested here. In approving of charging a corporation "with the collective knowledge of its employees," the court actually was speaking of the knowledge held by any given employee. The problem is that the phrase "collective knowledge" is readily interpretable to mean something far more than the knowledge of any given employee. And when so interpreted, whether intended by Judge Mukasey or not, "collective knowledge" is difficult to distinguish from the imputation of intent that the *Bank of New England* court ruled permissible, but which Judge Mukasey finds impermissible.

To be chargeable with collective knowledge means that if employee A knows something is untrue, and employee B knows the corporation has reported it as true (but is unaware that it is false), the corporation is chargeable with both items of knowledge. The corporation thus has knowledge that it has made a false statement. The line between this situation and imputed wrongful intent is quite thin. Counsel and courts would be well advised to use the phrase "knowledge of any given employee" and to avoid the slippery phrase "collective knowledge," even when that latter phrase is used as in *First Equity*.

CONCLUSION

Given that the case law does not strongly support a collective knowledge doctrine, and given the number of case directly addressing and rejecting that approach, it might be thought that the holding in *Bank of New England* was a narrow one. A review of the opinion shows that it was not.

> The acts of a corporation are, after all, simply the acts of all of its employees operating within the scope of their employment. The law on corporate criminal liability reflects this. Similarly, the knowledge obtained by corporate employees acting within the scope of their employment is imputed to the corporation. Corporations compartmentalize knowledge, subdividing the elements of specific duties and operations into small components. The aggregate of those components constitutes the corporation's knowledge of a particular operation. It is irrelevant whether employees administering one component of an operation know the specific activities of employees administering another aspect of the operation ... Since the Bank had the compartmentalized structure common to all large corporations, the court's collective knowledge instruction was not only proper but necessary.

821 F.2d at 856. (Citations omitted and quotation from *T.I.M.E.-D.C.* omitted). Two distinct questions are whether the instruction was proper and whether it was necessary.

In this author's view, the collective knowledge instruction was not proper, at least in terms of applying precedent. The preceding sections reveal that the *Bank of New England* decision is not well-grounded in case law. If anything, it runs directly contrary to cases in tort law refusing to "collectivize" employees' knowledge for purposes of determining a corporation's state of mind.

The cases discussed show how a doctrine can be created out of nearly whole cloth. First, one court establishes a narrow point, particular to its facts. Then another court makes a comment in dicta, broadly reading the first court's decision. The second court's dicta then gets treated as a statement of black letter law. As to the collective knowledge doctrine, the distortion of precedent has not yet solidified into widely accepted doctrine. Defense attorneys still have an opportunity to carefully educate the courts about how *Bank of New England* has misread and misapplied the prior cases.

As the *Bank of New England* court observed, one can ask not only whether the instruction was proper, but was it necessary. By 'necessary,' the court presumably meant was the instruction essential to promoting important policy concerns. This author submits that the collective knowledge instruction fails under this test as well.

Previously, this chapter discussed the cases under the Motor Carriers Act. The earlier cases, *Inland Freight*, *Riss & Co.*, and *Steere*, are truly not collective knowledge cases. But the later cases, *Sawyer* and *T.I.M.E.-D.C.*, were distinguished here because they interpreted that particular statute to impose an affirmative duty on the company to police its records. This is not necessarily that great a distinction from the doctrine *Bank of New England* would impose for all laws. The net effect, at least, frequently would be the same, whether the law is: (1) that a corporation has an affirmative duty to check for information that would reveal violations or (2) that the corporation is deemed to have the knowledge of all its employees.

However, the former approach has significant advantages. First, it makes explicit the burden to be imposed on companies. It is one thing to impose that burden as to a minor regulatory offense, involving a highly regulated industry directly affecting the public safety. It is quite another to impose that duty on all corporations, as to all possible violations that might occur throughout normal operations. When speaking of imposing a duty, it is clear that one is altering the elements of the crime (rather than simply modifying the method of determining knowledge for collective entities), arguably a task more clearly suited to legislatures than courts.

The courts have decided that in the Motor Carriers statutes, Congress has imposed such a duty. But can the courts with equal ease conclude that Congress has established the same rigorous standard for all criminal statutes across the board?

In addition, if corporate liability is altered by imposing an affirmative duty to collect information, failure to comply with that duty need not be a strict liability offense. The failure might be criminal when one is, for example, negligent, grossly negligent, or when the failure is reckless.

On the other hand, the second approach, imposing liability through collectivizing knowledge, creates strict liability. To impose the burden of strict liability ignores the realities of modern corporations, some with tens of thousands of employees, spread across the world, engaged in a myriad of activities. It is hard enough for corporations to ensure the information flow necessary to their normal operation. It would effectively be impossible to maintain the sharing of information necessary to prevent the occurrence of all events that, when one pools all the information within the corporation, yield a criminal state of mind.

Under the collective knowledge doctrine's strict liability standard, the company is guilty as long as an act, combined with the corporation's "collectivized" state of mind, satisfies the elements of a crime. This is so no matter how strenuously the company strives to assemble the information or to prevent the act.

To impose a criminal strict liability standard for failure to aggregate information risks imposing significant costs on corporations and thus society. Corporations would respond by incurring costs to stave off potential prosecution. Because even reasonable efforts at information collection would be no defense, corporations would have to incur more than reasonable costs, costs that would exceed those warranted by a normal cost-benefit analysis (including a cost-benefit analysis that internalizes the costs to society).

The specter raised is not an illusory one. Given the societal desire to point blame when the undesirable occurs, criminal prosecutions could be quite likely under a collective knowledge doctrine, even though no knowing or even unreasonable acts occurred. As the potential penalties increase, the costs corporations will incur to avoid those penalties likewise will increase. Under the strict liability standard imposed by *Bank of New England*, those costs will be commensurate, not with the potential harm from a violation, but from the potential cost to the corporation from a prosecution.

The most recent proposal for corporate sentencing involved fines ranging from two to three times the cost of the harm. Costs the corporation incurs to avoid such punishment will therefore potentially result in a net societal loss. This is the same point made earlier about imposing strict liability on corporate officers.

As with the problems some seek to address through the corporate officer doctrine, a genuine problem exists regarding the corporate state of mind. This problem is perhaps worthy of new developments in the criminal law. Corporations, given their unique nature, might require unique principles for determining state of mind.

The strict liability of *Bank of New England* was contrasted with the more common concept of unreasonableness. Perhaps negligence in ensuring an adequate flow of information among corporate employees is worthy of criminalization, given the potential harms that may result (witness the examples of dangerous discharges or false statements, related above). But if so, such significant changes in the law require careful drafting and thinking through all the ramifications. Should such a change apply to all laws, or only those protecting against certain types of harm? What should the level of negligence be, gross or simple? If the company is found negligent, does this simply render it guilty of a new crime, negligent failure to compile information? Instead, should the negligence allow a court to apply the collective knowledge doctrine, and find the company guilty of the substantive offense?

The problems involved in imposing even a negligence standard on corporations, in their obligation to collect employees' knowledge, require careful thought. For example, negligence applies a standard of reasonableness, but only based upon the facts known to the defendant at the time of the violation. *Manning v. Ashland Oil Co.*, 721 F.2d 192 (7th Cir. 1983) (applying Illinois law); W. Prosser, *Handbook of the Law of Torts* (4th ed. 1971), § 31 at 146. But incorporating the question of what facts were known risks a return to the entire collective knowledge problem. To resolve whether the corporation was unreasonable in ensuring that facts pertaining to potential violations were shared among employees, the jury must decide what facts about the sharing of information were known to the corporation.

If the corporation is to be considered negligent regarding the flow of information only if an individual employee were deemed negligent in that manner, there is no problem. But instead, should the jury be allowed to impute to the corporation all facts known to all employees, and to adjudge the corporation negligent if its actions would be considered unreasonable in light of all this information? In other words, can the jury apply a collective knowledge doctrine in deciding if the corporation is negligent in disseminating information? If so, the corporation would probably be deemed guilty any time the question is being asked.

The problem can be illustrated by the example of a corporation that files a discharge monitoring report. The signer believes that clean water was discharged. The tank operator knows the tank contains pollutants but does not know it was discharged. Under normal principles, no crime has been committed, but if this information is collected, the corporation has knowingly made a false statement. Suppose further that, as proposed above, the jury may aggregate all employees' knowledge only if the corporation is guilty of the negligent failure to collect information. If the report signer has made no efforts to determine the tank's contents from the operator, the signer acted negligently, which means under vicarious liability that the corporation acted negligently in collecting information. Under the hypothetical change in the law, the resultant use of the collective knowledge renders the corporation guilty.

But suppose that the corporation imposes and carefully enforces a strong policy requiring the sharing of information. On one occasion, the tank operator miscommunicates to the report signer but the miscommunication is non-negligent. Based on the information known to them, the information gatherers have acted quite reasonably. Therefore, the corporation is not vicariously negligent and the collective knowledge doctrine cannot be applied.

Under a hypothetical law, all the employees' knowledge may be pooled to determine what facts were known to the corporation, in deciding whether the corporation is negligently handling information flow. Then the knowledge that the tank contains pollutants, and the knowledge that the report is otherwise, are both known to the corporation, and it is negligent in not assuring that this information was transferred. In short, every time there is a failure to transmit information, the corporation will be deemed negligent, if we look, not to the negligence of individual employees, but instead to all facts known within the corporation. For the facts known by all individuals would reveal the lack of information flow and the fact that this lack has resulted in a potentially criminal act.

It thus appears that questions regarding negligent information flow (whether to establish a crime of its own, or as a prerequisite to using the collective knowledge doctrine) can only be asked through normal vicarious liability principles. Other problems arise if the jury may look, not just to the negligence of those employees entrusted with ensuring a proper flow of information, but the possible negligence of any employee.

The goal of this discussion was not to resolve the exact elements of the hypothetical new crime. Rather, it is to illustrate the complexities involved in revamping an entire body of law. If a decision were made to amend the criminal laws, such restructuring would require careful analysis. The courts, in their earnest desire to ensure and uphold a particular conviction, should not apply doctrines that may seem fair under the facts, but which threaten grossly unfair results under fact patterns not yet contemplated.

Endnotes

[1] *Riss* is notable for another reason. It frequently is cited, along with *United States v. Illinois Central R.R. Co.*, 303 U.S. 239 (1937) for the proposition that there need be no evidence of wrongful intent in malum prohibitum offenses, even though the statute requires proof of willfulness. *Riss* and *Illinois Central* do indeed lower the threshold for proof of willfulness, by eliminating the requirement that the government prove actual knowledge that the activity was prohibited. As the quoted language indicates, however, these cases merely lower the knowledge requirement, and slightly at that, but do not eliminate it. They require either an intentional disregard of a statute or plain indifference to its requirements. This latter standard is a far cry from what the government usually urges, namely eliminating from proof of willfulness any mental element regarding the statutory requirements. Included in the appendix are the defense and government briefs from *Schwitters*, which discuss in detail the meaning of "willfully."

□□□

IV. LITIGATION STRATEGIES

The problems inherent in corporate and other white collar criminal cases have become the frequent subject of continuing education seminars. Corporate counsel need to be attuned to various issues that may arise so they can turn to appropriate source material or a criminal defense expert when needed.

The potential issues are both myriad and complex. How, for example, should the corporation respond when a search warrant is executed at the company's premises? How does the company respond to grand jury subpoenas for corporate records? In particular, is there any way to assert Fifth Amendment privileges when faced with a records subpoena? When employees receive grand jury subpoenas, who, if anyone, can represent the employees? How should the corporation handle the issue of representation once particular officers become targets of the investigation?

If the company conducts an internal investigation, how can the attorney-client privilege be preserved? What tactics are appropriate to parallel proceedings, where the government is pursuing the company both civilly and criminally?

Each of these issues is fraught with peril, with significant consequences for the entire course of the proceedings. A slight mishandling of the internal investigation, for example, could result in a waiver of the attorney-client privilege, so that quite damning memoranda must be turned over to the government.

Corporate attorneys are trained in the world of civil litigation, where discovery is extremely broad, so they are likely to respond to a government investigation with openness. They later are shocked to discover that the government will turn over almost no discovery in return, even after charges are filed, and that the judge will not, and often cannot, order otherwise. Because the natural inclinations of civil lawyers may present exactly the wrong responses, these all are issues best handled by criminal defense experts.

This report will address a few aspects of litigation strategy that are peculiar to the government's attempts to expand the limits of corporate officer prosecution, as discussed in Chapter II. The collective knowledge doctrine is unlikely to have any particular implications for litigation strategies, other than making the defense much harder overall.

NEGOTIATING FOR THE OFFICER

To a great extent, negotiating with the prosecution on behalf of a corporate officer, when the prosecution invokes the responsible corporate officer doctrine, is no different from negotiating in any other case. A few aspects of negotiating do relate directly to the doctrines under discussion. For example, in its pursuit of individual defendants along with corporations, the prosecution frequently will assert that it will not allow the corporation to "buy off" the individual. At times, however, the government's negotiations belie this claim, and defense counsel should not ignore the possibility of pursuing a corporate guilty plea, with appropriate fines or other financial inducements, in exchange for dismissal or lesser charges against the individual defendants.

Where the proof against the officer is clear, a prosecutor who sincerely believes in emphasizing individual accountability will no doubt refuse to dismiss the individual's charges, no matter how attractive an inducement the corporation can offer. But counsel may be able to show the prosecution weaknesses in its case against the officers. Combining this with a guilty plea by the corporation, coupled with concessions that allow the government to claim a victory, may result in favorable treatment for the officers.

In a case where the government is pursuing the responsible corporate officer doctrine, part of defense counsel's negotiation posture will involve demonstrating a thorough grasp of these theories and awareness of their weaknesses. Convincing the government that it cannot establish culpability under traditional theories, combined with the ability to forcefully challenge the novel theories, certainly will help defense counsel.

An approach of "buying off" the individual should not breed cynicism. In fact, the prosecution's legitimate goals can be furthered by deals such as this. The resultant publicity can help with the government's deterrence mission. The mere fact of prosecution is sufficient to put fear into the hearts of most corporate officers, and one prosecution resulting in dismissal is unlikely to greatly reduce that fear.

A plea agreement can be structured to support the prosecution's aims even more directly. For example, in the *Pennwalt* prosecution, the corporation agreed to the maximum fine allowable by law, and in addition paid $600,000 into a trust fund to be used by the Coast Guard for enhancing radar imaging equipment in Puget Sound or purchasing spill response equipment. Thus, the case both generated significant publicity, supporting the goal of general deterrence, and directly contributed to the prevention of similar harms in the future.

It also is helpful if the offer is structured so that it does not resemble an attempt to "buy off" the individual defendants. If the offer is to provide some discrete benefit, rather than simply a sum of money, it has less of the appearance of using wealth to alter the justice system. For example, offering to endow a university chair in environmental law, or to supply a computer system needed for tracking laundered money, has far more psychological appeal than offering to pay $400,000 if the individual officer is dismissed. By acknowledging the validity of the prosecution's goals, and finding a way to advance those goals in a non-insulting way, counsel may be able to reach some accord that eliminates or limits the officers' liability.

The strict liability, or minimal liability, of the responsible corporate officer doctrine can be used advantageously in negotiating. Whenever defense counsel is negotiating, relative culpability is an issue. But it is particularly important here, for when counsel concedes that the government can find guilt under a responsible corporate officer doctrine, he is conceding little about his client's culpability. Luckily, the more traditional doctrines of criminal culpability comport with most people's innate sense of wrong. Thus, counsel may be able to make a psychological, as opposed to legal, appeal to the prosecutor, stressing how the client may be technically guilty, but not morally guilty.

In doing so, shifts are possible, such as conceding that the court will accept the validity of the responsible corporate officer doctrine. This allows an admission of guilt while still arguing how minimal that guilt is. The prosecutor may well believe he can convict under traditional doctrines, regardless of the responsible corporate officer doctrine. But by taking this approach, attorneys may shift the terms of the debate in their favor.

In addressing this issue, all the normal tools are used in establishing relative culpability: level of involvement, lack of prior involvement, objective indications of a good faith attempt to obey the law generally, and so forth. Such an approach may not result in a dismissal, but when combined with some of the suggestions made above, may have a significant effect on the plea bargain that can be reached.

NEGOTIATING FOR THE CORPORATION

The last point raised in relation to negotiating for the officer applies equally well in representing the corporation: Corporate counsel may be able to turn the strict liability of a corporation to their advantage. A corporation may be rendered guilty by an employee's crime, despite its best efforts to promulgate and enforce a policy of compliance. However, most prosecutors will not be immune to a demonstration that the corporation did everything possible to maintain a lawful operation. Once again, prosecutors generally entertain the same concepts of "fault" as everyone else, and if a disparity can be demonstrated between the client's legal culpability and its "moral" guilt, significant ground may be gained in negotiating a disposition.

The point is heightened in a collective knowledge case. There, the assumption is that no crime was committed except through the legal fiction of aggregating knowledge. The potential gulf between legal guilt and blameworthiness should be stressed through a detailed presentation of the client's efforts to maintain the proper flow of information.

TRIAL STRATEGY UNDER THE RESPONSIBLE CORPORATE OFFICER DOCTRINE

If, despite the points raised in Chapter II, the court decides to allow some sort of responsible corporate officer theory, defense counsel faces a task unlike that faced at virtually any trial. Normally, defending a client involves establishing that some particular act did not occur, that the defendant is not the one who performed it, or that he lacked a certain state of mind. None of these three defenses may be viable under a responsible corporate officer instruction.

In most prosecutions that will arise under this doctrine, little doubt is likely to exist about whether the violation occurred. Most environmental violations, for example, are indisputable, especially given the broad reach of the regulatory statutes. And establishing that a client had no personal involvement or no "guilty" state of mind may be of no help, because the corporate officer instruction is intended to eliminate just these elements.

How then is such a case defended? It greatly depends on the charge to the jury. Because the government often has not been specific about what it contends the corporate officer doctrine entails, this report can offer no firm guidelines. But some of the instructions the government has proposed in the past can be used as a basis for discussion.

The court might give an instruction modeled on the language in *Park* or *Dotterweich*, which requires that the officer stand in a responsible relation to the incident. The *Dotterweich* opinion notes how vague a standard it imposes: "It would be treacherous to define or even to indicate by way of illustration the class of employees which stands in such a responsible relation ... In such matters the good sense of prosecutors, the wise guidance of trial judges, and the ultimate judgment of juries must be trusted." 320 U.S. at 285.

One might suggest that it is equally treacherous to put a defendant's fate in the hands of prosecutors, judges, and juries, without more explicit guidance than the "responsible relation" test provides. Chapter II suggests that the Supreme Court never intended this imprecise test to supplant the elements of the crime in a non-strict liability offense. Nevertheless, if the trial court does give such an instruction, the jury will ultimately put flesh on this vague standard. It is up to counsel to convince the jury that the defendant did not stand in a responsible relation to the violation.

The government's position is likely to be that any officer is liable under this theory if his place in the chain of command is in line with the employees who physically committed the violation. At first glance, the government's position has a logical appeal. This is particularly true once one accepts the legitimacy of the *Park* instruction, predicating liability on having a "responsible relation" to the violation. If the plant manager had the responsibility to prevent unlawful discharges, and if the manager answers to the vice-president of the division under which the plant operates, the vice-president would likely be found to stand in a responsible relation to the plant's violations. The same logic would seem likely to apply to the president of the division and the CEO of the company.

As a technical matter this may be true, but the practicalities of a large corporation certainly are far different. The problem is that a jury probably will be pre-disposed to think of things the way the government argues. This difficulty combines with a general problem in white collar criminal trials: When the government focuses its investigative magnifying lens on a particular event in the defendant's life, blemishes inevitably appear. The jury presumes that these blemishes would have stood out to the defendant in real life in the same glaring manner that they appear to the jury under the tight focus of the trial.

It is counsel's job to rebut this appearance by bringing the realities of corporate management into the courtroom. Jurors need to be shown that, although their attention is being focused day after day on the violation, the client's situation was far different. Perhaps a technique can be borrowed from the personal injury plaintiffs' bar: Present the jury with a "day in the life" of the client. Let them know just how many decisions he faces, how many people operate under him. Discuss how many pieces of paper he signs a day and how many pages he is given to read.

If the case involves a faulty tank, as did *Pennwalt*, describe how many such tanks are technically under the defendant's aegis and how many decisions get made about each tank during its life span. But do not let the government confine the focus to tanks. How many items comparable to tanks also are nominally within the defendant's power? How many valves, pipes, and employees? Remind the jury how many things could go wrong in a day, but how few fail in even a year. How many other officers have responsibilities that touch on the tank? How much of the information employees garner about the tank do they fail to pass on to their superiors, despite corporate policies directing them to do so? In short, demonstrate the unfairness of the idea that the defendant can be considered "responsible" for every event that occurs under his chain of command.

However, this approach poses risks. It may open the door to proof of other mishaps, acts that might not otherwise be admissible. The defense is, "How can the defendant be called responsible for this one tank leak, when he has 10,000 tanks throughout the world, all supposedly under his control?" The court could well allow the prosecution to respond, "Yes, and he has known that 10 to 15 suffer significant leaks every year." Careful briefing might explain that such evidence is not proper rebuttal because it does not respond to the point, which is that the breadth of the client's "responsibilities" means he cannot really be held responsible for an individual event at a plant far away. Nevertheless, counsel needs to weigh the risk that such a litigation strategy will be held to have opened the door for a more harmful response by the prosecution.

The instruction the court gave in *Schwitters* allowed conviction if the defendant had the power to prevent a violation. This instruction could limit the defense even more than a "responsible relation" instruction. Read strictly, the only question becomes the corporate organizational chart and what powers it gives a particular officer. But even with this instruction, potentially there is room to maneuver.

If an officer had no knowledge of a potential violation, did he as a practical matter have any power to prevent it? The concept of "power to prevent" is sufficiently vague that the answer could be either "yes" or "no," and it should be up to the jury to decide. If so, this leaves room for an even broader defense than the "no responsible relation" defense, and the actual knowledge (although not the actual intent) of the client becomes completely relevant. The same evidence as suggested above would be presented, but establishing two different lessons: First, because of the practical complexities of the corporation, it is unfair to consider the defendant as standing in a "responsible relationship" to the event. Second, the lack of information that results from those practicalities means that he did not have the power to prevent the violation.

If the judge truly is committed to creating a strict liability offense, then he might exclude any defense of this nature. Even those judges who would accept the strict liability notions of the responsible corporate officer doctrine probably would, however, be uncomfortable with making the strict liability implications so explicit. While they may give unfavorable instructions, they are not likely to prevent counsel from presenting at least some elements of its defense.

The facts will not always justify a defense that involves distancing the officer from the violation. In some cases, the defendant may instead try to establish that he is not responsible because he was trapped by corporate policies, that he would have done something to prevent the violation but was hamstrung by higher officers. It is not clear that this constitutes a legal defense, although it was somewhat successful in the Oliver North trial. It may fit quite well into a theory that the defendent had no effective power to prevent the violation, given his dependence on the exercise of power by those above him. Or it may support a defense that the defendent did not stand in a responsible relation to the violation, because the policies restricting him denied him sufficient responsibility.

Even when not technically a defense, this approach may appeal to a jury enough that it serves as a grounds for an acquittal, as long as counsel can find some part of the instructions under which he can argue these facts. In essence, counsel is telling the jury that his client's only practical alternative was to quit, and that failure to do so should not be considered criminal. The sentencing implications of this position are discussed later in this chapter.

Pursuing this defense carries two dangers. First, if it does not succeed, it may alone serve as grounds for conviction, because the officer effectively will be admitting he had knowledge of, and at least the ostensible power to deal with, the violation. In addition, even if the defense has the potential for success with the jury, it presents defense counsel with a precarious balancing act. Counsel needs to establish that because the officer cannot be blamed for violations, the company strongly resisted his desire to rectify problems. On the other hand, if counsel paints too black a picture of the corporation policy, the jury may decide that the defendant should have quit and that his failure to do so justifies conviction.

In *Schwitters* and in *Cattle King*, the court gave the standard instructions on elements of the crime but also gave special instructions pertaining to corporate officers. The government in *Schwitters*, and the Tenth Circuit Court of Appeals in *Cattle King*, took the position that somehow the corporate officer instruction was not intended to supplant the elements instruction. If the government or trial court makes the same contention when counsel objects to the responsible corporate officer instruction, that can be turned to counsel's advantage. Argue the elements instruction clearly and forcefully to the jury. Tell them that the responsible corporate officer instruction only helps them interpret the elements instruction, and that ultimately they must find that the defendant knowingly discharged a pollutant, or whatever the particular elements of the crime might be.

The prosecution is unlikely to object, because that would be inconsistent with their attempt to justify the responsible corporate officer instruction. Should the prosecution object, or the court intervene, that will help build a record for appeal, demonstrating that the responsible corporate officer instruction was indeed an alternative not just a supplement to the charge on the elements.

Joint Defendants

Most prosecutions of corporate officers will involve charges against the corporation as well. The corporation usually has a deeper pocket, and its nearly strict liability for its employees' offenses virtually guarantees the prosecutor at least one conviction. Questions of severance, multiple representation, and coordination of strategies all are critical points that counsel in joint defendant trials must consider.

The corporation and corporate officer charged jointly frequently will be able to coordinate their defenses to mutual advantage. Usually, the corporation will not be trying to assign guilt to the officer, because the officer's guilt normally will lead automatically to the corporation's conviction. The two exceptions are (1) where the corporation tries to portray the officer as a renegade, acting in violation of clearly established and well-enforced policies (*see Chapter V*) or (2) where the corporation recognizes that conviction is inevitable, and is aiming at sentencing. In anticipation of sentencing, the corporation might try to distance itself from the officer as much as possible, so that its perceived responsibility, and therefore its punishment, is minimized.

The officer's defense may or may not be consistent with the company's. Normally, the officer is interested only in distancing himself from the violation, to show that in that sense, he is not "responsible." However, as discussed elsewhere in this Chapter, he may wish to present a "trapped by corporate policies" defense.

The ability to coordinate defenses can be significant. Normally, each defense counsel in a multi-defendant trial will make an opening statement at the beginning of the trial. They are not willing to wait for the close of the government's case before presenting their defense to the jury, and the distinct approaches of each defendant usually precludes relying on another defendant's attorney to present one's own side of the story. But the corporation frequently will have no defense beyond that which the corporate officer is presenting (the converse rarely is true; usually the officer will have specific points to make beyond those that help the corporation). Under these circumstances, the defense team can get two cracks at the jury. The officer's attorney can present a coordinated opening statement and then, before the presentation of defense evidence, corporate counsel can tell the entire story again, this time taking into account how the prosecution's case went.

Obviously, defense counsel can cooperate in numerous other ways. Because they are not peculiar to the defense of a corporate officer along with a corporation, they are more appropriately addressed in works more generally discussing trial tactics.

The responsible corporate officer instruction can potentially be used in obtaining a severance. Severance may be requested under Fed. R. Crim. P. 14 when joinder is prejudicial to a defendant. A common basis for such a motion is that much of the evidence will not be admissible against one defendant, but that the jury will have difficulty compartmentalizing this information. The motion, when grounded on this contention, is almost always denied.

In a responsible officer case, however, defense counsel may have a better basis for arguing that the evidence is far more difficult than usual for the jury to segregate. In the typical case, evidence is admissible against an individual either because he was personally involved, or because he is linked under a traditional vicarious liability theory—either that the evidence involves someone he aided and abetted, or someone else with whom he conspired. But in a responsible corporate officer case, the vicarious liability concept is much more intangible. The jury arguably would have a lot of trouble distinguishing between evidence that does not involve the defendant, and therefore cannot be considered against him, and evidence that does not involve the defendant, but may be considered against him anyway, because he stood in a "responsible relation" to the violation. This was exactly the basis for the severance in *United States v. Protex Industries, Inc.*

If the severance motion is denied pre-trial, the defense should not despair. To the limited extent that severances are ever granted, they may be easier to obtain mid-trial, when the court has a clearer picture of the evidence and how it affects the various defendants. Counsel therefore would want to build its record toward this end. Little point lies in building a record for appeal, because Rule 14 motions are subject to an abuse of discretion standard. Usually the same record that could be used on appeal will help convince the trial court, but to the extent the two goals conflict, counsel has a far greater chance with the trial court than on appeal.

Defense counsel should use every opportunity to let the trial court see how much of the evidence cannot be used against the defendant. For example, in *Protex*, the individual defendant was able to obtain limiting instructions 25 different times, stating that evidence was admissible only against the company. (In *Protex*, much of the evidence was not admissible against the individual defendant because he was not charged in several critical counts. Under many responsible corporate officer cases, the corporate officer will be charged in all or most counts in which the company is charged, in which case all or most of the evidence will be admissible against him.)

Limiting instructions are of arguable utility, because it generally is hard for a jury to limit the effect of evidence to only one defendant. Such instructions may even harm the defense case by unduly emphasizing the evidence. At times, the advantages and disadvantages of limiting instructions may make the issue almost a toss-up. If so, the ability to keep reminding the judge how unfair a joint trial is may tip the scale in favor of continually pushing for the instruction.

Counsel in *Protex* even obtained the prosecutor's stipulation that the entire testimony of half the witnesses was inadmissible against his client. This stratagem could backfire: The prosecution could then argue that, because the evidence came in discrete clumps, i.e. with entire witnesses' testimony either admissible or inadmissible against the defendant, it would not be that hard for the jury to compartmentalize the evidence concerning the defendant. Requesting such a stipulation requires another careful balancing for defense counsel, deciding whether it is more interested in emphasizing to the jury how little evidence there is against the defendant or instead more interested in convincing the judge that the defendant cannot obtain a fair joint trial. There are no easy answers; one must carefully consider the impact of strategy on obtaining an acquittal, on convincing the court of some legal position, and on the record for appeal. When one of these goals is highly unlikely to succeed, that may suggest altering strategy to increase the chances of establishing another goal.

Aggressive Briefing

Competent counsel do not need to be told that a hallmark of good advocacy is thorough research and briefing. This can require going to great lengths to establish a position. Looking simply to some of the secondary sources cited in this report, one would have wrongly concluded that the responsible corporate officer and collective knowledge doctrines are firmly established. The same obviously applies to the assertions made by the government in its briefs.

The meaning of *Frezzo Bros.*, as it applied to the *Schwitters* prosecution, is an excellent example. As discussed in Chapter II, the government frequently cites this case as an endorsement of the responsible corporate officer doctrine. An initial reading of the brief passage in the court of appeals decision seems to seal the issue in the government's favor. A careful reading of the trial court's published opinion on the motion for new trial, however, reveals that the issue presented to the court of appeals was a totally different point.

In *Schwitters*, it appeared this question was put to rest by citing to the published opinion from the *Frezzo Bros.* trial court. Yet the government continued to insist on its interpretation in its brief on appeal, without any reference to the history of the case. On appeal, defense counsel was able to convince the court of its position only by obtaining the *Frezzo Bros.* brief on appeal and the transcript of the objections to the instructions. Counsel included them in the record on appeal, leading the court to state unequivocally that "the issue of 'strict liability' or the necessary mens rea of the corporate officer was not argued to the Third Circuit."

Even this minor skirmish was not over. In a subsequent prosecution, the government once again cited *Frezzo Bros.* in support of its corporate officer instruction. The government also relied on the court's decision in *Schwitters* as an endorsement of this instruction, even though the opinion found that instruction to be grounds for reversal.

In *Schwitters*, the government engaged in other briefing tactics that required a thorough and aggressive response. It defended various jury instructions by citing to their use in other trials, although no decision was reported discussing the instructions in question. Contact with the defense attorneys in those cases revealed that the instructions had neither been objected to nor briefed by the defense, because the issues they involved, such as the definition of negligence, were not deemed relevant to the facts in dispute. In some cases, both sides had submitted the instruction.

The unlitigated giving of these instructions thus should have had no influence in a case where these elements were in dispute. Counsel submitted an affidavit documenting this situation, and this probably did much to brunt the government's citation to these other cases.

The inclusion of such an affidavit, a matter that was not part of the record in the court below, normally is unacceptable, just as unacceptable as the government's citation—for the first time on appeal—to unreported actions by another court. In *Schwitters*, the government stipulated to adding the affidavit to the record. Absent such a stipulation, counsel could file a motion to strike the offending portions of the government's brief. The facts regarding the other unreported cases could be included in an affidavit in support of the motion, thus explaining why the court should strike parts of the government's brief. Even if the motion is denied, the court still would get to see the defense affidavit and know why the government's authority is unreliable.

Normally, counsel only would need to go outside the reported record, for example by contacting counsel from another case, when the government has relied on unreported cases itself, such as the citation to instructions given by other trial judges. Sometimes, however, counsel might wish to contact the trial attorneys in a reported case. For example, the *Cattle King* opinion did not quote the responsible corporate officer instruction at issue in that case. Defense counsel in *Schwitters* obtained a copy from the *Cattle King* counsel, in hopes that the actual language of the instruction helped distinguish that case. In fact it did not, but had the language been helpful, a motion to augment the record, accompanied by the official transcript from the trial, would have been helpful.

Litigation Strategies for Sentencing

No matter how able the defense attorney, the majority of charged cases end up in a conviction, whether by guilty plea or by verdict at trial. Where the defendant is a corporation, the likelihood of conviction is even greater, given the lowered levels of culpability the law applies. Attorneys need to start thinking about sentencing strategy from the first hint of an upcoming charge.

As discussed in the introduction, the discretion of judges, particularly federal judges, has been severely circumscribed by the recent wave of determinate sentencing laws, such as the Sentencing Reform Act of 1984 (18 U.S.C. § 3551 et seq.). Nevertheless, ample room still exists for creative and effective representation in preparation for sentencing.

Several themes are almost certain to arise at sentencing. A dominant consideration is likely to be the harm resulting from the crime. Many crimes involving corporations or corporate officers may not result in any harm; the act is criminalized because it poses the potential for harm.

LITIGATION STRATEGIES

If in fact no harm has been demonstrated, this needs to be made clear to the court. Even more effective would be demonstrating that no harm has occurred. Do not hesitate to hire experts. It may be an environmental auditor, who can demonstrate that the pollutant in question is not harmful in the quantities discharged. Or it may be a stock market analyst, who can show that the public losses occasioned by insider trading were minimal.

In this regard, counsel may want to point out to the court the technical nature of the crime. For example, the defendant may have violated the Clean Water Act by causing discharges of a pollutant without a permit. But the same pollutant may be permitted for discharge by like companies throughout the region. The defendant did no more harm than anyone else; his sole crime was the failure to obtain the permit.

Presenting the above argument takes great care. Effective sentencing certainly requires an emphasis on mitigating factors, but it is essential that the defendant demonstrate contrition and acknowledge the wrongfulness of his acts. Maintaining the proper balance between these two requires careful planning of both the written and oral submissions.

It is unwise to allow the impression that the defendant thinks it is acceptable to discharge as long as no harm results. Counsel should keep reminding the court that his client does not believe he is above the law: He fully accepts the legitimacy of requiring such permits and his wrongfulness in failing to obtain one, regardless of the harm. But it also is important to keep stressing as a sub-theme that the ultimate goal of such laws is to prevent harm, and that no harm occurred in this case.

Yet another theme involves the willfulness of the client's act. The particular law may not have willfulness as an element of the crime, and the defendant may be guilty even if he had no knowledge that his act was wrongful. But the issue of willfulness, even when irrelevant to guilt, is highly relevant in determining the appropriate sentence. If people may reasonably be unaware of the regulation, counsel should emphasize that the client had received no warnings regarding the regulation.

As with the issue of harm, make clear that the defendant accepts his guilt, regardless of the lack of warnings. But it is advisable to stress the ways in which he has tried to keep up with the maze of regulations governing his industry. Where appropriate, counsel should get letters from government regulators in other areas of the law to develop the theme that the client is no scofflaw, but a businessperson struggling to help his employer comply with all regulations.

A third common defense theme is the steps the client has taken since the government investigation began. If the client has responded with a determined effort to change policies, stress this point. Frequently, corporate prosecutions take a long time to develop, and years may pass between violation and sentencing. If the company has instituted significant corrective measures and has been in compliance for several years, this can be critical in lessening the sentence.

With any sentencing theme, apply the same advocacy skills that would be used at trial. Most especially, emphasize the visual. Sentencing in complex cases tends to have a heavy emphasis on lengthy written submissions from the government, defense, and probation officer. It is quite easy in those circumstances for the court to lose sight of critical points, perhaps even more so than in a trial, where the evidence is gradually developed.

For example, when demonstrating post-violation compliance, photographs of the plant can be critical. Instead, counsel may be trying to develop the theme that his client's business is no less in compliance than all others in the industry, to support a claim that the client is unfairly being singled out. This theme could backfire, as the judge may decide that industry conditions call for a major deterrent message through a harsh sentence for this defendant. If this theme is to be developed, a few photographs of each plant will accomplish far more than lengthy declarations from investigators.

One critical aspect of sentencing involves the question of comparable sentences. In many areas of corporate crime, the sentencing judge has little experience with sentencing for like offenses. While the court will have sentenced white collar defendants for familiar crimes such as fraud, the spate of felony prosecutions for such matters as environmental violations still is quite new.

LITIGATION STRATEGIES

Being well-imbued with the doctrine of stare decises, judges, faced with a new issue, tend to do what other judges have done. A favored practice in environmental cases has been to present the sentencing judge with a table of sentences imposed in comparable cases. For the convenience of the court, this table usually is broken down by various categories, such as local versus national, or by the statute involved. This practice often involves using, as a supplemental source, tables presented by other attorneys in other cases. Counsel who have handled high profile cases usually are quite willing to share their pleadings. If not, sentencing submissions normally are part of the public record and can be obtained from the court clerk. Once such a table is assembled, whether created for the case or obtained from other counsel, it is a relatively simple matter to update it and cull out the older or irrelevant cases.

The government's sentencing memoranda also are excellent sources. The government will have presented the facts of the other cases in an egregious light, which will help defense counsel support his point that the sentence in his case, which is arguably less egregious, deserves a lesser sentence than imposed in those previous cases. An example of a sentencing table is presented as Appendix A.

As in any good advocacy, counsel must avoid overreaching at sentencing. Omitting critical, comparable cases where high sentences were imposed means risking a strong response from the prosecution and a resulting loss of credibility with the court.

On the other hand, counsel should point out overreaching by the prosecution. Frequently, the prosecution asks for sentences far out of line with what the courts have imposed. Demonstrating this with data is important because of the possibility that the court would see both sentencing proposals, the prosecution's and the defense's, as reasonable ones, and attempt to find an appropriate middle ground. Counsel should seek to establish that the prosecution's recommendation is not even reasonable, as measured by the arguably objective standard of what other courts had done. The aim is to convince the court that the prosecution's recommendation is basically a ploy, an attempt to get the court to split the difference. When available, one could present the court with an appendix to one's sentencing memorandum comparing each of the government's sentencing recommendations in past cases with the sentence actually imposed.

Sometimes difficulties in defending the corporation or the corporate officer, arising from the state of the law, can work to counsel's advantage when facing sentencing. In the *Marine Power* case (See Case Studies, Chapter VI), the decision to plead was prompted largely by the court already having, in another case, issued various rulings on liability under the Clean Water Act, the statute at issue in *Marine Power*. These rulings precluded much of the proposed defense. Counsel also recognized that even if all the liability rulings had gone counsel's way, the corporate officers might be convicted under normal standards of liability. The guilty plea was expressly predicated on the responsible corporate officer doctrine. At sentencing, this position allowed the presentation of a full factual defense, demonstrating that the corporate officers had no personal liability for the violations that occurred.

Even where the client pleads, or is convicted, under a theory of personal complicity, the standard of liability is often far lower than the standard to which the sentencing judge is accustomed. Misdemeanors under the Clean Water Act require mere negligence,[1] and the Rivers and Harbors Act establishes a strict liability offense. These are types of malfeasance for which the normal theories of criminal punishment simply are inapplicable. The court may be nominally aware of, but not fully appreciate, the distinction between the defendant's crime and most crimes that come before the judge.

Even putting aside crimes that entail an obvious criminal intent, such as crimes of violence, most white collar crimes require proof of knowing or willful conduct, and many have an element of "specific intent," where a deliberate intent to violate the law must be shown. Clearly, a sharp distinction exists between these more typical criminal mental states and to what mental state the defendant may have admitted. For example, negligence involves mere unreasonableness; gross negligence requires awareness of substantial risk; and strict liability means the defendant is not guilty of any wrongful act or mind-set, but simply that some prohibited result has occurred.

Counsel needs to develop this theme fully and forcefully, to ensure that his client is punished only for the level of culpability he actually demonstrated. Remind the court how rare it is that negligence, for example, is criminalized.

However, the defendant's admission to negligence, or to a strict liability offense, does not mean that the court will accept this as the extent of his culpability. The court is directed to consider all relevant conduct of the defendant, not just that set forth in the counts underlying the conviction. Federal Sentencing Guidelines, § 1B1.3. By stressing the low level of culpability the statute entails, counsel invites the prosecution to demonstrate the higher level of culpability that it contends the defendant actually demonstrated.

Arguing the actual culpability of the defendant is part of any sentencing and needs no special attention in this report. The point is to be aware that, where the crime involves such a minimal threshold for guilt, the disparity between the elements charged and the act for which the client is sentenced may be far greater than in most criminal cases. One cannot rely upon the low culpability required for conviction, and must be prepared to address what the court will see as the actual crime.

Charges against middle-level managers present their own considerations. Previously in this chapter, the report discussed a potential trial strategy for such defendants, emphasizing their powerlessness to remedy the corporation's problems. Whatever weakness this strategy may have in seeking an acquittal, it offers a lot in approaching sentencing.

Properly presented with the dilemma between losing one's job and countenancing violations, convinced of the relative powerlessness of the manager in question, a court might well see such an individual as closer to an employee than a corporate officer, and exercise discretion in his favor.

To some extent, prosecutors exercise their discretion in recognition of the employee's potential dilemma. Prosecutions of lower-level employees are rare, except where the employee was clearly acting on his own. But middle-level managers may be faced with the same dilemma as lower-level employees. Unfortunately for them, while they may be powerless to actually change illegal company practices, they often possess sufficient trappings of responsibility to attract the prosecutor's attention.

Some prosecutors have a policy, explicit or implicit, that they will not prosecute someone who directly informs his superiors of violations and urges corrective actions. Clearly, this approach makes sense in terms of the prosecutor's goals. It creates an incentive for middle-level management to generate documents that present proof that higher-level management has knowledge of illegalities, proof that frequently is lacking or highly circumstantial.

Whether this position makes sense in terms of broader policy issues is more questionable. In many cases, it may not solve the manager's dilemma: Generating such documents may be nearly as likely to threaten his job as a direct resignation, and thus as difficult to contemplate. On the other hand, these documents may not only create the paper trail of establishing knowledge where knowledge already exists; they may also serve the socially beneficial goal of bringing knowledge of problems to those who do have the power to change them.

But because this prosecutive "policy," if it does exist, is not widely known, it can operate unfairly on the middle-level manager who is fully aware that upper-level managers know of the problem but have declined to correct it. Such a manager is no more culpable for failing to paper his files than a manager who does, yet the former is prosecuted while the latter apparently will not be. If counsel can point to such a policy, he should stress the unfairness of prosecuting the client based on a factor so unrelated to culpability.

Even where the issue of memos to supervisors does not arise, counsel frequently can assist the middle-level manager client by establishing his powerlessness to prevent the violations. In doing so, counsel runs into the same two problems noted in discussing this approach in the context of the trial: (1) Counsel must, in effect, admit that the client's knowledge of the potential violation to present this sentencing pitch;[2] and (2) The worse counsel makes the company look, in trying to show the client's inability to change things, the worse it looks to the judge that this client chose violations over quitting. If the client's knowledge of events cannot effectively be disputed, the first of these problems evaporates. The second requires maintaining a careful balance in all cases.

Sometimes the client's powerlessness is not a function of corporate intransigence but simply a matter of his job authority. In that case, no real negatives exist in pursuing this approach at sentencing.

REPRESENTING THE CORPORATE OFFICER AT THE CORPORATION'S GUILTY PLEA

As mentioned in the introduction, at least one federal judge has refused to accept a corporation's plea unless that plea was personally entered by the president of the company. The resulting nationwide publicity has led other judges to adopt a similar practice. (The case, *United States v. Pennwalt*, is discussed in more detail in Case Studies, Chapter VI.)

Normally, a corporation may appear through its counsel in a criminal case. Fed. R. Crim. P. 43(c)(1). The usual practice is for counsel entering a guilty plea on behalf of the corporation to present a ratification from the board of directors.

The court's decision to require a personal appearance by a high corporate official is understandable. The goals of both special and general deterrence are arguably furthered when an individual officer must publicly take responsibility for the corporation's acts. But significant potential exists for self-incrimination problems in such a personal appearance.

The problem lies in the language of Rule 11, Federal Rules of Criminal Procedure and Rule 410, Federal Rules of Evidence. Rule 11(e)(6) states that, with exceptions not relevant here:

> [E]vidence of the following is not, in any civil or criminal proceeding, admissible against the defendant who made the plea or was a participant in the plea discussions: (A) a plea of guilty which was later withdrawn; (B) a plea of nolo contendere; (C) any statement made in the course of any proceedings under this rule regarding either of the foregoing pleas; or (D) any statement made in the course of plea discussions with an attorney for the government which do not result in a plea of guilty or which result in a plea of guilty later withdrawn.

FRE 410 has comparable language.

In other words, everything the corporate officer says at the guilty plea would be admissible against him in other proceedings, unless the plea were later withdrawn.[3] Such other proceedings could include a civil suit, either brought privately or by the government, or criminal charges. A guilty plea requires that the court "mak[e] such inquiry as shall satisfy it that there is a factual basis for the plea," F.R.Cr.P. 11(f). Most certainly, then, the corporate officer may be asked questions about the violation. The possibility for making statements that will subject him to civil or criminal liability should be evident.

Certainly, corporate officers could seek some legal protections. Because the corporation is pleading guilty, a plea agreement presumably exists, and the prosecution may be willing, as part of that agreement, to promise not to prosecute the corporate officer. This would protect him from criminal prosecution but not from civil use of his admissions at the guilty plea. Civil protection possibly could be obtained through a grant of formal immunity, if the prosecution were agreeable to obtaining an immunity offer.[4]

While these procedures may be legally sufficient, from other perspectives they may be unpalatable to the corporation or the officer. Seeking immunity connotes guilt to many people. It may be personally disturbing to the corporate officer; it may significantly compound the public relations problems the plea itself poses for the corporation.

If faced with a judge who insists that some corporate officer personally enter a plea, it may be possible to reach some accommodation as to which individual will appear. The ideal choice would be someone unconnected with the violation, either personally or by position (lest his statements support later proceedings under a responsible corporate officer theory). Such a choice, however, may be antithetical to the goals of the judge. In trying to "put a face on corporate crime," (as *The New York Times* described the *Pennwalt* events), the judge may wish to expose the corporate officer most connected with the crime.

Through properly deferential maneuvering, counsel may be able to work around this conflict between the judge's goals and counsel's goal of protecting the corporate officer.[5] Point out to the judge the problem posed in this section; it may be that the judge simply did not consider the self-incrimination implications of requiring an officer to appear.

If the court is insistent on having an officer present, counsel may be able to convince the judge that the best face to put on corporate crime is the individual highest up the corporate ladder, rather than the one most connected to the violation.[6]

Ultimately, a defense attorney's greatest bargaining chip may be the choice between trial and a plea. Presumably, however much the court wants an individual to appear for the plea, the court wishes even more to avoid a trial. So does the corporate client, so in negotiating with the courts, counsel must be careful not to squander the plea bargain possibility.

The prosecution, for once, can be an ally, or at worst, an innocent bystander. Having negotiated a plea with the corporation, the prosecution will not be inclined to gear up again for trial. Presumably they will have decided that, regardless of the judge's goals, their goals of general and special deterrence are sufficiently served by the plea agreement. At this stage of the proceedings, their major interest will be in protecting the plea agreement, regardless of who appears.

Endnotes

[1] It is still an open question whether the act requires gross negligence or garden-variety tort negligence. Tort negligence is simply the failure to protect others against unreasonable risk of harm, applying the standard of conduct of a reasonable person under like circumstances. Restatement (Second) of Torts, § 282, 283. Gross negligence involves awareness of a substantial and unjustifiable risk. "The risk must be of such a nature and degree that the defendant's failure to perceive it, considering the nature and purpose of his conduct and the circumstances known to him, involves a gross deviation from the standard of care that a reasonable person would observe in the defendant's position." Model Penal Code, § 2.02(d) (American Law Institute, 1985). The differences between these two standards are significant.

While the court ruled in *Schwitters* that proof of simple negligence sufficed, that decision has no precedential value, and to the author's knowledge, no other court has ruled on the question. Strong arguments are to be made that Congress intended to require proof of gross negligence, which is the standard for criminal negligence under the laws of most jurisdictions. See Appendix, the government's and defendant's *Schwitters* briefs, which discuss this issue in detail.

[2] Technically, defense counsel need not admit the client's knowledge to make this sentencing presentation. But it is quite difficult to deny knowledge of the violation and at the same time stress how the client could not have prevented the violation, even if he had known about it. The "lack of knowledge" defense makes the "inability to prevent" defense seem irrelevant, and reliance on the "inability" defense suggests to the judge that counsel does not expect the court to believe the "lack of knowledge" defense.

[3] Even if the plea were later withdrawn or were a nolo contendere plea, the statements might be admissible against the corporate officer in an action brought personally against him. The rule, in making evidence inadmissible against the defendant, appears to be talking about the defendant who is pleading guilty, not the defendant in the later civil or criminal proceeding. (If the rule were referring to the defendant in the later proceedings, the rule would not address the issue of evidence admitted against the individual, were he to become a civil plaintiff.) However, it is the corporation, not the corporate officer, who is the criminal defendant in the situation we are assuming. Thus, the corporate officer may not receive the protections of the rule even in the limited circumstances it covers. Presumably, the authors of the rule never contemplated the situation of an individual speaking on behalf of another defendant. Yet that is the situation created by judges following the *Pennwalt* precedent.

[4] Title 18 U.S.C. § 6002 allows grants of immunity to a "witness." It is not clear that an officer speaking on behalf of a corporation in a plea of guilty constitutes a "witness." However, since Rule 11 authorizes the court to ask questions in establishing a factual basis, one could argue that the officer is a witness in this circumstance.

[5] An obvious potential for conflict exists between the corporation's interests in ensuring a successful guilty plea and the corporate officer's interests in protecting himself from future liability. Counsel for the corporation should be extremely leery of representing the officer's interests; obtaining separate counsel seems a most prudent step.

[6] Under a broad view of the responsible corporate officer doctrine, someone at the apex of the corporate pyramid is "responsible" for everything occurring below, so presenting the highest officer as spokesman at the plea may not insulate him from prosecution.

□□□

V. PREVENTIVE MEASURES

In many realms of the law, one of the attorney's most worthwhile functions is advising the client on how to avoid future problems. Criminal defense lawyers, however, usually are called in only after the problem has arisen, when their task is to try to get the client out of trouble. However, given the highly regulated nature of most industries, violations of the law are virtually certain to occur. And given the state of the criminal law as it pertains to corporations, a defense to violations frequently is difficult to mount. It thus behooves the corporation to take steps to detect violations and to correct them.

Advice as to potential law violations is not so much an issue of criminal law, but a question of the substantive law in the particular area of regulation, be it defense contracting, banking, hazardous wastes, or anti-trust. Thus, advice at this stage normally will come from corporate counsel with expertise in the industry in question. But the criminal defense lawyer also can provide important input because detecting violations can have an impact on any criminal prosecutions that might develop.

The advantages of a compliance audit extend far beyond the potential for avoiding criminal prosecution. The risks of tort liability—civil penalties, costs of correction, and bad public relations—all are important considerations in motivating a corporation to ensure compliance with the law.

However, from the criminal defense perspective, a compliance audit poses significant dangers. If such an audit ends up in the hands of the government, it may be the method by which the prosecution learns of a criminal violation and decides to pursue the case. Even if the prosecution discovers the violation through another source, the written compliance audit could become "exhibit A" at trial—direct proof that the corporation was aware of the violation. Because the mental element of the crime often is the only possible source of a defense to a corporate criminal charge, an admissible compliance audit could determine the course of the prosecution.

The most viable method of protecting the audit is through the attorney-client privilege. The leading case is *Upjohn Co. v. United States*, 449 U.S. 383 (1981), which itself involved a compliance audit, this time of an investigation into possible illegal payments by foreign subsidiaries to foreign officials. The court rejected the "control group" test that had been applied by most courts of appeals, and instead concluded that the attorney-client privilege held by a corporation can include conversations with any employees.

While declining to set down a broad rule, *Upjohn* discussed a number of factors relevant to resolving the privilege question. In *Upjohn*, the communications were made (1) by corporate employees, (2) at the direction of their superiors, (3) to corporate counsel, acting as attorneys, (4) in order for the corporation to obtain legal advice from the attorneys, (5) with the employees' knowledge of this purpose, (6) involving matters within the scope of the employees' corporate duties, and (7) confidentially and kept that way.

The lower courts, in applying *Upjohn*, have not treated these factors as dispositive, and have upheld the privilege as long as the totality of the circumstances suggested the investigation was undertaken to render legal advice to the corporation. Nevertheless, it is best to document the purpose of the inquiry in a letter to counsel, and to instruct employees in writing regarding their obligation to talk with counsel and to keep the communication confidential. Care should be taken to distinguish this advice from an instruction not to discuss the underlying facts. The latter instruction might be viewed as obstruction of justice or witness tampering.

While it may not be necessary for purposes of establishing the privilege, it might be best to advise employees that they hold no personal privilege for the communication to counsel and that management may disclose the employees' comments if desired. This helps make clear that the employees know that counsel is serving only as corporate counsel, and not as the employees' own counsel.

While the range of people whose communications are covered by the privilege is large, the range of those who, by disseminating the communication, can waive the privilege also is large. Presumably, only those in management would be deemed to have authority to waive the privilege, but the corporation would be advised to carefully limit the audience for the compliance audit, and to expressly instruct recipients that they may not divulge its contents without explicit permission from the board of directors.

It probably is best to have the audit conducted by outside counsel. Because in-house counsel frequently hold other corporate positions, having outside counsel makes it more clear that the audit is being conducted by counsel only in his capacity as legal counsel. While it may seem obvious when stated, counsel and management should be aware that if new management is installed, it will hold the sole power to waive the privilege, even over the objections of the previous management.

A host of related issues pertain to how the civil regulatory agency will respond to the compliance audit. Will it, for example, seek to obtain access to audits, or, on the other hand, agree to reduce oversight or enforcement actions in order to encourage self-auditing? For a discussion of these questions as they relate to environmental audits, see C. Price, and A. Danzig, "Environmental Auditing: Developing a 'Preventive Medicine' Approach to Environment Compliance," 19 *Loyola of Los Angeles Law Review* 1189-1212 (June 1986). Several books also discuss environmental compliance audits, primarily from the practical, rather than the legal standpoint. These include H. Blakeslee & T. Grabowski, *A Practical Guide to Plant Environmental Audits* (1985); J. Greeno, G. Hedstrom & M. DiBerty, *Environmental Auditing-Fundamentals and Techniques* (1985); L. Harrison, *The McGraw-Hill Environmental Auditing Handbook* (1984); T. Truitt, D. Berz, D. Weinberg, J.B. Molloy, G. Goldman, G. Price, and B. Florence, *Environmental Audit Handbook — Basic Principles of Environmental Compliance Auditing* (2d ed. 1983).

The issue we discuss should not be confused with normal recordkeeping. Many regulatory statutes have provisions requiring in-house monitoring, recordkeeping, and self-reporting, and also allowing agency access. Records generated pursuant to such requirements would certainly not qualify for a privilege. It is only the special audit, conducted for the purpose of obtaining legal advice, which could be protected.

PROTECTING THE CORPORATION WITH CORPORATE POLICY

The second area in which defense counsel can possibly provide prophylactic advice pertains to one viable defense: that the employee's criminal act was in violation of corporate policy. As discussed in Chapter III, a corporation is not exonerated just because the employee's acts are contrary to stated company policy.

However, corporate policy may be relevant to the "intent to benefit" prong of corporate vicarious liability. The most explicit statement in that regard is in *Beusch*, 596 F.2d at 878. In that case, the corporation challenged a jury instruction on the ground that it imposed strict liability for the employee's acts. The court observed as follows:

> [The instruction] does not impose strict liability on [the corporation] without proof of intent. Rather, it suggests that a corporation may be liable for acts of its employees done contrary to express instructions and policies, but that the existence of such instructions and policies may be considered in determining whether the employee in fact acted to benefit the corporation. Merely stating or publishing such instructions and policies without diligently enforcing them is not enough to place the acts of an employee who violates them outside the scope of his employment. It is a question of fact whether measures taken to enforce corporate policy in this area will adequately insulate the corporation against such acts, and we see no reason to disturb the jury's finding in this regard.

Accordingly, if a corporation has indeed diligently enforced its instructions and policies, it should be entitled to defend on the ground that the employee acted outside the scope of his employment. It also should be entitled to a jury instruction setting forth the principles of *Beusch*. Cf. *Hilton Hotels*, 467 F.2d at 1007:

> For these reasons we conclude that as a general rule a corporation is liable under the Sherman Act for the acts of its agents in the scope of their employment, even though contrary to general corporate policy and express instructions to the agent .... Appellants could not gain exculpation by issuing general instructions without

undertaking to enforce those instructions by means commensurate with the obvious risks.

The clear import of *Beusch* and *Hilton Hotels* is that, when a corporation does undertake to enforce a policy, it should be allowed to present such evidence, to aid the jury in applying the law that says the corporation need not be held liable for acts done contrary to policy.

The Fourth Circuit also has endorsed the *Beusch* approach. In *United States v. Basic Construction Co.*, 711 F.2d 560 (4th Cir. 1983), the district court gave an instruction virtually identical to that given in *Beusch*. The company contended on appeal that the jury should consider its compliance policy in determining whether the company had the requisite intent. While the court rejected that position, it held that "the district court properly allowed the jury to consider Basic's alleged antitrust compliance policy in determining whether the employees were acting for the benefit of the corporation." 711 F.2d at 573. However, the Third Circuit approved a jury instruction that expressly stated that corporate directives were not a defense. *United States v. American Radiator & Standard Sanitary Corp.*, 433 F.2d 174, 204-05 (3d. Cir. 1970), cert. denied, 401 U.S. 948 (1971). The decision precedes *Beusch* and *Hilton Hotels*, and does not really discuss this aspect of the instruction, so possibly could be viewed as not being binding precedent on the issue.

The model instructions that have addressed the issue have been far more pro-prosecution than the case law on which they rely. For example, Seventh Circuit Model Instruction 5.03 (a) contains the following sentence in parentheses:

> If the agent was acting within the scope of his employment, the fact that the agent's act was illegal, contrary to his employer's instructions, or against the corporation's policies will not relieve the corporation of responsibility for it.

Even without this parenthetical addition, the instruction appears to make the corporation's liability result automatically if the agent's acts are within his authority and with the intent to benefit the corporation. Similarly, former Model Ninth Circuit Instruction 5.10[1] did not inform the jury that corporate policies and instructions are relevant to deciding whether the corporation is vicariously liable for the agent. The instruction therefore eliminated the defense that *Beusch* specifically allowed. The instruction in *Beusch* stated:

> A corporation may be responsible for the acts of its agents done or made within the scope of its authority, even though the agent's conduct may be contrary to the corporation's actual instruction or contrary to the corporation's stated policies.
>
> You may, however, consider the corporate policies and instructions as one of the circumstances along with any other circumstances that you find to be significant in determining what the authority of the agent actually was and whether the agent was acting on behalf of the corporation.
>
> In order to be acting within the scope of his authority, the employee must be found to be acting on behalf of the corporation with the purpose of benefiting the corporation or serving some corporate purpose.

The Ninth Circuit's commentary did not even address the inconsistency between the Model Instruction and *Beusch*. The commentary to the Seventh Circuit instruction, however, concedes that the circuit...

> has never considered the question whether or to what extent a corporation should have a defense if it could show that the agent's conduct had been contrary to corporate policy. (The Seventh Circuit may construe at least some criminal offenses as imposing a duty upon the corporation to prevent intentional offenses by its employees and that [sic] it may further hold that a corporation will not satisfy the duty by merely instructing its agents not to commit the prohibited acts. Naturally, this instruction should be modified if any criminal offense is interpreted differently.)

The Seventh Circuit is at least more open than the Ninth about the lack of case authority for its model instructions. In the early 1980's, several circuits established committees that developed model instructions, supposedly to simplify and clarify the instructions then in use. The two examples cited typify the extent to which this activity was as much an attempted revamping of criminal law as it was a simplification of jury instructions. However, the model instructions are not binding precedent, and can be resisted when their substance is not supported by precedent.

Although many district court judges seem strongly wedded to the Model Instructions, proper briefing on *Beusch's* holding may get counsel an instruction consistent with its principles.

Of course, promulgation of policies mandating compliance with the law has two distinct benefits. First, it is a legitimate part of the corporation's goal of avoiding violations and prosecutions. But should violations occur anyway, these actions may provide a legal buffer between the corporation and the employee-violator, thus possibly protecting the corporation from conviction. If, despite the thesis of Chapter II, the strict liability version of the corporate officer doctrine gains in application, acquitting the corporation may be the only way to protect the corporate officer from conviction.[2]

Hiring of Independent Contractors

Another area in which the criminal defense attorney can provide the corporation with prophylactic advice is the hiring of independent contractors.

A relatively unlitigated issue is when a corporation may be liable for the acts of others beyond its employees, e.g., independent contractors. This question is likely to arise with more frequency in the future, given the prosecutorial trends discussed in this report and the greater political value of targeting a corporation rather than its independent contractors. When some small contractor allegedly commits a violation, an indictment against the hiring corporation is likely.

Seventh Circuit Model Instruction 5.03 states that corporations are liable for the acts of agents, and defines agents as "the officers, directors, employees, or other persons who may be authorized to act for the corporation." This would appear to include all independent contractors, who are of course authorized to act for the corporation. Former Ninth Circuit Model Instruction 5.10 (1985 edition) made corporations vicariously liable for the acts of "agents, that is, its employees, officers or other authorized representatives" without ever defining the term "authorized representatives."

If it is valid to render a corporation vicariously liable for the acts of employees, then a corporation also would at times be liable for the acts of others, such as independent contractors. The mere form of the relationship presumably should not control. But what principles should govern in instructing a jury on this issue?

As discussed above, the doctrine of corporate criminal liability is grounded in the analogy to tort law. *New York Central,* 212 U.S. at 493-94. The general principle in tort law is that "the critical factor in making this determination [as to liability of the contractor's hirer] is the authority of the principal to control the detailed physical performance of the contractor." *Logue v. United States,* 412 U.S. 521, 527-28 (1973).

Applying this tort approach in criminal law makes sense from a policy standpoint. If the principal has authority to control the contractor in the areas that led to the alleged violation, the principal had the ability to prevent the violation and, from a deterrence or punishment standpoint, is one deserving to take the blame. (By analogy to corporate employees, see Chapter II, the contractor presumably could not escape liability on the grounds that the principal could have prevented the violations, or even that the principal authorized the violations.)

But where the contractor has the expertise and the authority to control the details that result in the violation, no solid ground exists for making the principal liable. The government's current approach would seek liability here, too, because the government appears to believe that placing liability on as many parties as possible increases the chances that some party will prevent the violation. This approach ignores the costs involved in putting potential liability on so many parties: Corporations will become unduly hesitant to undertake worthwhile activities involving independent contractors, because the risk of criminal penalties, a risk the corporation cannot control, threatens the activity's economic viability.

United States v. Georgetown University, 331 F. Supp. 69 (D.C. Cir. 1971) is the only reported case to tackle this issue. The university was charged with a violation of the Rivers and Harbors Act, a strict liability offense, based upon the discharge of oil from a heating system that was being installed. The work was performed by independent contractors. The court acquitted the university, holding,

> When one is not in control of facilities which lead to a violation of statutes like those in the case at bar, ultimate result or damage to persons or property should be examined in the light of the Congressional policy to impose strict liability upon only those corpora-

tions or individuals who have it peculiarly within their power through the exercise of due diligence to protect the public. To stretch the instant statutes to their logical extreme would be to allow the Government to criminally indict even the most unrelated persons in business entities instead of the real perpetrator.

331 F. Supp. at 73.The court looked to the Restatement Second of Agency, § 220 and Comment B to that section, which explains that not all independent contractors are agents, and looked to the element of control. The court analogized the university's situation to that of an owner who contracts with a builder to construct his house, where the work is controlled by the contractor.[3]

The issue was squarely presented in *Schwitters,* discussed in Chapter II and in Case Studies, Chapter VI. There, the crime was the discharge of sandblasting grit, where some of the sandblasting had been done by an independent contractor. The trial court refused to define the term "authorized representatives" from former Ninth Circuit Model Instruction 5.10. On appeal, the court did not resolve the broader question of how an appropriate jury instruction should read. Instead, the court held that there was no error on the facts of the case, given that all the sandblasting violations involved use of the corporation's dock and materials. But the ruling ignores that the jury was not allowed to decide if those facts mean that the corporation had the necessary control over the contractor.

Thus, the law in this area is somewhat uncertain. How, then, should corporations respond? A court, before which a corporation might stand as a defendant, could choose between two approaches. If it adopts the government's approach, it will simply make corporations liable for all acts of independent contractors. In that case, the corporation can do nothing in advance, other than to try to prevent the occurrence of violations.

> On the other hand, if a court carefully analyzes this issue, using the tort law analogy, it will submit a jury instruction that predicates liability on the extent of control exercised by the hiring corporation. This might seem to put the corporation on the horns of a dilemma: The more control it exercises, the more it can ensure no violation exists, but the more control it exercises, the more likely that it will be found liable for any violation.[4]

However, this dilemma may not actually exist. It assumes a corporation that normally would have had the authority to control the contractor's work has released that authority in order to reduce the corporation's criminal exposure. In such circumstances, the court would look askance at, and probably completely reject, the proposed defense. That would be a correct result from the perspectives of both policy and precedent. In terms of the principle relied on in *Georgetown University*, namely the hiring firm's authority, the court surely would interpret this to mean the initial authority.

The voluntary relinquishment of that authority, especially for such questionable motives, would not undo the fact that the corporation did in fact have that authority, at least at one point. And where a contractor normally has his employer exercise control, shifting control to the contractor probably would increase the likelihood of improper methods, so from a policy standpoint, such a stratagem should be discouraged.

It thus seems extremely risky for a corporation to alter its dealings with independent contractors, simply in anticipation of a *Georgetown University* defense. Still, counsel can give some prophylactic advice. In all circumstances, the relationship between the corporation and the contractor should be documented as carefully as possible. The corporation should take care not to assume authority over the contractor that normally would not exist. This includes both the explicit assertion of authority and the informal exercise of control, even by low-level employees. Employees should be instructed to allow the contractor to carry out his tasks without interference, except in emergencies.

PROTECTING CORPORATE OFFICERS WITH CORPORATE POLICY

Corporate policy, as established before the alleged crime, could be relevant to the criminal trial in one other way. As discussed in Chapter II, some prosecutors seek to make a corporate officer culpable, not based on anything the officer did, but based on his status in the corporation. It follows that corporate policy regarding an officer's status could play a significant role in determining guilt.

Whether formally or informally, corporate policies normally will define the areas of responsibility for each corporate officer. Corporate counsel should carefully review these, perhaps with the guidance of criminal counsel, to anticipate how these policies would implicate a criminal trial. For one thing, counsel should ensure that the policies reflect reality: If a corporate officer plays no practical role in ensuring environmental compliance, his duties most definitely should not be defined as including that role. In addition, duties probably should be defined as narrowly and as precisely as possible. If every officer's duties can be read as encompassing nearly everything, then every officer risks reading his name on an indictment, based solely on his status as a "responsible" officer.

Such an approach has one disadvantage. It clearly will single out one or more persons as responsible. This will focus the prosecution's attention during the charging decision, and will make it far harder for that officer to deny responsibility (in this broad sense of the word) at trial. However, in the absence of such clearly defined policies, the current climate risks the prosecution and the jury finding nearly every officer "responsible." Adopting clear role definitions has far more potential for rightly exculpating some than for helping to inculpate any, rightly or wrongly.

From a policy standpoint, as opposed to a criminal defense perspective, it probably is to the corporation's (and society's) benefit that the responsibility of the appropriate officer be highlighted. This makes it more likely that he will carefully scrutinize everything under his realm of responsibility, thus reducing the risk of violations. As discussed, the corporation probably will be held liable for any such violations, no matter how careful it, as an institution, has been. Instilling due care with the appropriate officer thus benefits the corporation.

While this approach can serve the useful function of dividing responsibility horizontally, it may be less efficacious in limiting responsibility vertically. In other words, the corporation may clearly designate who, among middle-level management, is responsible for environmental compliance. But the corporation may have far more trouble convincing a prosecutor or a jury that that officer's supervisor is not a "responsible" officer, no matter how strongly corporate job descriptions may seek to establish otherwise.

The prosecution is likely to evince an attitude that ultimate responsibility rests at the top of the corporate ladder. As discussed in Chapter II, this position is of questionable foundation from a policy perspective, but it certainly serves the prosecutorial goal (legitimate and illegitimate) of making convictions easier and of maximizing publicity.

Chapter IV addressed some of the trial strategies counsel can apply in responding to this attitude. While those strategies may be quite effective in helping the jury limit the concept of "responsible officer," the mere existence of a corporate policy excusing higher-level officers from responsibility probably would carry little weight with jurors.

One other point should be made regarding preventive measures, although it presumably does not involve corporate policy. Corporate officers, in attempting to create a legal protection for themselves, must not be led to believe that they can insulate themselves from criminal prosecution by reducing the flow of information they receive from lower-level employees. Such a belief reflects a gross misconception about the state of the law.

Under normal circumstances, lack of knowledge would be a valid defense to a crime that has a "knowing" element, as most crimes do. But if an individual takes deliberate steps to insulate himself from knowledge, such action can itself serve as a substitute for the knowledge element. See, e.g., *Jewell*, 532 F.2d at 704; *United States v. Aleman*, 782 F.2d 492 (11th Cir. 1984).

Indemnifying Corporate Officers

The criminal lawyer also can advise the corporation in ways that can do much to ease the minds of corporate management, although this will not protect the corporation from prosecution or conviction. This advice relates to the issue of indemnification for defense in a criminal case. Most states have their own particular rules governing when a corporation can indemnify officers or other employees in a criminal case.

It may not always be in the corporation's interest to indemnify an officer's legal fees. For public relations purposes, the corporation may not wish to be linked to an officer charged in a notorious case. Indemnification can be expensive, as well. High-profile, federal criminal cases frequently are massive undertakings in which the defense fees can run into the hundreds of thousands, or even millions of dollars. Finally, in some cases, it may not be in the corporation's interest for a particular defendant to be well-represented, and the corporation might prefer to leave him to his own resources.

This situation is the unusual one, however. In most cases, the corporation will be charged along with the officer. Under the doctrines reviewed earlier in this chapter, the corporation will almost always be convicted if the officer is. It thus behooves the corporation to ensure that the officer has competent counsel. Furthermore, as any attorney who has participated in a multi-defendant case can attest, it is imperative to have a team of defense counsel who can work together in a cooperative manner, even if their defenses are not totally consistent. Good teamwork is far more likely to occur if the corporation is assisting the officer in obtaining and paying for his attorney.

Finally, indemnification is important to corporate officers' peace of mind. As the government steps up its high-profile prosecutions of corporate officers, those officers will become increasingly aware of their precarious position. Even the lack of culpability on an officer's part is not a guarantee against conviction, and it surely is no bar to prosecution. Under these circumstances, corporations may decide that indemnification is a necessary part of compensation packages.

The corporation need not always authorize indemnification prior to indictment. Nevertheless, counsel become aware of the relevant state's provisions so that decisions can be made promptly if an indictment suddenly surfaces.

Endnotes

[1] The current Model Ninth Circuit Instructions (1989 edition) contain no instruction on corporate liability.

[2] Many states have codified corporate criminal liability, enacting rules that are more protective of corporations than the federal doctrine. Many of these codifications are based on the Model Penal Code, which provides:

> Section 2.07. Liability of Corporations, Unincorporated Associations and Persons Acting, or Under a Duty to Act, in Their Behalf.
>
> 1) A corporation may be convicted of the commission of an offense if:
>
> > (a) the offense is a violation or the offense is defined by a statute other than the Code in which a legislative purpose to impose liability on corpora-

tions plainly appears and the conduct is performed by an agent of the corporation acting in behalf of the corporation within the scope of his office or employment, except that if the law defining the offense designates the agents for whose conduct the corporation is accountable or the circumstances under which it is accountable, such provisions shall apply; or

b) the offense consists of an omission to discharge a specific duty of affirmative performance imposed on corporations by law; or

c) the commission of the offense was authorized, requested, commanded, performed or recklessly tolerated by the board of directors or by a high managerial agent acting in behalf of the corporation within the scope of his office or employment.

...

4) As used in this Section:

...

b) "agent" means any director, officer, servant, employee or other person authorized to act in behalf of the corporation or association and, in the case of an unincorporated association, a member of such association;

c) "high managerial agent" means an officer of a corporation or an unincorporated association, or, in the case of a partnership, a partner, or any other agent of a corporation or association having duties of such responsibility that his conduct may fairly be assumed to represent the policy of the corporation or association.

5) In any prosecution of a corporation or an unincorporated association for the commission of an offense included within the terms of Subsection (1)9a) or Subsection (3)(a) of this Section, other than an offense for which absolute liability has been imposed, it shall be a defense if the defendant proves by a preponderance of evidence that the high managerial agent having supervisory responsibility over the subject matter of the offense employed due diligence to prevent its commission. This paragraph shall not apply if it is plainly inconsistent with the legislative purpose in defining the particular offense.

For a discussion of the law in states which apply a version of the Model Code, see Brickey, "Rethinking Corporate Liability Under the Model Penal Code," 19 Rutgers L.J. 593 (1988). The Code thus differs from the federal law in two critical respects: 1) it requires approval or reckless toleration by high officials for many crimes and 2) it allows a "due diligence" defense for many crimes. This latter factor is what *Beusch* explicitly, and *Hilton Hotels* implicitly, allows, but which has been ignored in many other decisions.

[3] The situation in *Georgetown University* is complicated by the fact that an employee of the university turned on the pump that led to the discharge. Because that employee was operating under the direction of the contractor, with no knowledge of the probable consequences of his acts, the court applied the borrowed servant doctrine, so that the employee's master was the contractor rather than the university.

[4] It might be submitted that this point actually supports the government's policy argument: The more inclusive the criminal law, the less likely a violation. However, that argument would be fallacious. It assumes that the corporation's exercise of control would in fact reduce the chances of a violation. The situation raised in the text is that the corporation, because of fears that it will be held criminally liable for acts of one it does not control, will attempt to exercise control. But this attempt may actually increase the likelihood of a violation because the contractor is presumably more experienced at ensuring that his actions are done properly. So in fact this example shows the harm in the government's policy: When the laws are over-inclusive, they may motivate behaviors that are counter-productive.

☐☐☐

VI. CASE STUDIES

The following case studies examine some of the problems that arise under the new wave of corporate prosecutions and some of the strategies used by defense counsel. Some of the lessons of these cases go beyond the particular focus of this work but are included because they contribute to understanding the wide range of issues in corporate criminal defense.

SEA GLEANER MARINE, INC.

Paul Schwitters was the owner of Sea Gleaner Marine, Inc., a small ship repair yard operating on Lake Union in Seattle, Wash.[1] A minor component of his work involved sand-blasting paint off boat hulls. For a period of time he hired an independent contractor to do the sand-blasting, but eventually, as a cost-cutting measure, he trained his staff to do the work. Schwitters followed the practices of his former contractor, who had told him that various environmental enforcement officers had reviewed his work without making any complaints.

Sea Gleaner's proximity to a yacht club generated complaints to authorities about the dust resulting from the sand-blasting. Schwitters was charged with four misdemeanor violations of the Clean Water Act for willful and negligent discharges into the navigable waters without a National Pollution Discharge Elimination System (NPDES) permit. The trial might never have occurred, because the search of Schwitters' yard also revealed a leaky tank that could have been charged as a felony RCRA count. Had he been charged under RCRA, Schwitters almost certainly would have pleaded guilty to the misdemeanors in exchange for dismissal of the felony. The failure to file the felony was attributable to a prosecutor who recognized that the tank violation was inadvertent. The prosecutor was unwilling to use a charge in which he did not believe to extract a conviction on the original charge.

The prosecutor's attitude was greatly affected by Schwitters' decision to appear for an interview, without counsel, and fully and frankly discuss the violations. Defense counsel may bemoan that the defendant's willingness to waive his right to counsel could weigh so heavily in his favor. But such an outcome is analogous to a street criminal's demeanor with the police favorably affecting the disposition of his case. Unfortunately, it is difficult to determine so early in a case whether a client is better off maintaining his rights and his silence or instead ingratiating himself to the authorities.

Both sides recognized that this trial presented one of the first opportunities to flesh out the meaning of the Clean Water Act. Counsel extensively briefed numerous issues pre-trial, including the meaning of the responsible corporate officer doctrine. Other issues included the meaning of "willfully,"[2] whether negligence meant gross negligence or simple unreasonableness, and the liability of corporations for the acts of independent contractors.

In a pre-trial hearing, the magistrate declined to fashion jury instructions in detail but ruled on the general implications of the corporate officer doctrine. He ruled for the government on every point of contention. Essentially, this eliminated any possible defense because discharges by employees had, in fact, occurred, which made the corporation guilty. Schwitters, as president, would fall within the magistrate's interpretation of the corporate officer doctrine, so the corporation's guilt would lead automatically to his guilt. Not surprisingly, the jury found both Schwitters and Sea Gleaner guilty.[3]

Schwitters received probation and was fined $5,000; the corporation was fined $30,000, a fairly substantial amount for a business grossing approximately $1 million and with little, if any, net profit.

The defense filed massive appellate briefs attacking the corporate officer jury instruction, among others, because it created an essentially strict liability. The government's brief contained a minimal defense of the corporate officer theory. Instead, the government argued that because the "elements" instruction required a finding of willfulness or negligence, the instructions as a whole did not allow a conviction under a strict liability theory.

Because defense counsel found the government's briefs vague in their interpretation of the responsible corporate officer doctrine, counsel at first found it difficult to respond. The government appeared to take the position on appeal that there had been no attempt to impose strict liability. But the prosecutor's closing argument clearly espoused a theory that Schwitters was vicariously liable for the acts of his employees.

The defense relied upon a line of cases that created a fairly low burden: Could the jury have understood the corporate officer instruction to create strict liability, despite the presence of the correct "elements" instruction? Chapter II also details some of the other briefing battles the case presented, where the government's citation to authority required more than the usual response.

In reliance on these points, the district court[4] reversed Schwitters' conviction but affirmed the instructions given on corporate liability. The prosecutor sensed that Schwitters was far more concerned with his own conviction than with that of the corporation. He transformed this position into a negotiating strength, and offered to drop any appeal of the reversal for Schwitters if Sea Gleaner would drop its appeal. Schwitters agreed.

Counsel extracted only one other agreement from the government: It would not argue that a Rule 35 motion by the corporation was barred by changes to that rule that accompanied the Sentencing Reform Act. That motion was based on the company's worsened financial condition, and the fine eventually was dropped to $5,000, with near acquiescence from the government.

Endnotes

[1]Both Schwitters and Sea Gleaner were represented by Dan Dubitzky and this author, of Dan R. Dubitzky, P.S., Seattle.

2 This term was removed from the Clean Water Act in the 1986 amendments. The term remains in numerous federal statutes. Counsel should take pains to unlearn the maxim that "ignorance of the law is no excuse": Extensive case law

supports the view that the term "willfully" nearly always denotes an awareness that the defendant acted with the knowledge that his actions were prohibited by law. This appears to be particularly so in regulatory crimes (other than those that deal exclusively with inherently dangerous items, such as guns), where one's apparently innocent activities can turn out to be prohibited ones. These matters were briefed extensively in *Schwitters*, and the briefs are included in the Appendix.

[3] The defendants were acquitted on one of four counts, where there was disputed evidence that the son of the vessel owner, rather than Sea Gleaner employees or contractors, had done the sand-blasting. In concentrating on larger issues, such as a full-scale legal attack on the corporate officer doctrine, it is quite easy to lose sight of such other defenses.

[4] Because trial was to a magistrate, appeal was to a district court, with additional appeal allowed to the Court of Appeals. (Rules of Procedure for the Trial of Misdemeanors Before United States Magistrates 7(b).)

□□□

MARINE POWER, INC.

Marine Power, Inc. was a large shipbuilding company with two yards in Seattle, Wash. On Feb. 25, 1985, the government executed a search warrant on both yards. They essentially closed down the business for a day, while going through the bulk of the company's records.

Defense counsel was informed that among the seized files could be numerous attorney-client privileged documents that might relate directly to the case. Counsel obtained a hearing before a magistrate as the search continued. The magistrate ordered that the records be sealed and not examined by government attorneys or investigators. Defense attorneys were given access to the records so that potentially privileged documents could be set aside for in camera review.

The quantity of documents identified was significant. Rather than subject the court to a laborious task of determining privilege for each document, defense counsel and the government adopted a procedure whereby one assistant U.S. Attorney, unconnected with the case, reviewed the documents for which a claim of privilege had been asserted. He agreed to erect a "Chinese Wall" between himself and those involved in the case. He examined the arguably privileged documents to see if any were related to the case, and if so, whether the government disputed the claim of privilege. Only those few documents would have to be examined by the court, while the rest were to be returned to the corporation.

Ultimately, the government obtained an indictment charging 113 violations of the Clean Water Act and two strict liability Rivers and Harbors violations (for transporting a navigation-disrupting barge without a permit). Charged along with the company were its president, vice-president, and environmental officer.[1] The violations all resulted from Marine Power lowering its drydocks without cleaning off spent sandblast grit. This resulted in the discharge of the grit into the navigable waters without an NPDES permit.

The case was assigned to the same magistrate who had presided in *Schwitters*. Once he issued his rulings in that case, it appeared that the defendants would have no defense to the law as the magistrate was interpreting it.

Clearly, discharges had occurred, and the corporation was liable for its employees' acts. Under the responsible corporate officer doctrine as applied in *Schwitters*, the officers of Marine Power surely would be found guilty. While a strong chance existed for reversing this instruction on appeal, going to trial just to preserve the issue was hardly an enviable course to pursue.

The government's theory was not limited to the corporate officer doctrine, but attempted to show that two defendants had hands-on involvement in the drydock operation. As to the company president, the government contended that his office location over the drydocks gave him clear notice of the violations.

The magistrate's interpretation of the term "willfully" excluded an entire line of defense aimed at this alternate prosecution theory. A major contention of the defendants was that they were lulled into believing their acts were lawful. Significant debate exists within the industry as to whether drydocks constituted "point sources" for purposes of the Clean Water Act. (The act, in prohibiting unpermitted discharges, defines "discharge" to mean the addition of pollutants to the navigable waters from a point source. 33 U.S.C. § 1362(12). "Point source" is defined as a "discernible, confined and discrete conveyance." 33 U.S.C. § 1362(13).)

While pretrial research revealed that drydocks clearly would be considered point sources under governing case law, so that NPDES permits were required before pollutants could be discharged, the confusion in the industry led many to believe their practices were legal. In addition, regulators had completely ignored the practice of lowering uncleaned drydocks. It was an open and standard procedure within the industry. No company had been cited, civilly or criminally, by either state or federal authorities, and none had even been warned. In fact, state Department of Ecology workers had conducted a walk-through of the Marine Power site, pointing out discharges that would require an NPDES permit, and agreeing that if those problems were corrected, no permit was necessary. Never was it suggested that the sandblasting grit on the drydocks necessitated a permit.

These facts represent mitigating circumstances, but they would not be exonerating facts under the court's interpretation of the law. In *Schwitters*, the magistrate had prevented the defendants from presenting any evidence that they lacked awareness they were violating provisions of the act. The Marine Power officials entered pleas to two counts. The pleas were expressly predicated on the magistrate's interpretation of the responsible corporate officer doctrine, so there was no admission of personal culpability.

Both sides conducted a massive sentencing effort. The submissions were close to a foot high. Besides establishing the mitigating factors, counsel challenged the philosophy underlying the government's indictment, in which criminal charges were used as a substitute for civil enforcement. Defense counsel argued that this was an unfair procedure because it exposed each company to a risky calculus. The chance of being singled out as the prosecutor's "example" meant the officers risked jail if they did not comply fully with the law. But the regulatory climate allowed all the company's competitors to continue doing business as usual, so that the costs of full compliance could be the financial undoing of the company.

Defense counsel contended that the fair and effective route to environmental improvements was uniform and industry-wide enforcement. The improvements did not have to be gradual, but the government should not select an individual and severely punish him for failing to do what no one else had even been asked to do.

Significant factual disputes also arose. While the government simply pointed to photographs of dirty drydocks in arguing that significant discharges had occurred, defense counsel retained hydraulics experts to compute the likely quantities of discharges. When the government divers contended that there was a huge wall of sand under a drydock, counsel obtained Army Corps of Engineers plans that showed this was the result of permitted dredging years earlier. The government only conceded its error on this point many months after the sentencing.

Sentencing presented what has become a classic dilemma in white collar guilty pleas. The defense seeks to demonstrate an attitude of contrition, which is virtually essential to getting a sympathetic ear from the judge, while at the same time disputing the claims of the government, which are far broader than the narrow crime to which the defendant pleaded.

Achieving both these goals always involves a delicate balancing act. In *Marine Power*, it required admissions that the officers were culpable, in the sense that they did not more thoroughly research the law or put themselves on the vanguard of changing the environmental practices in the industry. This was accompanied by continual reminders that the officers were not terribly culpable, because of the activities of regulators that contributed to legitimate confusion about the law, and because the discharges were far less in scope than the government claimed.

This approach was largely successful. Although the magistrate's sentencing oration displayed a belief in the need for harsh punishment, he imposed a total of five days work release, about 3 percent of the six-month sentence the prosecution requested.

Endnotes

[1] The company was represented by Ruth Nelson, in-house counsel; the president by Dan Dubitzky and this author, of Dan R. Dubitzky, P.S.; the vice-president by David Bukey, of Bukey & Bentley; and the environmental officer by Katrina Pflaumer, all of Seattle.

PENNWALT CORP.

Pennwalt Corp.[1] operates a chlor-alkali manufacturing plant in Tacoma, Wash., one of many plants owned by the company worldwide. The Tacoma plant manufactures chemicals used in the pulp-producing industry, including sodium chlorate. The plant had an NPDES permit, although that permit did not allow the discharge of these chemicals. Sodium chlorate is manufactured with an additive, sodium dichromate.[2]

On Jan. 2, 1985, a 180,000 gallon tank unexpectedly ruptured, spilling sodium chlorate. Because much of the chlorate entered the sewer and spilled into the neighboring waterway, the plant manager promptly reported the spill to the local Coast Guard authorities and the state Department of Energy. Employees were directed to wash the remaining chlorate off the plant's roads because of the chlorate's flammable nature. This resulted in additional liquid entering the waterway.

The state authorities ordered a cleanup, which was performed by Pennwalt. The state then closed its file and concluded in a memorandum that no criminal sanctions were warranted and that no negligence had occurred. Nevertheless, on Oct. 10, 1985, federal officials executed a search warrant.

Almost three years after the spill, an indictment was filed. The plant manager, along with the company, was charged with one felony count of filing false statements under 18 U.S.C. § 1001, because his report of the spill characterized the substance as sodium chlorate, without disclosing that the chlorate contained sodium dichromate, which is the actual reportable substance. In addition, he provided a rough estimate of 20,000 gallons spilled, when the final calculations suggested approximately 75,000 gallons. The company and the manager also were charged under CERCLA—42 U.S.C. § 9603(b)(3), failure to report discharge of a hazardous substance, based upon the same incomplete report.

The company and the manager were charged with four counts of Clean Water Act violations, based on the negligent discharge of chlorate. The company was charged with one additional discharge.

Copyright © 1990
The Bureau of National Affairs, Inc.

The charges of negligence were based on the history of the tank. The tank had suffered significant corrosion because of the action of the sodium dichromate on the steel. Six months before the spill, the company had decided to contain the liquid within bag liners, supported by the structure of the tank.

The most striking aspect of the Pennwalt indictment was the charging of three Pennwalt executives, who all had worked at corporate headquarters in Pennsylvania at the time of the spill. All three had signed the appropriation authorizing the bag liners. The three were the manager of manufacturing for the inorganic chemicals division, the president of that division, and the corporate vice-president for chemicals.[3]

The parties engaged in far more than the normal pre-trial legal skirmishing. One legal challenge was based on the conduct of government counsel. One of the managers had retired from Pennsylvania and was living in Oregon. The case agent telephoned the manager to ensure that he was home, hanging up as soon as there was an answer. He and the prosecutor then drove six hours to the manager's home, were invited in, and conducted a two-hour interview. Testimony differed about whether the prosecutor discussed the issue of contacting an attorney. But in any event the visit occurred after business hours. Only after the interview did the prosecutor return to his car, obtain a grand jury subpoena and produce a typewritten letter informing the manager that he was a target of the grand jury inquiry. A motion to suppress based upon allegations of misconduct was denied.[4]

Another major challenge was based on the provisions of 33 U.S.C. § 1321(c)(3) and 42 U.S.C. § 9603(b)(3), which provide immunity for notifications of hazardous substance discharges. The plant manager's counsel challenged the entire indictment as being derived from the report made to the Coast Guard.[5] The judge denied this motion summarily without allowing an evidentiary hearing. The manager then filed an interlocutory appeal, asserting that a trial would be a violation of his Fifth Amendment self-incrimination protections.

Another motion to dismiss was based on the corporate officer doctrine. If the government had instructed the grand jury based on this doctrine, and if those instructions misstated the law, presumably the entire indictment was void. Again, the judge denied the motion without giving the defense discovery of the instructions to the grand jury, and without any explanation. All defendants filed an interlocutory appeal on this ground.

The case thus entered the thicket of the case law regarding interlocutory appeals. The judge denied a stay of trial, and the defendants went to the court of appeals requesting a stay. The stay was granted in spite of the government's opposition. The case was briefed with particular regard to the implications of *United States v. Mechanik*, 475 U.S. 66 (1986), for interlocutory appeals relating to grand jury issues. At this time, *Midland Asphalt Corp. v. United States*, 109 S.Ct. 1494 (1989), another major case on interlocutory criminal appeals, was awaiting a decision by the Supreme Court.

The day before oral argument on the merits was scheduled before the court of appeals, the parties reached a plea agreement. The charges against all three Pennsylvania managers were dismissed. The plant manager pleaded guilty to two misdemeanor counts. The corporation pleaded to all of the misdemeanor counts and agreed to a fine of $500,000, the maximum allowed by law. The corporation also entered into a contract with the government to pay $600,000 into a trust fund to be administered by the Coast Guard for environmental safety in the Puget Sound area.

The final event in the Pennwalt saga generated nationwide press coverage. The corporation appeared through counsel at the hearing for change of plea. The judge refused to accept the guilty plea. He stated that if corporations are allowed to plead guilty through their attorneys, rather than their officers, deterrence would be insufficient.

At the next scheduled hearing, Pennwalt flew out the head of the inorganic chemicals division, which operated the Tacoma Plant. Also present was the senior vice president in charge of chemicals. Counsel had given the judge written notice of which individuals would be present for the corporation. Nevertheless, the judge again refused to accept the plea, insisting that the "top officer" be present.

Finally, when the chief executive of Pennwalt came to enter the plea on Pennwalt's behalf, the plea was accepted. While it seemed clear that the court had no authority to impose any conditions, let alone a sentence, upon the corporate officers, counsel was ready to file an immediate appeal, with an emergency motion for stay of execution, if necessary. These events led to a flurry of news reports on the issue of corporate accountability.

Endnotes

[1] Pennwalt is now known as Atochem North America, Inc.

[2] In its dry state, sodium dichromate has been described as a suspected carcinogen if inhaled. There is no evidence that it is carcinogenic in its liquid state when, as was the case here, it is added to sodium chromate solution.

[3] These three individuals were represented, respectively, by Jonathan Goldstein and Richard D. Shapiro, of Hellring, Lindeman, Goldstein, Siegal, & Stern, of Newark; Richard Sprague and Pam Higgins of Sprague, Higgins, & Creamer, of Philadelphia; and Larry Finegold and Jon Zulauf of Finegold & Zulauf, of Seattle. The company was represented by Thomas E. Kelly, Jr. of Preston Thorgrimson Shidler Gates & Ellis, and Scott Engelhard, presently of Finegold & Zulauf, both of Seattle. The plant manager was represented by David Bukey and Allen Bentley, of Bukey & Bentley, of Seattle.

[4] The prosecutor was subpoenaed by the defense as a witness for the suppression hearing. Although the subpoena was quashed in *Pennwalt*, this points out the hazards involved when counsel blur the distinction between advocate and investigator. See *Barbera v. Smith*, 836 F.2d 96 (2d Cir. 1987) (absolute immunity for prosecutors does not apply to actions of an investigatory or administrative nature).

[5] This issue is similar to that unsuccessfully raised by counsel for Captain Hazelwood in his prosecution in Alaska, arising out of the *Valdez* oil spill.

□□□

PROTEX INDUSTRIES

Protex Industries is a family-owned business in Denver, Colo., involved in manufacturing materials for use in concrete construction.[1] Government inspection of the yard revealed various chemicals classified as hazardous waste. Most of the chemicals were linked to the company's drum recycling activities. The government claimed that three employees suffered possibly irreversible psycho-organic symptoms resulting from solvent poisoning.

The government filed a 19-count indictment alleging conspiracy and various substantive violations under RCRA and the Clean Water Act, in addition to false statements counts under 18 U.S.C. § 1001. The company was charged in all 19 counts, including three charges under RCRA § 6928(e). That section, generally referred to as "knowing endangerment," involves knowingly placing a person in imminent danger of death or serious bodily injury. This was the first prosecution in the United States under the knowing endangerment statute.

The company controller was charged with 15 counts and the vice-president/general manager was named in 11 counts.[1]

Prior to trial, the controller entered into a plea agreement with the government in which he pled guilty to two misdemeanors and agreed to testify against the remaining defendants. He received a minimal fine and probation.

One major pre-trial issue centered around 42 U.S.C. § 6927. That section grants the government the right to enter hazardous waste establishments for purposes of inspection and obtaining samples. But it requires the government to give the owner a split sample (an equal quantity of a sample, so that independent tests can be performed). Results of any analyses also must be promptly furnished to the owner. In Protex's case, the company did not receive split samples during the execution of the search warrant.

Although samples eventually were provided, the company presented expert evidence that the passage of time had rendered the samples useless. As to the original visits, the company presented testimony that it had declined split samples

Copyright © 1990
The Bureau of National Affairs, Inc.

upon the assurance that it would be notified if problems were detected, but that such notification never came.

The section does not specify the remedy for failure to provide analyses or split samples. Defense counsel used as an analogy comparable provisions from the FDA, 21 U.S.C. §§ 372(b) and 374(d). The case under that section made clear that if the government did not turn over samples or analysis, sanctions could result, including suppression or dismissal. (The case law under the FDA provides a classic example of miscitation to precedent. The first case, *Triangle Candy Co. v. United States*, 144 F.2d 195, 199 (9th Cir. 1944) dismissed a case, holding that provision of a split sample "is a condition precedent to prosecution," because, "if those accused under the Act are not given a portion of the sample, their power to make a complete defense is substantially curtailed." Now however, the case is cited for the proposition that failure to turn over samples precludes prosecution only if the ability to defend is curtailed. *United States v. Cassaro, Inc.*, 443 F.2d 153, 157 (1st Cir. 1971).)

The *Protex* defense had several hurdles to overcome. The two pre-search warrant inspections had been conducted by the Colorado Department of Health, accompanied by an EPA criminal investigator on the second inspection, which presented the issue of whether the statutes covered these inspections. The samples taken pursuant to the search warrant were arguably not governed by the provisions of § 6927. In this regard, the defense introduced an internal EPA memo requiring that split samples be preserved from warrant executions and be turned over to the defense. Such internal policies often may not be binding, but may certainly help establish an air of government lawlessness that could help win the judge over.

The defense motion to suppress or dismiss, in all practicality, had to be grounded on the statutory provision, because the constitutional law pertaining to lost evidence requires the defense to demonstrate that they have been prejudiced by the loss, a burden usually made impossible to meet by the very loss that is the subject of the motion. *California v. Trombetta*, 467 U.S. 479 (1984). The motion was denied.

The general manager's other major pre-trial motion was for a severance. The essence of the motion was that the overwhelming bulk of the government's evidence pertained only to the company, and only to the knowing endangerment charges.

Copyright © 1990
The Bureau of National Affairs, Inc.

The defense argued that the jury could not compartmentalize this evidence and that the potential prejudicial spillover effect mandated severance. The motion was denied, primarily on the government's representation that it would present evidence of the manager's direct involvement in many of the violations charged.

As it turned out, however, the evidence, especially as brought out on cross-examination, demonstrated the manager's overall lack of involvement. Because the manager was not charged in the knowing endangerment counts, which were the subject of most of the testimony, the defense was able to obtain limiting instructions 25 different times. Testimony from half the witnesses was stipulated as completely inadmissible against the manager. Only six of 32 witnesses discussed the manager's activities.

When the government rested, the court granted the severance it previously had denied. The court held that the jury would not be able to segregate the evidence that was admissible against the manager from that which was not. This was particularly true because the government was proceeding on a responsible corporate officer theory.

Normally, a jury can use common sense in segregating the evidence that directly involves a defendant from that which does not. But, in this case, the government was asking the jury to apply against the manager evidence that did not directly involve him. This made it harder for the jury to distinguish between some evidence that, while not involving the manager, was usable against him, and other evidence, also not involving the manager, that had to be ignored.

The company ultimately was convicted. It was fined $7.53 million (with $7.09 million suspended), required to establish a $950,000 trust fund for the employees who suffered ill effects from the plant's chemicals, and ordered to fund a $2.1 million clean-up of the site.

The manager moved for a dismissal, on the grounds that retrial would violate double jeopardy. *Oregon v. Kenny*, 456 U.S. 667, 679 (1982) requires that the defendant, to win such a motion, demonstrate that the prosecutor subjectively intended to obtain a mistrial, in order to reap the benefits of a mistrial. This is another example of a nearly impossible burden. The manager relied on the radical disparity between the government's claimed evidence, when opposing the pre-trial severance motion, and the actual evidence at trial. The motion was denied.

The manager then appealed. Double jeopardy is one of the few issues that can be appealed interlocutorily. *Abney v. United States*, 431 U.S. 651 (1977). Before the court of appeals could rule, the government agreed to a plea to misdemeanor charges. The manager received probation and a $25,000 fine.

The company's appeal was unsuccessful. *United States v. Protex Industries, Inc.*, 874 F.2d 740 (10th Cir. 1989). The court held that §6927 provides no defense to RCRA charges.

Endnotes

[1] The company was represented by David G. Palmer of Gibson, Dunn & Crutcher, the controller by Richard S. Vermeire, and the vice president/general manager by Robert T. McAllister, of Martin & McAllister, all of Denver.

BANK OF NEW ENGLAND

The Bank of New England was indicted along with two head tellers, a branch manager, and a commercial customer.[1] One count charged a scheme to conceal the customer's currency transactions under 18 U.S.C. § 1001; 36 additional counts charged specific failures to file currency transaction reports under 31 U.S.C. § 5322. The branch manager and one teller were each charged with one count of perjury.

The perjury count against the branch manager involved a faulty collateral issue: She had testified before the grand jury that she never was reprimanded by management regarding the handling of currency transaction reports. She was severed from the case. The perjury charge against one teller, based on testimony regarding a Christmas gift from the customer, was likewise severed. Although the court is almost never obligated to sever counts or defendants under federal law, sympathetic facts may lead a trial court to exercise its discretion in favor of severance. Here, the relatively trivial subject matter of the alleged perjury no doubt had a significant influence on the trial court's view of these charges.

One major pre-trial issue was whether there was any obligation to file reports when no individual transaction exceeded the $10,000 threshold. The various circuits had split on this issue, with some applying the law to any structured transactions, but with others holding that no report must be made unless the multiple transactions in some way could be considered one transaction, for example if they were at the same branch on the same day. (Congress has since added 31 U.S.C. § 5324. This statute prohibits the structuring of transactions in an attempt to evade the reporting requirements.) In this case, multiple transactions occurred in a single visit by the customer. The district court held that such transactions were within the scope of the statute, and the court of appeals ultimately concurred.

The tellers' defense was straightforward: they did not know of any obligation to report transactions of less than $10,000, even if the transactions were structured in the way these were. Such knowledge was required to establish the element of willfulness. Although a bank manual discussed the law, there was no showing that the manual had been distributed to the tellers.

Given the court's intent to give a collective knowledge instruction, the bank was fairly hamstrung in presenting a defense. Under normal corporate liability principles, it could simply have joined in the tellers' defense, supporting their contention that they lacked the requisite willfulness.

Their acquittal would likely have resulted in the bank's acquittal. But with an instruction pooling knowledge, the mere fact that others in the bank knew what the regulations required, combined with the fact that no reports were made, almost guaranteed conviction.

The customer's defense was the same as the tellers'; he lacked any knowledge that structured transactions required a CTR. In order to undercut jury suspicions about the reasons for his cash transaction, he admitted to being a bookie. He established, through government witnesses, that he had fully disclosed his status as a bookie, paying the requisite occupational tax and excise tax.

The two tellers and the customer were acquitted, while the bank was convicted on 31 counts. After the trial, the severed perjury charges against the teller and manager were dismissed. The bank was fined $1,240,000.

Endnotes

[1] The Bank was represented by Amos Hugh Scott and Mark Michelson of Coate, Hall & Stewart, Boston; the tellers by Michael Collora of Dwyer, Collora & Gertner, Boston and Richard K. Donahue of Donahue & Donahue, Lowell; the branch manager by D. Lloyd MacDonald of McDermott & Rizzo, Boston; and the customer by Willie J. Davis of Davis & Robinson, Boston.

□ □ □

Copyright © 1990
The Bureau of National Affairs, Inc.

VII. CONCLUSION

The trend is evident: Corporations and their officers increasingly will become targets of criminal prosecutions. The phenomenon cannot be prevented, and it should not have to be, because corporate crimes pose significant threats to the public welfare.

This report attempts to address whether the rules of the battle being waged by prosecutors will be radically transformed — whether the government will be able to convict corporate defendants with even lesser proof of fault than previously necessary.

The report's author has endeavored to demonstrate that the attempts to give the prosecution dramatically more powerful weapons are subject to serious criticism as a matter of policy.

But regardless of one's view of whether the prosecution's powers should be increased, the courts cannot view these powers as established doctrines flowing from either congressional enactment or case law precedent, the author submits. Prosecutors are attempting to establish new doctrines, and their efforts must be recognized as such.

Fundamental shifts in the concept of criminal culpability do pose significant policy questions. Before these doctrines are adopted, the implications of a change in criminal law should be thought out thoroughly, and by legislators and policy analysts, not prosecutors and judges.

This report attempts to present sufficient weapons, in terms of case law and statutory analysis, to help practitioners prevent judges from enacting these doctrinal changes by fiat. But not all judges will take a pro-defense stance, even when precedent, logic, and policy all support that position. So this report addresses steps counsel can take if confronted with the doctrinal changes.

Copyright © 1990
The Bureau of National Affairs, Inc.

Any drive to protect society from criminal misdeeds is worthwhile. But the author submits that goal of protecting the wrongfully accused, while a much-maligned and frequently Sisyphean task, is equally worthwhile. So the goal is to maintain some semblance of a fair balance of power between the forces pursuing these two missions.

☐☐☐

APPENDICES

Appendix A — Sample Appendix to Sentencing Memorandum Discussing Comparable Sentences in Environmental Cases...A-1

Appendix B — Materials from *United States v. Schwitters*...B-1

Published by The Bureau of National Affairs, Inc.

APPENDIX A

Sample Appendix to Sentencing Memorandum Discussing Comparable Sentences in Environmental Cases

Published by The Bureau of National Affairs, Inc.

APPENDIX A

APPENDIX B

Western District of Washington Cases

United States v. Marine Power, CR 86-128S. The defendants, Marine Power & Equipment, its president, and two vice-presidents, were charged with 113 counts of Clean Water Act violations. Pursuant to plea agreement, they pled guilty to 2 counts each, alleging several days of violation.

The charges arose out of the company's regular practice of sandblasting ship bottoms on drydocks, then lowering the drydocks without removing the spent sandblast grit and/or the particles of sandblasted paint and other materials. The government stated that "it is logical to conclude the waste did (and still does) cause some harm in the Duwamish River and Lake Union," because "the wastes involved uniformly killed test organisms which were exposed to it during EPA bioassays" and because other evidence made this a commonsense conclusion. The government's position was that "defendants demonstrated a remarkable, totally arrogant, disregard for the law, including committing blatant violations of the same nature within a day after United States Environmental Protection Agency ("EPA") criminal agents sharply reconfirmed the law for defendants . . ." The case was compounded by "obstruction and falsities" committed by the defendants. [Quotations from Government's Sentencing Memorandum]

Each individual was sentenced to five days work release with fines ranging from $1,000 to $5,000. The company was fined $200,000.

United States v. Squyres, No. 88-74FDB

Mr. Squyres was general manager of the George Scofield Co. Both he and the company pled guilty to violations of the Clean Water Act. For a number of years, the plant had regularly been discharging waste water from concrete trucks to the Tacoma City Waterway. Mr. Squyres, as manager, had an active role in supervising and preventing pollution. Mr. Squyres did not inform higher management of the problem, because he believed the funds were lacking. Mr. Squyres received probation, with a $10,000 fine imposed on him only because the company would be taking responsibility for the fine. The company was fined $40,000, pursuant to a plea agreement.

[Source: personal knowledge and government's oral presentation at sentencing.]

United States v. Schwitters, No. 86-129S

Sea Gleaner Marine, Inc. and its president, Paul Schwitters, were convicted of three counts of Clean Water Act violations. The discharges involved sandblasting the side of ships directly over the waters of Lake Union. Witnesses testified that Mr. Schwitters was directly involved in instructing employees how to do the sandblasting. The government presented evidence that Mr. Schwitters was directly informed by a DOE employee that his activities should be stopped.

Mr. Schwitters received probation and was fined $10,000. The company was fined $30,000, ultimately reduced to $5,000.

[Source: review of transcript]

United States v. Cairns, et al., No. CR 84-167V.

The Wyckoff Company and its president pled guilty to one count each of RCRA felony and Clean Water Act misdemeanor violations. These pertained to the storage of hazardous wastes in an unlined pit. These activities were accompanied by what the government called "fraudulent conduct." Three other management level employees pled guilty to conspiring to violate the Clean Water Act by discharging hundreds of thousands of gallons of wood preserving chemical wastes into the Duwamish River. The president was sentenced to sixty days incarceration and fined $25,000. The other officers received probation with fines ranging from $2,500 to $10,000. They were to provide community service ranging from 100 to 200 hours. The company was fined $1,000,000.

[Source: Summary provided by government in Marine Power; government's sentencing memorandum in Cairns.]

United States v. Hoflin, CR 85-82T.

The Director of Public Works for the City of Ocean Shores was convicted of RCRA and Clean Water Act violations. The RCRA offense related to the burial of fourteen drums of ignitable and toxic hazardous wastes in soils next to a Pacific Ocean beach and a state wildlife refuge. The wastes were high in toxic heavy metals and mixed with toxic solvents. The method of burial caused their contents to flow into the soils. The Clean Water Act violation involved the disposal of 300,000 gallons of untreated liquid sewage in permeable soils next to the beach.

APPENDIX A

Mr. Hoflin received probation, with 200 hours of community service imposed.

[Source: Government's Sentencing Memorandum]

United States v. Hedegard, et al., CR 85-342PKS.

JANCO-UNITED, Inc., its president, and its vice-president were sentenced for conspiracy to violate the Clean Water Act and for willful substantive violations. These related to the virtually daily discharge, over several years, of the chemical residues from the manufacture of various cleaners, including solvents. The wastes were discharged into the Duwamish River via a hidden pipe. The officers were sentenced to five days imprisonment, 300 hours of community service, and a $5,000 fine each. The corporation was fined $30,000.

[Source: Summary provided by government in Marine Power; government's sentencing memorandum in Hedegard.]

United States v. Blackstone, CR 86-12T.

The owner of a body shop paid an individual to remove 12 barrels of hazardous, flammable material shortly before his shop was about to be inspected and to place them in a deserted locale. There was some leakage after disposal. He had identifying labels removed to prevent the barrels being traced to his shop. He received a year and a day sentence and was ordered to pay $7,500 in restitution.

United States v. Argent, et al., No. CR 88-__D.

The company, its president and vice-president pled guilty to violations revolving around the sdale of unregistered pesticides, some of which were alleged to be carcinogens. The sales continued over a several year period despite repeated warnings by Food and Drug Administration and EPA. Both defendants made false statements, certifying that the sales were not continuing. The company pled to felony violations of 18 U.S.C. § 1001 and the two individuals pled to misdemeanor violations involving the sale of fish food and chemicals containing the prohibited material. The president of the company received 6 months work release. The vice-president was given probation.

Other Districts

Toxic Substances Control Act ("TSCA") Cases

In United States v. Derecktor (D.R.I. 1986), a shipyard company admitted to 24 discharges of sandblasting debris and other pollutants, in violation of the Clean Water Act. It also admitted to failing to notify EPA when removing asbestos, in violation of the Clean Air Act, or the release of asbestos, in violation of CERCLA. The company's owner admitted to four violations of the Toxic Substances Control Act, for removing three PCB-contaminated transformers from the shipyard and burying them at his residence. The company was fined $600,000, with $200,000 suspended upon paying of $200,000 restitution. The owner was fined $75,000.

The State of Rhode Island v. E.W. Audet & Sons, Inc., No. P2/86-1519 (Providence Sup. Ct. 1986) was initiated as an investigation of violations under TSCA and state statutes regulating the disposal of PCBs conducted by a joint task force of state and federal officials from the Department of Environmental Management ("DEM"), the Environmental Protection Agency ("EPA") and the United States Attorney's Office. The company had illegally stored over 100 transformers, some of which were leaking and discharging fluid. Samples taken by the government indicated that the transformers and the soil were contaminated with PCBs. In addition, the defendants had cannibalized some of the transformers and poured the contents, contaminated motor oil, into a cesspool. The defendant pled nolo contendere to ten counts involving the illegal storage of PCBs. The corporation was sentenced to a fine of $75,000 to be paid over a five year period. As part of the settlement the company agreed to pay cleanup costs for the site. The principal of the company was given a suspended sentence of five years and placed on probation for a period of five years. It was agreed by the government that there would be no federal prosecution.

In United States v. Baseman, (D.N.M. 1983), Vernon L. Baseman pled guilty to two counts under TSCA, one for the interstate transportation of PCBs and PCB containers and one for the disposal of PCB materials. Baseman was sentenced to a fine of $2,000. Charges against the other defendant, David R. Faulkner, were dismissed on the condition that he successfully complete one year of probation.

In United States v. Holley Electric Corp. (M.D. Fla. 1983), the corporation and its president, Onis Lynwood Holley, were charged in a ten count indictment with six counts under TSCA for the illegal disposal of PCBs. Holley pled guilty to the failure to mark PCB drums and to making false statements. He was sentenced to a fine of $25,000 and placed on two years probation. The corporation, which pled

APPENDIX A

guilty to the unlawful disposal of PCBs and making false claims to the government, was fined $35,000 and placed on probation for a period of two years.

In United States v. Transformer Services, Inc. (N.D. Ohio 1983), the corporation and its president, G.A. Booth, and warehouse and operations manager, R.W. Rafferty, were charged in a seven count indictment with unlawful disposal of PCBs in violation of TSCA, conspiracy, fraud and the making of false statements. The individual defendants pled guilty to violations of TSCA and to wire fraud. The charges against the corporation were dismissed. Neither imprisonment nor fines were imposed on the defendants. They were sentenced to seventeen days in a halfway house on work release, two years probation and community service.

In United States v. Pacific Hide & Fur Depot, Inc. (D. Idaho 1984), the company and William Knick were convicted at trial on three counts under TSCA. Knick and the corporation were each sentenced to pay a fine of $8,000 on each of the three counts.[1]

In United States v. Zeldenrust (N.D. Ill 1984), the defendant pled guilty to one count under TSCA involving the illegal disposal of one drum of pure PCBs in a forest preserve. Zeldenrust was sentenced to pay a fine of $3,000 and to probation for a period of one year.

United States v. Drum Recovery, Inc. (D. Or. 1984) involved violations of several environmental statutes, including TSCA, by a corporation engaged in the business of transporting hazardous waste, which also arranged for the disposal of such wastes on behalf of its clients. Charles Tuttle, the sales manager of the company, pled guilty to one count under TSCA. Eugene Tienken, a part-owner and general manager of Drum Recovery, pled guilty to four counts under TSCA for the illegal storage of PCB materials. Tuttle was sentenced to five years probation and 100 hours of community service and was required to pay one-third of the costs of the cleanup of the site by the government. Tienken was sentenced to serve ninety days in prison and to probation for a period of five years and was also required to pay one-third of the costs of cleanup.

United States v. Ward, 676 F.2d 94 (4th Cir. 1982), involved particularly egregious violations of TSCA. The defendant arranged for the disposal of more than 10,000 gallons of PCB-contaminated oil from transformers stored at

---

[1] The convictions were reversed on appeal on the basis of an improper instruction to the jury on deliberate avoidance. United States v. Pacific Hide & Fur Depot, Inc., 768 F.2d 1096, 1099 (9th Cir. 1985).

the Ward Transformer Company by spraying the oil along roadways in North Carolina from a specially outfitted truck. The spraying was done in rural regions, deliberately avoiding "inhabited or well-lit areas." United States v. Ward, 618 F. Supp. 884, 891 (E.D.N.C. 1985). Ward was indicted and subsequently convicted at trial on eight counts of knowingly and willfully causing the illegal disposal of PCBs. He was sentenced to pay a fine of $200,000 and to eighteen months imprisonment.

In United States v. Electro Sales Co., Inc. (D. Mass. 1984), the company pled guilty to two counts under TSCA for the improper storage and marking of capacitors containing PCBs. The company was sentenced to pay a fine of $25,000.

In United States v. Rockwell International (D. Colo. 1986), the corporation was cited for the improper disposal of PCBs. PCB-contaminated fluids had leaked from six electrical transformers in concentrations ranging from 50-500 ppm to 30,000 ppm. EPA proposed an administrative penalty of $111,000. The EPA attorney with responsibility for the case stated, "The proposed fine is somewhat larger than would be proposed for a first time violation of TSCA. The penalty was increased because of a history of TSCA violations by Rockwell. If someone had never violated TSCA before, the proposed penalty could have been $60,000." 17 Env't. Rep. (BNA) 585 (August 15, 1986).

Clean Water Act ("CWA") Cases

In United States v. K.W. Thompson Tool Company, Inc. (D.N.H. 1985) the corporation, its president and two vice presidents were charged with violations of environmental statutes, including the CWA. The charges against the individual defendants were dismissed. The corporation pled guilty to fifteen violations of the CWA. It was sentenced to pay a fine of $4,000 on each count, for a total of $60,000.

In United States v. Venus Laboratories (N.D. Ill. 1985), the corporation was charged in a twenty-two count indictment with the negligent discharge of chemical wastes without a permit in violations of the CWA. The company pled guilty to four counts under the CWA and was sentenced to pay a fine of $2,500 on each count, for a total of $10,000.

In United States v. Georgia Bonded Fibers (W.D. Va. 1985), the corporation pled guilty to one count of discharging pollutants in violation of the CWA and to two counts of making false statements. The company was sentenced to pay a fine of $25,000 on the count under the CWA and to reimburse the costs of the investigation. The president of the company, Kostelni, pled guilty to three

APPENDIX A

counts, two under the CWA, and was sentenced to pay a fine of $10,000 on each count, all of which, except for $5,000, was suspended.

In United States v. Ocean Reef Club, Inc. (S.D. Fla. 1986), the corporation and two of its officers, Claude H. Gehman, vice president, and Mark Malka, utilities supervisor, were charged in a 346 count indictment with violations of the CWA. The corporation, a real estate development firm in the Florida Keys, had dumped a monthly average of one to three million gallons of partially treated or untreated sewage from its North Key Largo residential community from 1979 through 1982. The court noted in its findings of fact that the discharges were harmful to the environment in the surrounding Keys area. The firm was sentenced to pay a fine of $600,000. (The maximum under the agreement was a fine of $1,000,000 against the firm.) The individual defendants were sentenced to fines of $5,000 and $2,000, respectively, and to probation for a period of one year. The firm also agreed to pay a $60,000 fine to the State of Florida for violations of state environmental laws.

In United States v. Ganon (E.D. Pa. 1985), a former company president pled guilty to a violation of pretreatment standards for discharges to a publicly owned treatment works under the CWA. He was sentenced to pay a fine of $2,500 and to a period of three years probation, with community service.

In United States v. Maritz Corp. (E.D. Mo. 1984), the corporation was charged with three counts of exceeding permit discharge limitations and one count of making false statements under the CWA. The company was sentenced to pay a fine of $15,000 on each count of violating permit limits, which was suspended pending the submission of a community work plan. The president of the corporation, W. Piefer, pled guilty to two counts of exceeding permit limitations and was sentenced to a period of thirty months probation, community service and payment of a $2,500 fine.

In United States v. Ralston-Purina Co. (Ky. 1982), the corporation pled guilty to charges under several environmental statutes, including the CWA, for discharging hexane into the Louisville, Kentucky sewer system without a permit. The discharges resulted in explosions which destroyed part of the city's sewer system. The company pled guilty to four misdemeanors and was fined $62,500.

In United States v. Louisville and Nashville Railroad (W.D. Ky. 1982), the corporation was charged with two counts under the CWA for discharging pollutants without a permit and for violating pretreatment standards. The company pled guilty and was sentenced to pay a $38,000 fine.

Published by The Bureau of National Affairs, Inc.

In *United States v. A.C. Lawrence Leather Co., Inc.* (D.N.H. 1982), the company and several of its officers were charged in a sixty-eight count indictment with forty-three violations of the CWA. The charges were reduced at trial to five counts for discharges, in violation of NPDES permit conditions, directly to navigable waters by bypassing a treatment plant. The company was fined $10,000 on each of the counts under the CWA, for a total of $50,000, and was placed on probation for a period of five years. Five company officers, who pled guilty to from five to ten violations of the CWA, were sentenced to suspended terms of imprisonment for one year, probation for a period of two years and the payment of fines of $2,500 for each CWA count.

In *United States v. Frezzo Bros., Inc.*, 602 F.2d 1123 (3d Cir. 1979), cert. denied, 444 U.S. 1074 (1980) the corporation and several of its officers were convicted at trial on six counts of discharging pollutants from a storm water run-off system on the company's mushroom farm. The corporation was fined $50,000. The individual defendants were sentenced to thirty days imprisonment and fined, in the aggregate, $50,000.

Comprehensive Environmental Response, Compensation and Liability Act ("CERCLA") Cases

In *United States v. K.W. Thompson Tool Co.* (D.N.H. 1985), the company pled guilty, among other counts, to the failure to report the existence of a hazardous waste facility under section 103(c) of CERCLA. The company was sentenced to a fine of $7,500.

In *United States v. R.J. Clements, Inc.* (E.D. Va. 1985), the company pled guilty to one count charging a failure to report a release under section 103(b) of CERCLA. The company was sentenced to a fine of $4,000.

In *United States v. Fried Industries, Inc.* (D.N.J. 1985), the company pled guilty to a two count information, consisting of one count under RCRA and one count under section 103(b) of CERCLA. The company was sentenced on both counts to pay a fine of $40,000.

In *United States v. Franco* (E.D. Va. 1985), a company vice president and project manager, Alan Franco, pled guilty to a failure to report a release of friable asbestos in violation of CERCLA. The charge arose in connection with a Department of the Navy contract for the removal of asbestos pipe insulation at the Naval Observatory in Washington, D.C. Franco was given a suspended sentence of thirty days, placed on probation for a period of sixty months and required to pay a fine of $150.

APPENDIX A   A-11

In United States v. Mills (M.D. Tenn. 1985), (S.D. Ala. 1985), the defendant, George Mills, pled guilty to three counts under section 103(c) of CERCLA. He was given a suspended sentence of three years, placed on probation for a period of five years and required to pay a fine of $30,000.

In United States v. SCA Chemical Services, Inc. (D. Mass. 1984), the corporation pled guilty to one count of charging a failure to report a release under section 103(b) of CERCLA. The company was sentenced to pay a fine of $7,000.

In United States v. Quality Research Labs, Inc. (E.D. Pa. 1983), the corporation and two individual defendants were charged with violations of RCRA and section 103(b) of CERCLA. The individual defendants, M. Yaron and B. Yaron, were sentenced, respectively, to probation for a period of five years and a $5,000 fine and to probation for three years and a $2,000 fine on the count under CERCLA.

In United States v. Drum Recovery, Inc. (D. Or. 1984), which involved a thirty-nine count indictment under several environmental statutes, one individual defendant, Gary Van Lom, pled guilty to one count of violating the Hazardous Materials Transportation Act and one count for failure to report a release under CERCLA. He was sentenced on both counts to one year of imprisonment and a period of five years probation and was required to pay one-third of the costs of cleanup for the site. Violation of the HMTA is a felony offense.

In United States v. Lackawanna Refuse Removal, Inc. (M.D. Pa. 1983), a corporate defendant, Northeastern Land Development Company, and an individual defendant were charged with one count under CERCLA for the failure to report the existence of a hazardous waste facility. The corporation pled guilty and was sentenced to pay a $10,000 fine. The charges against the individual defendant were dismissed.

In United States v. A.C. Lawrence Leather Co., Inc. (D.N.H. 1983), which involved a sixty-eight count indictment charging violations of several environmental statutes, the corporation pled guilty to two counts under sections 103(b) and 103(c) of CERCLA. The corporation was sentenced to pay a fine of $5,000 on each count. Two individual defendants, Stone and Goodspeed, pled guilty to two counts under CERCLA and were given suspended sentences of one year, placed on probation for a period of two years and required to pay fines of $2,500 and $5,000, respectively, on each count. A third individual defendant, Marshall, pled guilty to one count under section 103(c) of the statute and was given a suspended sentence of one year, placed on probation for a period of two years and required to pay a fine of $5,000, of which all, except for $2,500, was suspended.

Resource Conservation and Recovery Act ("RCRA") Cases

In United States v. Greer, (M.D. Fla. 1986), the proprietor of a hazardous waste handling facility was convicted of illegal discharge of hazardous waste, one count of failing to report the discharge, and 13 counts of mail fraud. Charges of knowing endangerment, mislabeling hazardous chemicals, requiring employees to test waste drums by sniffing them and falsifying identification test reports were either dismissed or resulted in a hung verdict. Although the prosecution said the incidents "were among the most serious set of facts we encountered in the environmental crime area," the defendant received 90 days incarceration, 1,000 hours of community service, five years probation and a $23,000 fine.

Clean Air Act ("CAA") Cases

In United States v. Hope Resource Recovery, Inc., (E.D.N.Y. 1986) a refuse incinerator company operated an air contaminant source without a certificate, in violation of the Clean Air Act. The company received a $10,000 fine.

In United States v. Waterbury House Wrecking Co., Inc. (D. Conn. 1985), which involved a five count indictment under the CAA, the president and contractor for the corporation pled guilty to one count for the violation of regulations for the removal of asbestos promulgated under the CAA. The president of the company, Maurice Fabrini, was sentenced to imprisonment for one year, all of which, except for thirty days, was suspended, to probation for a period of five years, with community service, and was required to pay a fine of $25,000. The contractor, Peter Vileisis, was given a suspended sentence of one year, placed on probation for a period of five years, with community service, and required to pay a fine of $25,000.

APPENDIX B

APPENDIX B

Materials from *United States v. Schwitters*

Opening Brief of Appellants ...(B-3)
Brief of Appellee ...(B-79)
Reply Brief of Appellants ...(B-152)
Order on Appeal ...(B-196)

Published by The Bureau of National Affairs, Inc.

APPENDIX B

UNITED STATES DISTRICT COURT
FOR THE WESTERN DISTRICT OF WASHINGTON AT SEATTLE

UNITED STATES OF AMERICA,)	
Plaintiff-Appellee,)	NO. CR 86-129
v.)	
PAUL D. SCHWITTERS and)	
SEA GLEANER MARINE, INC.,)	
Defendant-Appellants.)	

OPENING BRIEF OF APPELLANTS

Published by The Bureau of National Affairs, Inc.

I. **STATEMENT OF THE ISSUES PRESENTED FOR REVIEW**

II. **STATEMENT OF THE CASE**

III. **STATEMENT OF FACTS**

IV. **ARGUMENT**

   A. INTRODUCTION AND SUMMARY OF ARGUMENT

   B. STANDARD OF REVIEW

   C. THE COURT APPLIED STRICT LIABILITY PRINCIPLES TO DEFENDANT SCHWITTERS, IN VIOLATION OF THE CLEAR STATUTORY LANGUAGE ALLOWING CONVICTION ONLY FOR WILLFUL OR NEGLIGENT ACTS

      1. <u>The Unambiguous Language of the Clean Water Act Dictates That Corporate Officers, Like All Other "Persons," May be Convicted Only If They Act Willfully or Negligently</u>

      2. <u>The "Responsible Corporate Officer" Doctrine Is Applicable Only to Strict Liability Offenses</u>

      3. <u>A Congressional Intent to Impose Strict Liability Must be Clearly Expressed</u>

      4. <u>The Legislative History of the Clean Water Act Does Not Contradict the Clear Language of the Statute</u>

      5. <u>Applying Strict Liability Under the Terms of the Act Would Deny Defendant His Due Process Right to Clear Notice of What Acts Are Made Criminal</u>

      6. <u>Conclusion</u>

   D. A CRIMINAL CONVICTION FOR NEGLIGENCE MAY NOT BE BASED ON THE MINIMAL SHOWING NECESSARY FOR TORT NEGLIGENCE

      1. <u>A Criminal Conviction for Negligence Requires Proof of a Gross Deviation From a Reasonable Standard of Care</u>

APPENDIX B

2. Negligence Under Both Tort and Criminal Law May Be Judged Only By the Circumstances Known to the Defendant

3. Conclusion

E. A CORPORATION IS NOT VICARIOUSLY LIABLE FOR THE ACTS OF INDEPENDENT CONTRACTORS WHO ARE NOT ITS AGENTS

F. PROOF OF "WILLFULNESS" REQUIRES THAT DEFENDANTS WERE AWARE THEY VIOLATED THE CLEAN WATER ACT

1. Introduction

2. The Legislative History of the Clean Water Act Demonstrates Congress's Intent to Require Awareness That a Violation Has Occurred

3. The Language "Willfully Violates" Has Consistently Been Used by Congress to Require Awareness That a Violation Has Occurred

4. Where a Statute Prohibits Conduct Which Would Not Alert Citizens To the Likelihood of Criminal Regulation, the Term "Willfully" Requires Awareness of the Regulation

5. The Cases Interpreting the Clean Water Act Do Not Support the Prosecution's Interpretation of "Willful"

6. This Circuit Requires an Instruction on Willfulness When Congress Makes Willfulness an Element of the Crime

7. Conclusion

G. WHERE THE CLEAN WATER ACT PROHIBITS "NEGLIGENTLY VIOLAT[ING]" PROVISIONS OF THE ACT, CONVICTION REQUIRES PROOF OF A NEGLIGENT STATE OF MIND AS TO THE FACT THAT A VIOLATION IS OCCURRING

H. THE TRIAL COURT'S REFUSAL TO ADMIT ANY DEFENSE EVIDENCE ON AN ESSENTIAL ELEMENT WAS ERROR

I. THE COURT'S REFUSAL TO DEFINE THE MENTAL ELEMENT REQUIRED FOR CONVICTION AS AN AIDER AND ABETTOR WAS ERROR

V. <u>CONCLUSION</u>

APPENDIX B

B-7

TABLE OF AUTHORITIES

CASES CITED

American Federation of Labor and Congress of Industrial Organizations v. Federal Election Commission, 628 F.2d 97 (D.C. Cir.), cert. denied, 449 U.S. 982 (1980)

Benchwick v. United States, 297 F.2d 330 (9th Cir. 1961)

Cabana v. Bullock, ___ U.S. ___, 106 S.Ct. 689, 88 L.Ed.2d 704 (1986)

Dennis v. United States, 341 U.S. 494, 71 S.Ct. 857, 95 L.Ed. 1137 (1951))

Dickerson v. New Banner Institute, Inc., 460 U.S. 103, 103 S.Ct. 986, 74 L.Ed.2d 845 (1983)

Dumansky v. United States, 486 F. Supp. 1078 (D.N.J. 1980)

Fenton v. Freedman, 748 F.2d 1358 (9th Cir. 1984)

Garcia v. United States, 469 U.S. 70, 105 S.Ct. 479, 83 L.Ed.2d 472 (1984)

Grayned v. City of Rockford, 408 U.S. 104, 92 S.Ct. 2294, 33 L.Ed.2d 222 (1972)

Ivers v. United States, 581 F.2d 1362 (9th Cir. 1978)

Leary v. United States, 395 U.S. 6, 90 S.Ct 642, 24 L.Ed.2d 610 (1970)

Liparota v. United States, 471 U.S. 419, 105 S.Ct. 2084, 85 L.Ed.2d 434 (1985)

Logue v. United States, 412 U.S. 521, 93 S.Ct. 2215, 37 L.Ed.2d 121 (1973)

Manning v. Ashland Oil Co., 721 F.2d 192 (7th Cir. 1983)

Marshall v. Root's Restaurant, 667 F.2d 559 (6th Cir. 1982)

Minnehaha Creek Watershed Dist. v. Hoffman, 597 F.2d 617 (8th Cir. 1979)

Moragne v. States Marine Lines, Inc., 398 U.S. 375, 90 S.Ct. 1772, 26 L.Ed.2d 339 (1970)

Nabob Oil Co. v. United States, 190 F.2d 478 (10th Cir.), cert. denied, 342 U.S. 876 (1951)

Nat. Steel, Etc. v. Occupational Safety and Health Comm'n, 607 F.2d 311 (9th Cir. 1979)

Rewis v. United States, 401 U.S. 808, 91 S.Ct. 1056, 28 L.Ed.2d 493 (1971))

Sewell v. United States, 406 F.2d 1289 (8th Cir. 1969)

Spies v. United States, 317 U.S. 492 (1943)

State of La., ex rel. Guste v. M/V Testbank, 564 F. Supp. 729 (E.D. La. 1983)

Trexler v. Tug Raven, 290 F. Supp. 429 (E.D. Va. 1968), rev'd on other grounds, 419 F.2d 536 (4th Cir. 1969)

Turner v. United States, 396 U.S. 398, 89 S.Ct. 1532, 23 L.Ed.2d 57 (1969)..........................

United States v. $122,043 in U.S. Currency, 792 F.2d 1470 (9th Cir. 1986)

United States v. Albertini, 472 U.S. 675, 105 S.Ct. 2897, 86 L.Ed.2d 536 (1985)

United States v. Allied Chemical Corp., 431 F. Supp. 361 (W.D.N.Y. 1977)

United States v. Andreen, 628 F.2d 1236 (9th Cir. 1980)

United States v. Anzalone, 766 F.2d 676 (1st Cir. 1981)

United States v. Austin, 462 F.2d 724 (10th Cir.), cert. denied, 409 U.S. 1048 (1972)

United States v. Avila-Macias, 577 F.2d 1384 (9th Cir. 1978)

United States v. Balint, 258 U.S. 250, 42 S.Ct. 301, 66 L.Ed.2d 604 (1922)

APPENDIX B

United States v. Barker, 546 F.2d 940 (D.C. Cir. 1976)

United States v. Barker, 735 F.2d 1280 (11th Cir. 1980), cert. denied, 105 S.Ct. 329 (1984)

United States v. Barnett, 507 F. Supp. 670 (E.D. Ca. 1981) rev'd on other grounds, 667 F.2d 835 (9th Cir. 1982)

United States v. Bass, 404 U.S. 336, 92 S.Ct. 515, 30 L.Ed.2d 488 (1971)

United States v. Benally, 756 F.2d 773 (10th Cir. 1985)

United States v. China Daily News, 224 F.2d 670 (2d Cir. 1955)

United States v. Combs, 762 F.2d 1343 (9th Cir. 1985)

United States v. Dotterweich, 320 U.S. 277, 64 S.Ct. 134, 88 L.Ed.2d 48 (1943)

United States v. Dye Construction Co., 510 F.2d 78 (10th Cir. 1978)

United States v. Eastern Airlines, 192 F. Supp. 187 (S.D. Fla. 1961)

United States v. Flores, 753 F.2d 1499 (9th Cir. 1985)

United States v. Frade, 709 F.2d 1387 (11th Cir. 1983)

United States v. Freed, 401 U.S. 601, 91 S.Ct. 1112, 28 L.Ed.2d 356 (1971)

United States v. Freeze, 707 F.2d 132 (5th Cir. 1983)

United States v. Frezzo Bros. Inc., 461 F. Supp. 266 (E.D. Pa. 1978)

United States v. Frezzo Bros., Inc., 546 F. Supp. 713 (E.D. Pa. 1982)

United States v. Frezzo Bros. Inc., 602 F.2d 1123 (3rd Cir. 1979)

United States v. Georgetown University, 331 F. Supp. 69 (D.C. Cir. 1971)

United States v. Granda, 565 F.2d 922 (5th Cir. 1978)

United States v. Guilbert, 692 F.2d 1340 (11th Cir. 1982), cert. denied, 460 U.S. 1016 (1983)

United States v. Hamel, 551 F.2d 107 (6th Cir. 1977)

United States v. Harris, 713 F.2d 623 (11th Cir. 1983)

United States v. Indelicato, 611 F.2d 376 (1st Cir. 1979)

United States v. International Minerals and Chemical Corp., 402 U.S. 558, 91 S.Ct. 1697, 29 L.Ed.2d 178 (1971)

United States v. Ives, 609 F.2d 930 (9th Cir. 1979), cert. denied, 445 U.S. 919 (1980)

United States v. Johnson, 221 U.S. 488, 31 S.Ct. 627, 55 L.Ed. 823 (1911))

United States v. Launder, 743 F.2d 686 (9th Cir. 1984)

United States v. Lizarraga-Lizarraga, 541 F.2d 826 (9th Cir. 1976)

United States v. Mandujano, 499 F.2d 370 (5th Cir. 1974)

United States v. Marshall, 532 F.2d 1279 (9th Cir. 1976)

United States v. Maverick, 601 F.2d 921 (6th Cir. 1979)

United States v. MCC of Florida, Inc., 772 F.2d 1501 (11th Cir. 1985)

United States v. Montoya, 739 F.2d 1437 (9th Cir. 1984)

United States v. Newman, 490 F.2d 139 (3rd Cir. 1974), cert. denied, DeLetelier v. Republic of Chile, 471 U.S. 1125 (1985)

United States v. Otley, 509 F.2d 667 (2nd Cir. 1975)

APPENDIX B

United States v. Pardee, 368 F.2d 368 (4th Cir. 1966)

United States v. Park, 421 U.S. 658, 95 S.Ct. 1903, 44 L.Ed.2d 489 (1975)

United States v. Porter, 591 F.2d 1048 (5th Cir. 1979), cert. denied, Freedlander v. United States, 449 U.S. 952 (1980)

United States v. Prince, 529 F.2d 1108 (6th Cir.), cert. denied, 429 U.S. 838 (1976)

United States v. Raper, 676 F.2d 841 (D.C. Cir. 1981)

United States v. Simpson, 561 F.2d 53 (7th Cir. 1977)

United States v. Sirhan, 504 F.2d 818 (9th Cir. 1974)

United States v. Talbot, 460 F. Supp. 253 (S.D. Oh. 1978)

United States v. United States Gypsum Co., 438 U.S. 422, 98 S.Ct. 2864, 57 L.Ed.2d 854 (1978)

United States v. Varbel, 780 F.2d 758 (9th Cir. 1986)

United States v. Westbrook, 502 F. Supp. 588 (E.D.Mi. 1980)

United States v. Wilford, 710 F.2d 439 (8th Cir. 1983), cert. denied, 464 U.S. 1039 (1984)

United States v. Winston, 558 F.2d 105 (2d Cir. 1977)

United States v. Wise, 370 U.S. 405, 82 S.Ct. 1354, 8 L.Ed.2d 590 (1962)

United States v. Zemek, 634 F.2d 1159 (9th Cir. 1980), cert. denied, 450 U.S. 916 (1981)

Wilson v. Good Humor Corp., 757 F.2d 1293 (D.C. Cir. 1985)

Published by The Bureau of National Affairs, Inc.

STATUTES CITED

2 U.S.C. § 437

7 U.S.C. § 2024

15 U.S.C. § 1990

18 U.S.C. § 1112

18 U.S.C. § 3401

18 U.S.C. § 922

21 U.S.C. § 331

22 U.S.C. § 1934

29 U.S.C. § 216

29 U.S.C. § 439

29 U.S.C. § 666

31 U.S.C. § 5316

31 U.S.C. § 5317

31 U.S.C. § 5322

33 U.S.C. § 1251

33 U.S.C. § 1311

33 U.S.C. § 1319

33 U.S.C. § 1321

33 U.S.C. § 1362

42 U.S.C. § 1395

45 U.S.C. § 152

47 U.S.C. § 501

49 U.S.C. § 1809

49 U.S.C. § 1472

50 U.S.C. App. § 16

APPENDIX B

OTHER AUTHORITIES CITED

K. Brickey, *Corporate Criminal Liability* (1984)

J. Hall, *General Principles of Criminal Law*, 137 (2d ed. 1960)

W. LaFave and A. Scott, Substantive Criminal Law (2d ed. 1986)

W. Prosser, *Handbook of the Law of Torts* (4th ed. 1971)

Wharton, *Criminal Law* (1978)

5th Circuit Pattern Jury Instructions

Manual of Model Jury Instructions for the Ninth Circuit (1985)

11th Circuit Pattern Jury Instructions

Model Penal Code (American Law Institute, 1985)

Restatement (Second) of Agency (1958)

A Legislative History of the Water Pollution Control Act Amendments of 1972, Congressional Research Service of the Library of Congress, Serial No. 93-1 (1973)

I.

STATEMENT OF THE ISSUES PRESENTED FOR REVIEW

1. May a corporate officer be held strictly liable for violations of the Clean Water Act, even though the Act explicitly states that only willful and negligent discharges may be prosecuted?

2. May a person be convicted of negligence under doctrines of tort negligence rather than the criminal requirement of a gross deviation from the standard of due care?

3. May a person be convicted of negligence without the standard requirement of both criminal and tort negligence that the standard of care must be determined in light of the circumstances as known by him to exist?

4. Where the Act criminalizes "willfully violating" provisions of the Act, may a person be convicted when he has no awareness that his actions constituted violations of those provisions?

5. Where the Act criminalizes "negligently violating" provisions of the Act, may a person be convicted when he was not negligent as to the fact that his actions constituted violations of those provisions?

6. May a corporation be held criminally liable for the acts of individuals who are not employees or agents of the corporation?

7. May a person be convicted of willfully causing another to act, without any instruction to the jury on the mental elements required?

APPENDIX B

II.

STATEMENT OF THE CASE

A. SUBJECT MATTER JURISDICTION

Subject matter jurisdiction of the magistrate's court was pursuant to 18 U.S.C. § 3401.

B. APPELLATE JURISDICTION IN THE DISTRICT COURT

Jurisdiction in this Court is pursuant to Rules of Procedure for the Trial of Misdemeanors before United States Magistrates, 7(b).

C. APPEALABILITY OF THE ORDER

Appeal is from the judgment and order of probation of each defendant, which are final orders.

D. TIMELINESS OF THE APPEAL

The judgment and order of probation as to each defendant was filed on October 21, 1986 [CR 55, 56]. The notices of appeal were filed on the same date [CR 57, 58]. The appeals are therefore timely. RPTM 7(b).

E. BAIL STATUS OF THE DEFENDANTS

Both defendants received probationary sentences.

F. NATURE OF THE CASE

This case involves the criminal prosecution of Paul D. Schwitters ("Schwitters") and Sea Gleaner Marine, Inc. ("Sea Gleaner") for the discharge of pollutants into the waters of the United States without a permit, in violation 33 U.S.C. § 1319(c)(1) of the Clean Water Act.

G. STATEMENT OF PROCEEDINGS

On May 8, 1986, defendants Schwitters and Sea Gleaner were named in an information charging each with four counts of violations of the

Clean Water Act [CR 1]. On May 15, 1986, both defendants pled not guilty [CR 2, 3].

Trial by jury was held August 11 - August 14, 1986 [CR 41, 42, 43, 49] before Magistrate Philip K. Sweigert. Prior to the start of trial, the court heard argument regarding the mental elements necessary for violations of the Clean Water Act. These issues had been extensively briefed by defendants and the prosecution [CR 27, 30, 35, 36]. In accordance with the court's conclusions on those issues, the court granted the government's motion in limine to exclude any evidence as to defendants' knowledge or lack of knowledge that they were violating provisions of the Clean Water Act [CR 41]. Defendants filed an offer of proof as to the testimony which would have been presented on this issue, set forth within their Sentencing Recommendation [CR 68, 10/6/86 RT 8-9].[1]

The jury returned a verdict of guilty on Counts 2, 3 and 4 as to each defendant, and not guilty on Count 1 as to each defendant [CR 49]. Defendants were adjudged guilty and given probationary terms. Defendant Schwitters received a fine of $10,000, with $5,000 suspended, and defendant Sea Gleaner was fined $60,000, with $30,000 suspended [CR 54, 55, 56]. Timely notices of appeal were filed [CR 57, 58].

---

[1] References to the three volume Reporter's Transcript, covering August 11 through August 14, will be "RT ___". Reference to the pre-trial colloquy on issues of intent will be "8/11/86 RT ___". References to the sentencing hearing will be "10/6/86 RT ___".

APPENDIX B

III.

STATEMENT OF FACTS

The issues on appeal relate almost exclusively to the trial court's instructions as to the elements of the crime charged, not to evidentiary rulings. These issues can be resolved without a detailed recitation of the specific facts of the case. However, a brief review of those facts will be helpful.

Defendant Sea Gleaner is a ship repair facility on the shore of Lake Union, in Seattle, Washington. It is a small family operation run by defendant Paul Schwitters and his brother Dan. Paul Schwitters is an officer of Sea Gleaner. Sea Gleaner repairs and refits vessels and a small portion of that work requires sandblasting. The essence of the prosecution's evidence was that when Sea Gleaner or its independent contractor engaged in the sandblasting of vessels, some paint and sandblasting grit was discharged into Lake Union. Neither defendant held an NPDES [National Pollutant Discharge Elimination System] permit allowing these discharges with either EPA or the Washington State Department of Ecology (which administers the NPDES system for EPA) [RT 72-75, 236-238].

The information charged violations on four occasions: Count I: May 30, 1984 (involving the vessel COASTAL TRADER); Count II: October 19, 1984 (MARK I); Count III: March 2, 1985 (PAT SAN MARIE); and Count IV: March 10, 1985 (PAT SAN MARIE). The prosecution also introduced evidence regarding the sandblasting practices at Sea Gleaner in general. Defendants were acquitted of Count I.

The Proposed Defense:

There was no dispute that discharges of pollutants occurred. The defenses were that 1) defendants lacked the requisite **mens rea** and 2) whatever discharges did occur were caused by individuals for whom defendants were not legally responsible. Defendants were excluded from presenting most of their evidence on the first issue and, as the subsequent sections will demonstrate, the instructions precluded the jury from properly considering either issue.

Defendants made an offer of proof regarding the excluded testimony, set forth within their Sentencing Recommendation [CR 68, 10/6/86 RT 8-9]. That evidence would have established that Paul Schwitters had been involved with shipyard work for fifteen years. Throughout those years, he maintained a cooperative relationship with all environmental and other regulatory agencies and promptly corrected all problems they identified. He had never been charged with any crime before.

Schwitters had never heard of any permit requirement for sandblasting vessels over the water until the day Sea Gleaner was searched. There were several factors which gave him every indication that open sandblasting was totally permissible. Throughout his years in shipyard work, he was exposed to the practices of other boat yards in the region, and the common procedure was to sandblast directly over the water. He had never heard of anyone obtaining a permit for this. At no time did any agency suggest to him that such a permit was necessary.

This state of affairs was due to lax enforcement from the Washington Department of Ecology and the Environmental Protection

APPENDIX B   B-19

Agency. Because DOE was understaffed, it had taken virtually no action to educate the ship repair industry regarding permit requirements. Although the Clean Water Act requires EPA to develop effluent limitations for point sources, that step had never been completed for the ship repair industry. A draft document was never finalized due to lack of funds.

Schwitters immediately ceased all sandblasting as soon as he was informed of the permit requirement. He cooperated fully with the prosecution in the investigation of this case.

Evidence as to Sea Gleaner in General:

Mr. Ron Zylstra, former Commodore of the Puget Sound Yacht Club, testified that sandblasting was done at Sea Gleaner throughout 1984. The Yacht Club was located next to the Sea Gleaner facility. Material from the blasting occasionally covered the docks and some of the boats at the yacht club and landed in the water. Paint from the blasting would also end up in the water. Zylstra observed no attempts to keep material from going into the water. The blasting of a vessel's hull exterior was generally done from a raft which was too small to catch all the material. The blasting generated a large amount of noise because of the compressor used to blow the grit [RT 99-103, 109-110]. Zylstra also observed spray painting of vessels; overspray would land in the water [RT 119]. On visits to Sea Gleaner's facilities, he observed a great deal of sandblast grit on the dock [RT 123].

The prosecution presented similar evidence from Tom Poinier [RT 151-186], Dean Genandt [RT 191-207] and Eleanor Genandt [RT 207-214], all members of the Yacht Club.

Published by The Bureau of National Affairs, Inc.

Michael Matta, an agent with EPA, participated in the execution of the search warrant as a diver. He observed gritty material on the lake bottom, similar to the grit observed on the docks. He was unaware that blasting had been done at those facilities before Sea Gleaner arrived, and was unsure if the debris he found could have been from that earlier activity [RT 380-395]. Charles Morgan, another diver, gave similar testimony [RT 395-399].

Count I: The COASTAL TRADER

Ron Zylstra was in the process of selling his boat on May 30, 1984. He observed someone shoveling debris off of the Coastal Trader, which was tied to Sea Gleaner's docks. The material was spent sandblasting grit which was being swept into piles on the deck of the vessel [RT 89-98]. He observed a slick on the water and identified photographs which showed a similar slick [Exs. 7.6, 7.7; RT 106-107]. He did not know who the individuals were on the Coastal Trader or for whom they worked [RT 107, 147-148]. Gary Hansen confirmed this testimony [RT 186-190].

Count II: The MARK I

Seattle Police Officer Robert Avery visited the Puget Sound Yacht Club on October 20, 1984 in response to a complaint. He observed large amounts of black dust on the dock and the vessels at the club. The MARK I was being sandblasted at Sea Gleaner's facilities [RT 65-68]. Poinier also recalled blasting on approximately October 19 [RT 166-167].

Counts III and IV: The PAT SAN MARIE

Mr. Zylstra was present on March 2, 1985, when there was a great deal of spent grit at the Yacht Club. He identified photographs

APPENDIX B

depicting the PAT SAN MARIE being worked on [Exs. 6.1 - 6.5; RT 111-113]. The vessel was being sandblasted and also sanded with a hand sander. He did not know whether the person depicted in Exhibit 6.1 was a Sea Gleaner employee or Chris Peterson, the son of the owner of the vessel [RT 148-149].

Zylstra was also present at the Yacht Club on March 10, 1985. On this date, there was blasting of the stern ramp area of the PAT SAN MARIE [RT 119].

Poinier generally confirmed Zylstra's testimony, although he testified there was grinding and spraypainting, but no sandblasting, on March 2 [RT 169]. Genandt observed paint overspray on his boat on March 2. He took pictures of the work being done on the PAT SAN MARIE [Exs. 6.1-6.5; RT 201]. An individual was using a grinder on the PAT SAN MARIE and there was material in the water [RT 200-205].

Statements and Testimony of Sea Gleaner Personnel:

Gus Holman was formerly employed as a laborer for Sea Gleaner. He testified that Paul Schwitters did not remain in the office at all times, but spent some of his time on the Sea Gleaner dock. Schwitters sometimes painted or worked on fitting and welding. When blasting was first done at Sea Gleaner, it was done by one J.W. Bateman. Sometime later, it was performed by Sea Gleaner employees. Schwitters taught Holman how to use the sandblasting equipment. Holman participated in clean-up of the Sea Gleaner facility on an occasional basis after sandblasting [RT 217-234; 239-272].

Eugene Kelly was a Sea Gleaner employee. Kelly testified that both Paul and Dan Schwitters were his bosses. Kelly was asked by Paul Schwitters to sandblast a portion of the deck and interior of the hull

Published by The Bureau of National Affairs, Inc.

of the PAT SAN MARIE on a Sunday. Schwitters taught Kelly how to sandblast and did some of the sandblasting himself. The area blasted by Schwitters was approximately four feet by three and a half feet, all on the inside of the stern ramp. The lip of the ramp kept 95% of the material from leaving the vessel, so that only approximately two shoeboxes full became airborne. The vast majority was left on the deck to be cleaned up later.

Kelly confirmed that the individual depicted in Exhibits 6.1 and 6.2 grinding the outside of the PAT SAN MARIE was Chris Peterson. Peterson was the son of the owner of the vessel and not a Sea Gleaner employee. As of the date of the photographs, there had been no sandblasting of the PAT SAN MARIE. The material shown on the surface of the water in Exhibits 6.1 - 6.5 was paint from the grinding and not sandblasting grit. There was no sandblasting grit accumulated on the windows of the vessel, as there would have been if blasting had taken place [RT 276-306].

Ira Stevenson was a Sea Gleaner employee. He observed Chris Peterson using an electric hand grinder on the exterior of the PAT SAN MARIE. He did not recall any sandblasting by Sea Gleaner employees on the exterior of the hull [RT 426-446].

Juanita Lindros was the secretary for Sea Gleaner. She identified invoices reflecting Sea Gleaner's work on the COASTAL TRADER, documents relating to the contract to work on the MARK I, and the contract for modification of the PAT SAN MARIE [RT 324-340].

Agent Gert Hattwig of the EPA identified Sea Gleaner documents showing Schwitters to be incorporator and president of Sea Gleaner. Hattwig participated in the execution of a search warrant at Sea

APPENDIX B

B-23

Gleaner. When interviewed by Hattwig, Schwitters spoke openly and without hesitation, appearing to have nothing whatsoever to hide. Schwitters informed Hattwig that until three weeks earlier, all sandblasting had been done by Bateman. After that, Sea Gleaner employees performed the work. Schwitters confirmed that work had been done on the COASTAL TRADER, and that the owner of the vessel contracted separately for sandblasting with Bateman. Schwitters also stated that Sea Gleaner employees had sanded, sandblasted and painted the PAT SAN MARIE.

Hattwig relayed that Schwitters had been aware of complaints from the Yacht Club. Schwitters stated that he had not taken any precautions to prevent sandblasting material from being discharged into the water because he had not been aware of any requirement to do so. Schwitters had been told by the sandblasting subcontractors that they were not in violation of any city, state or federal laws. He had been visited by the Seattle police, the State Department of Ecology, the U.S. Coast Guard and possibly the EPA, and after each of those visits his subcontractor told him that everything was all right.

Hattwig acknowledged that Schwitters later called the prosecutor and asked to come down and talk with him. He came without an attorney and was interview by the prosecutor and Hattwig. He stated in that interview that Bateman had been working on the waterfront for ten years and that Schwitters thus thought everything about his work was fine regarding the Department of Ecology [RT 340-353; 373-380].

The prosecution, by a motion in limine, obtained an order preventing the defendants from presenting any evidence that they did not know their activities were in violation of the Clean Water Act.

However, the prosecution attempted to show that defendants did have such knowledge. Barbara Smith, an employee of the Washington State Department of Ecology, telephoned Sea Gleaner in October, 1984, in response to complaints. She asked to speak to the person in charge, and was transferred to an individual identifying himself as such. She told that person that sandblasting debris could cause problems with water quality and asked him to try to stop the material from entering the water. The individual stated that they would try [RT 75-85]. She did not advise him that an NPDES permit was necessary before material could be discharged into the water [RT 88].

Ms. Smith did not know the identity of the individual with whom she spoke [RT 80]. She was shown a copy of a memorandum prepared by EPA agents who had interviewed her seven months after the phone call. She had stated at that time that she believed it was Schwitters she had spoken with, but she had not been certain and was not certain now [RT 81, 86-87]. She was not aware that Schwitters' brother, Dan Schwitters, was a general supervisor at Sea Gleaner who frequently answered the phone. She had taken notes of her phone conversation, but neither Paul nor Dan Schwitters' name appeared in those notes [RT 86].

The court refused to allow evidence that Bateman had been informed twice by EPA officials that his operation was in compliance with the law [RT 130, 134].

APPENDIX B

IV.

ARGUMENT

A. INTRODUCTION AND SUMMARY OF ARGUMENT

This appeal raises several issues regarding the interpretation of the Clean Water Act, 33 U.S.C. § 1251 et seq. Most of the issues have not yet been considered by any other court. In fact, the trial court conceded that it was breaking new ground in its rulings [8/11/86 RT 27, RT 354]. The prosecution admitted that several of the issues posed "troublesome questions" with little controlling authority [RT 411, 418, 421-422].

The Clean Water Act is a comprehensive law governing various aspects of water quality. For the purposes of this appeal, the relevant portions prohibit the discharge of any pollutants into the navigable waters of the United States. 33 U.S.C. § 1311. There are exceptions for those who obtain NPDES permits, which allow for the regulated discharge of pollutants. Section 1319(c)(1) states that any person who willfully or negligently violates Section 1311, various other sections of the Act, or the conditions of permits issued under the Act, shall be guilty of a misdemeanor.[2]

The reach of the Act is incredibly broad. "Any addition of any pollutant," no matter how slight, constitutes a prohibited discharge. 33 U.S.C. § 1362(12). More importantly, the term "pollutant" is defined expansively. It includes

---

[2] The Act was amended in 1987, altering the mens rea requirements and the penalties. Pub.L. 100-4. These changes, discussed at nn. 3,4,14 and 17, infra, have no direct bearing on this case except to the extent that they reflect on the Congressional intent in enacting the earlier version.

dredged spoil, solid waste, incinerator residue, sewage, garbage, sewage sludge, munitions, chemical waste, biological materials, radioactive materials, heat, wrecked or discarded equipment, rock, sand, cellar dirt and industrial, municipal and agricultural waste.

33 U.S.C. § 1362(6).

Other portions of the Act specifically address hazardous substances,[3] but the prohibition of Section 1311 requires no evidence that the discharged pollutant have any deleterious effects, either alone or in conjunction with other discharges. Minnehaha Creek Watershed Dist. v. Hoffman, 597 F.2d 617, 627 (8th Cir. 1979).

As a result, although the Act encompasses some behaviors uniformly condemned by society, it also prohibits acts which most people would be surprised to discover are crimes.[4] For example, a person who skips a rock over a lake has violated Section 1311. Unless the rock reaches the opposite shore, it is a pollutant which has been discharged into the waters of the United States. A picnicker whose cup blows from a table top into a stream has similarly caused the discharge of a pollutant. A bather who brushes sand off himself violates Section 1311 if any of the sand lands in the water. In fact, any bather violates the Act, unless the water is warmer than body temperature, because the bather will be discharging body heat, a pollutant under Section 1362(6), into the water. It is only the mens rea requirements of the Act which prevent these acts from always being crimes.

---

[3] The 1987 amendments also add specific criminal penalties for violations which threaten death or serious bodily injury. Section 1319(c)(3)(A).

[4] Under the 1987 amendments, these actions are felonies if committed knowingly.

APPENDIX B   B-27

   So far, prosecutorial restraint has not resulted in any published opinions involving acts as innocuous as these, although one court has confirmed that cutting seagrass with a boat propeller and redepositing it violates the Act. United States v. MCC of Florida, Inc., 772 F.2d 1501 (11th Cir. 1985).[5] But as demonstrated below, Part IV.F.4, the courts consistently look to the full potential reach of the statute, not just those acts which prosecutors say they might prosecute, in discerning Congressional intent, especially on the mens rea required for conviction.

   The evidence presented at trial, in conjunction with that the trial court excluded, showed that Paul Schwitters reasonably believed he was in full compliance with the law. He had complied completely with all regulations of which he was aware, such as fire, occupational safety, and air pollution. He had been visited frequently by officials from various regulatory agencies and on no occasion was he advised of the necessity of an NPDES permit or of any violation of the Act. In fact, his subcontractor specifically informed him after those visits that his work was in compliance with the law. Schwitters' long history of ship-repair work had never given him any indication that a permit was required for this work. None of the other shipyards had such a permit to his knowledge and in fact, due to lax enforcement by EPA, he had never even heard of an NPDES permit.

   The broad reach of the statute, together with these facts, provides the backdrop for most of the mens rea issues raised by this

---

[5] In that case, the defendant acted particularly egregiously, continuing in violation of a Corps of Engineers Cease and Desist Order and the district court's express directions. The lack of such blatant behavior would of course provide no judicial check, should a prosecutor choose to indict one who cuts seagrass more innocently.

appeal. Do the intent elements found by the trial court provide the protections which Congress intended against overly broad application of the statute? For example:

1) the Act makes clear that corporate officers, like other persons, are guilty only if they act willfully or negligently. Despite this, the trial court allowed conviction of Schwitters under strict liability. Even if the Act had been ambiguous as to its *mens rea* requirement, application of strict liability would require an explicit directive from Congress.

2) the trial court defined negligence in simple tort terms. The common law of negligence, as that term is used in criminal law, demonstrates that Congress intended to follow the Model Penal Code, allowing conviction only for gross deviations from the standard of care.

3) the trial court omitted an essential element of both tort and criminal negligence, by instructing the jury to consider all the circumstances proven at trial in determining if the standard of care had been violated. The law is clear that the jury may consider only the circumstances known to the defendant at the time he acted.

4) the instructions made defendants vicariously liable for individuals who were neither employees nor agents (as that term is properly defined) of defendants. Case law clearly shows that defendants are not liable for the acts of independent contractors, when defendants do not control the specific methods by which those contractors work.

5) the term "willfully violates," as used in the Act, requires knowledge that one is violating some provision of the Act. There is

APPENDIX B

direct legislative history to this effect. Congress uses this specific language when it is requiring *mens rea* as to the fact of violation. Finally, the term "willfully" has been interpreted with regularity to require such knowledge in regulatory laws such as the Act. The instructions eliminated this element.

6) the term "negligently violates" requires a negligent state of mind as to the fact of a violation. This follows the same argument as that regarding the term "willfully violates." This element, too, was kept from the jury.

7) the trial court excluded any evidence that defendants were unaware they were violating the Act. Such evidence goes directly to the *mens rea* elements established by Congress.

8) the trial court refused to define the mental elements required for aiding and abetting, and in particular left the term "willfully" unexplained. Case law makes clear that such definition is mandatory.

B. STANDARD OF REVIEW

Each of the issues raised below, except in Part IV.H, involves the refusal of the trial court to properly instruct the jury regarding the elements of the crime.[6] This Court interprets the statute and determines what elements it requires on a *de novo* basis. United States v. Varbel, 780 F.2d 758, 761 (9th Cir. 1986); United States v. Launder, 743 F.2d 686, 688-689 (9th Cir. 1984) (determining elements of criminal intent).

"A jury's verdict cannot stand if the instructions provided the jury do not require it to find each element of the crime under the

---

[6] The standard of review for Part IV.H is set forth therein.

proper standard of proof." *Cabana v. Bullock*, ___ U.S. ___, 106 S.Ct. 689, 696, 88 L.Ed.2d 704 (1986). The trial court has no discretion to define the crime without all of the essential elements. *United States v. Combs*, 762 F.2d 1343, 1346 (9th Cir. 1985).

C. THE COURT APPLIED STRICT LIABILITY PRINCIPLES TO DEFENDANT SCHWITTERS, IN VIOLATION OF THE CLEAR STATUTORY LANGUAGE ALLOWING CONVICTION ONLY FOR WILLFUL OR NEGLIGENT ACTS

The trial court's instructions allowed Paul Schwitters to be convicted on any of three different theories. The first required proof that Paul Schwitters discharged pollutants willfully or negligently. This instruction, and the definitions the court applied in explaining that instruction, are discussed further in Parts IV.D, F and G, *infra*. The second theory was that he aided and abetted violations. Error in that instruction is addressed in Part IV.I.

The third route to conviction was predicated on Schwitters' corporate position. The jury was instructed that:

> The Federal Clean Water Act specifically provides that "responsible corporate officers" can be held responsible criminally for the acts of their corporation. Not every corporate officer is a "responsible" officer or one in a "position of authority" upon whom Congress has placed the burden of vigilance and foresight. A "responsible corporate officer," or one in a "position of authority" for criminal purposes, has been defined as one who has a responsible share in the furtherance of the transaction or occurrence which the statute forbids. Another way of defining this is as follows: if a corporate officer has the responsibility, and powers equal to that responsibility, to devise whatever measures are necessary to ensure compliance with the Clean Water Act, then he is a responsible corporate officer.
>
> If you find that SEA GLEANER, INC., is guilty of the crime charged in any of these counts, and if you find beyond a reasonable doubt that defendant PAUL D. SCHWITTERS had, by virtue of his position in the corporation, the power to prevent or correct such a violation, and if you find that he failed exercise that power to prevent or correct the

APPENDIX B

wrongdoing, then you may find him guilty. [Instruction No. 20, RT 473-74].

Defendant submits that this instruction is contradicted by the plain reading of the statute, principles of statutory construction, and well-entrenched doctrines of criminal responsibility. It is supported by neither its legislative history nor case law.[7]

1. **The Unambiguous Language of the Clean Water Act Dictates That Corporate Officers, Like All Other "Persons," May be Convicted Only If They Act Willfully or Negligently**

The court's instruction was based on 33 U.S.C. § 1319(c)(3). That section states that the term "person", in addition to the definition in Section 1362(5)[8], shall include "responsible corporate officers." Since "responsible corporate officers" are simply incorporated within the definition of "persons," the statute thus provides that "Any responsible corporate officer who willfully or negligently violates Section 1311 . . . shall [be guilty of a misdemeanor]." By its very terms then, the statute makes the liability of such officers no different than that of other individuals.

The trial court's instruction, however, required no negligence or willfulness on Paul Schwitters' part. It instead required only that defendant Sea Gleaner be convicted and that Schwitters have held a responsible position within the corporation. This instruction thus

---

[7] Defendants objected to the trial court's instruction [RT 457].

[8] Section 1362(5) provides, "The term 'person' means an individual, corporation, partnership, association, State, municipality, commission, or political subdivision of a State, or any interstate body."

entirely eliminated the mens rea so clearly required before corporate officers may be convicted.[9]

In fact, during the colloquy regarding this provision, both the court and the prosecution recognized the clear import of this language [RT 8/11/86 24-26, 27-28].

> THE COURT: I do have a question of Mr. Marshall, just briefly. As I read the statute, all the responsible corporate officer -- the only place it's referred to, of course, is in the definition where it says an individual includes, isn't that right?
> MR. MARSHALL: That's right, Your Honor.
> THE COURT: So that just means then we take the word responsible corporate officer and transpose it over to individual, isn't that right, so that we would say in reading what is done wrong any responsible corporate officer who intentionally or negligently. How else could you read that?
> MR. MARSHALL: I don't think there is any other way to read it.
> THE COURT: Well, then wouldn't it require that he have the same intent that any other individual has, whether that intent is to do the act or violate the law, isn't that correct, wouldn't he have to have that intent?
> MR. MARSHALL: I think that's quite clear. I don't think there is any way -- the way this statute reads as defining the term person to include that phrase and if you substitute --
> THE COURT: Then what does it add?
> MR. MARSHALL: I think it adds a concept --
> THE COURT: In other words, he's the same as any other individual. He has to either do the act with intent or negligently, right, or violate the law with intent or negligently, one or the other.
> MR. MARSHALL: I think what it adds is Congress' intent that officers who are not directly involved in the conduct be reached. There is legislative history on the floor of the Congress where they encourage prosecutors to file cases. In fact, this language, if I understand correctly, came out of the Kepon case in the James River or followed -- my counsel is shaking her head so I will retract that.
> In any event, I think what it does is it simply helps explain what we are arguing negligence includes. That's what I was saying earlier, that responsible corporate officer liability really isn't much different from negligence and

---

[9] The statute does not immunize the supervisor who directs the discharge of pollutants, but avoids acting as a principal. Such a person faces full criminal exposure under the law governing aiders and abettors.

possibly the right way to handle it is to move the two together into one instruction, that it's part of the concept of negligence, they read very similarly.

We haven't done that previously, candidly, because we haven't tried too many of these cases and we're fortunately learning to some degree, as with the courts. I agree with Your Honor.

THE COURT: <u>He has to have the same intent that an individual has, doesn't he?</u>

MR. MARSHALL: <u>I think that's right.</u>

THE COURT: He either has to -- if he doesn't know about it, somebody else did it, he obviously can't intentionally do the act.

MR. MARSHALL: Right.

THE COURT: Or violate the law.

MR. MARSHALL: I think it really makes sense in light of the negligence standard. It doesn't help you very much in light of the willful standard. As you say, it's difficult for a person -- I guess it is possible because someone doesn't need to personally do it, they can just intend it to happen. I'm not making sense. Let me try to explain that. I think that if a person knows that they have a way of getting rid of waste and he is not actually involved in the activity, he's not intentionally doing the discharge, <u>he is just aware of it</u>, I think in that context willfully might apply to a responsible corporate officer and it might make sense.

I just think in summary, without wasting more of the Court's time, I think the concept responsible corporate officer simply helps a little in understanding or defining negligence in the context of a corporate case. That's how we view it. [RT 8/11/86 24-26][emphasis added]

THE COURT: . . .As to the second issue, I still haven't clarified in my own mind just how that's going to come down, except that it seems to me that where we say -- the statute says a responsible corporate officer is the same as an individual, individual includes responsible corporate officer. All you do is say a responsible corporate officer discharging a pollutant negligently or intentionally. It requires the same kind of intent, it seems to me, and that's where negligently comes in. That <u>if as a responsible corporate officer he should have known that pollutants were going into this water</u> by the kind of operation that was going on, then it seems to me with the appropriate instructions the jury can find him individually liable, as well as the corporation, and that's basically where I come down. And that's the way it's going to be in this case anyway. I can appreciate that may be an issue that is going to be thrashed out on appeal, but whatever. That's the way I'm going to do it. [emphasis added][RT 8/11/86 27-28]

Unfortunately, the trial court and the prosecution eventually backtracked from this position [8/11/86 RT 33-34] and the jury instruction on this issue did not apply the elements so clearly required by the statute. That instruction instead allowed a finding of guilt upon two specific findings by the jury: 1) that the corporation be guilty and 2) that Paul Schwitters, by virtue of his corporate position, had the power to prevent the violation. Thus the instruction did not require, as the court and the government conceded it should, that Schwitters act either intentionally or negligently.

As the court initially suggested, a negligence standard would require that the officer "should have known that pollutants were going into this water." [RT 8/11/86 27] The level of willfulness suggested by the prosecution was that the corporate officer be aware of the corporate violations [RT 8/11/86 26].[10] All such elements, however, were absent from Instruction No. 20. By its instruction, the court erroneously applied a strict liability standard to Paul Schwitters.

2. The "Responsible Corporate Officer" Doctrine Is Applicable Only to Strict Liability Offenses

In submitting an instruction similar to that given by the court, the prosecution relied upon United States v. Dotterweich, 320 U.S. 277, 64 S.Ct. 134, 88 L.Ed.2d 48 (1943) and United States v. Park, 421 U.S. 658, 95 S.Ct. 1903, 44 L.Ed.2d 489 (1975). Those cases held that when

---

[10] As discussed in Parts IV.D and G, defendants submit that negligence under Section 1319(c) requires proof of more than simple civil negligence. Since the court's instruction did not even require proof of this lowest definition of negligence, Schwitters' conviction must be reversed regardless of the resolution of those other issues. Similarly, the question of just what willfulness entails [Part IV.F] does not affect Instruction No. 20, since no standard of willfulness was required.

a business enterprise violates the Federal Food, Drug and Cosmetic Act, "[t]he offense is committed . . . by all who do have such a responsible share in the furtherance of the transaction which the statute outlaws . . ." Dotterweich, 320 U.S. at 284.

The FDCA is a strict liability offense. 21 U.S.C. § 331(k). Shipments are "'punished by the statute if the article is misbranded [or adulterated], and that the article may be misbranded [or adulterated] without any conscious fraud at all.'" 320 U.S. at 281 (quoting United States v. Johnson, 221 U.S. 488, 497-498, 31 S.Ct. 627, 55 L.Ed. 823 (1911))

> Such legislation dispenses with the conventional requirement for criminal conduct--awareness of some wrongdoing. In the interest of the larger good it puts the burden of acting at hazard upon a person otherwise innocent but standing in a responsible relation to a public danger.

Id.

As stated in Park, 421 U.S. at 672,

> the Act imposes not only a positive duty to seek out and remedy violations when they occur but also, and primarily, a duty to implement measures that will insure that violations will not occur.

Given this broad reach, the FDCA necessarily encompasses not only those who directly ship the goods, but all those who bear a responsible relationship to the shipping. Since the FDCA requires no mental element with regard to the adulterated quality of the shipped goods, the responsible corporate agent approach imposes the same standard of liability on corporate officers as that established for other defendants under the Act.

But this principle has no place in Clean Water Act prosecutions. This Act does not impose strict liability. Even under the government's interpretation of "willfully" and "negligently" (see Parts IV.F and G, infra), Section 1319 requires some proof of the defendant's mens rea. As discussed in Comment, Limits on Individual Accountability for Corporate Crimes, 67 Marquette Law Review 604, 618 n. 85 (1985), the doctrine of Dotterweich and Park has only been applied to strict liability offenses.

The trial court's interpretation of the law thus created a most anomolous result. Without any basis in the statutory language, it imposed a far stricter standard of liability on corporate officers than on any other individuals. Where Congress made clear that corporate officers must be treated no differently than others, Instruction No. 20 treated Paul Schwitters far, far worse.

There are further problems with the prosecution's attempt to import the Park doctrine into the Clean Water Act. For example, does some employee of the corporation have to act willfully or negligently before the corporate officer can be convicted, or may there simply have been some discharge of pollutants by the corporation or its agents? Although the instruction given by the court required a finding that the corporation was guilty, there is no basis in the statutory language for such a conclusion. The Clean Water Act in Section 1311 forbids any discharge of pollutants. If such a discharge has occurred, then the officer has had "a responsible share in the furtherance of [a transaction or occurrence which the statute forbids]," regardless of whether the acting employee was willful or not.

This ambiguity only highlights how misplaced the strict liability corporate officer doctrine is in the non-strict liability Clean Water Act. This problem does not arise under the FDCA because that is a strict liability statute; any prohibited transaction, regardless of intent, makes the employee, the corporation, and the officer all guilty.

The only case to discuss the responsible corporate officer provision of the Clean Water Act is United States v. Frezzo Bros. Inc., 602 F.2d 1123, 1130 n. 11 (3rd Cir. 1979). That decision, however, does not resolve the implications of Section 1319(c)(3), since the defendants did not object to how liability for corporate officers was defined. Defendants instead complained that, although they had been charged in the indictment as corporate officers, the jury was told defendants could be found guilty as individuals. The defendants' objections to the jury charge are discussed in more detail in United States v. Frezzo Bros. Inc., 461 F. Supp. 266, 272-273 (E.D. Pa. 1978). The sole issue was the claimed discrepancy between the indictment and the instruction, not the specifics of the corporate officer instruction.

3. **A Congressional Intent to Impose Strict Liability Must be Clearly Expressed**

In United States v. United States Gypsum Co., 438 U.S. 422, 436, 98 S.Ct. 2864, 57 L.Ed.2d 854 (1978), the Supreme Court reiterated "the familiar proposition that '[t]he existence of a mens rea is the rule of, rather than the exception to, the principles of Anglo-American criminal jurisprudence.'" 438 U.S. at 436 (quoting Dennis v. United States, 341 U.S. 494, 500, 71 S.Ct. 857, 95 L.Ed. 1137 (1951)). Strict liability offenses have a "generally disfavored status," and "intent generally remains an indispensable element of a criminal offense," 438 U.S. at 437.

In accordance with these principles, the Supreme Court "has on a number of occasions read a state-of-mind component into an offense even when the statutory definition did not in terms so provide." Id. Gypsum thus insists on a clear mandate from Congress before strict liability may be applied.[11] Accord, Liparota v. United States, 471 U.S. 419, 105 S.Ct. 2084, 85 L.Ed.2d 434 (1985). To apply the Park principle to the Clean Water Act would stand this approach on its head. It would remove intent requirements specifically provided by Congress.

Another principle of statutory construction also governs here. Defendant Schwitters submits that the Act is clear in prohibiting only "willful" and "negligent" violations by corporate officers. The most that could be said for the government's position would be that the provision is unclear. The Gypsum decision adheres to the "injunction that 'ambiguity concerning the ambit of criminal statutes should be resolved in favor of lenity.'" 438 U.S. at 437 (quoting Rewis v. United States, 401 U.S. 808, 812, 91 S.Ct. 1056, 1059, 28 L.Ed.2d 493 (1971)). Liparota, too, recently applied this principle in the context of determining intent requirements. Under these circumstances, where there are simple and explicit ways Congress could have altered the liability for corporate officers, the lenity principle mandates that this Court apply the straight-forward, common sense reading of Section 1319(c)(3) urged by defendants.

4. **The Legislative History of the Clean Water Act Does Not Contradict the Clear Language of the Statute**

---

[11] Gypsum also suggests that due process may limit strict liability to offenses involving items which, by their inherently dangerous nature, put one on notice of likely regulation. The Clean Water Act, with its broad reach, is not such a statute. See Part IV.A.

APPENDIX B   B-39

As previously mentioned, the reading of Sections 1319(c)(1) and (3) makes clear that corporate agents, like others, violate the law only if acting willfully or negligently. The Supreme Court has consistently stressed that under such circumstances, resort to legislative history is inappropriate. Under such circumstances, this Court must follow the plain meaning of that language. "Courts in applying criminal laws generally must follow the plain and unambiguous meaning of the statutory language. [Citations omitted] '[O]nly the most extraordinary showing of contrary intentions' in legislative history will justify a departure from that language." United States v. Albertini, 472 U.S. 675, 105 S.Ct. 2897, 2902, 86 L.Ed.2d 536 (1985), quoting Garcia v. United States, 469 U.S. 70, 75, 105 S.Ct. 479, 83 L.Ed.2d 472 (1984). This circuit pays close and strict adherence to the plain meaning rule. Varbel, 780 F.2d at 761.

Even if this Court were to look beyond the statute's plain wording, there is no legislative history to support the court's instruction. In fact, there is no legislative history regarding Section 1319(c)(3) at all.

A provision identical to Section 1319(c)(3) was added to the Clean Air Act five years later in 1977. The sole comment regarding that amendment states:

> The Committee intends that criminal penalties be sought against those corporate officers under whose responsibility a violation has taken place, and not just those employees directly involved in the operation of the violating source.

Report of the Committee on Environment and Public Works, United States Senate, Report No. 95-127, 51, reprinted at 6 A Legislative History of the Clean Air Act Amendments of 1977, 1371, 1425.

This comment is susceptible of several interpretations. It can be read to mean that such officers need have no personal culpability, just "responsibility" for the operation in question. But another fair reading is those officers who are "responsible," in the sense of having caused the violation, should be just as subject to prosecution as the individuals who physically operate the equipment.[12] This comports with the holding in United States v. Wise, 370 U.S. 405, 82 S.Ct. 1354, 8 L.Ed.2d 590 (1962). In Wise, the defendant contended that, since the Sherman Act lists corporations, but not corporate officers, as potential violators, it does not govern an officer who acts solely for the corporation. The Supreme Court rejected that contention. Congress, which had included corporations as persons in Section 1362(5), was ensuring in Section 1319(c)(3), that the Wise conclusion would apply to the Clean Water Act.

Even if this language were thought to indicate an intent to impose strict liability in the Clean Air Act, this brief passage regarding a different statute, enacted by a totally different Congress, is too slim a reed to support the trial court's interpretation of the Clean Water Act. This is not "a clearly expressed legislative intent" as to the Clean Water Act. Only such a definitive statement might be sufficient to overcome the "conclusive" effect of the statute's unambiguous

---

[12] Other reasonable readings of this comment would be in accord with the levels of culpability suggested by the trial court and the prosecutor in the colloquy quoted above. The Committee could have been referring to an officer who is responsible in that he is aware of the discharge, but in no way has caused it [8/11/86 RT 26]. Or the reference could be to an officer who is responsible in that he should have known of the discharge [8/11/86 RT 27]. Defendant submits that neither of these meanings comports with the clear language of the statute that the "person" must willfully or negligently discharge himself. Nevertheless, these interpretations would still mandate a higher level of proof than that required by Instruction No. 20.

APPENDIX B

language. Varbel, 780 F.2d at 761, quoting Dickerson v. New Banner Institute, Inc., 460 U.S. 103, 110, 103 S.Ct. 986, 74 L.Ed.2d 845 (1983). This is especially so given the courts' and Congress's "inhospitable attitude to non-mens rea offenses." United States Gypsum Co., 438 U.S. at 438.

Further support for defendant's interpretation comes from another portion of the legislative history of the Clean Air Act. H.R. 294, 1977 U.S. Code Cong. & Ad. News 1077, 1148-1149, describes Congress's desire to impose the standards of Park and Dotterweich to civil liability. The committee rejected an amendment which would have injected a scienter requirement, "knowingly," into the civil penalty scheme. The discussion makes clear that any such scienter requirement would be inconsistent with Park and Dotterweich. Accordingly, Congress's inclusion of scienter requirements for corporate officers' criminal liability rebuts any reading of the Park doctrine into the Clean Water Act criminal actions.

5. **Applying Strict Liability Under the Terms of the Act Would Deny Defendant His Due Process Right to Clear Notice of What Acts Are Made Criminal**

Should this Court conclude that Congress did intend to make corporate officers strictly liable, the conviction would be void on another ground. A fundamental of due process is that "laws [must] give the person of ordinary intelligence a reasonable opportunity to know what is prohibited, so that he may act accordingly." Grayned v. City of Rockford, 408 U.S. 104, 108, 92 S.Ct. 2294, 33 L.Ed.2d 222 (1972). As noted in United States v. Anzalone, 766 F.2d 676 (1st Cir. 1981), the rationale for this rule dovetails with the principle of lenity:

"A fair warning should be given to the world in language that the common world will understand of what the law intends to do if a certain line is passed. To make the warning fair, so far as possible, the line should be clear". . . . This policy embodies "the distinctive distaste against men languishing in prison unless the lawmaker has clearly said they should."

766 F.2d at 680-681 (quoting United States v. Bass, 404 U.S. 336, 348, 92 S.Ct. 515, 30 L.Ed.2d 488 (1971).

Throughout the preceding sections, defendants have demonstrated that corporate officers are not strictly liable under the Clean Water Act. This section becomes relevant only if this Court should conclude otherwise. Even with such a conclusion, it must be conceded that Congress chose an incredibly obscure, ambiguous, one might even say bizarre, method of expressing its intent. Instead of simply stating, "a corporate officer is liable for all criminal acts he had the power to prevent," Congress stated "a corporate officer is liable if he willfully or negligently violates provisions of this Act."

It simply cannot be contended that a strict liability standard was made clear through this language. Under those circumstances, despite Congress's supposed intent, due process would bar prosecution.

6. Conclusion

The trial court's instruction borrowed a doctrine from a totally different statutory scheme, and placed it within a framework where it simply does not fit. That instruction negated clear statutory language and important principles of mens rea. By eliminating a critical element of the crime, the court allowed Paul Schwitters to be improperly convicted. That conviction must be reversed.

APPENDIX B

D. **A CRIMINAL CONVICTION FOR NEGLIGENCE MAY NOT BE BASED ON THE MINIMAL SHOWING NECESSARY FOR TORT NEGLIGENCE**

In instructing the jury that defendants could be convicted for negligently discharging pollutants, the trial court defined negligence to mean "failure to use reasonable care." [Instruction Nos. 9,10, RT 470-471] Defendants objected to this instruction [RT 453] on the ground that it applied straight tort law concepts rather than a definition more appropriate to criminal cases. Defendants submitted a jury instruction taken almost verbatim from the Model Penal Code, § 2.02(d) (American Law Institute, 1985). That instruction provided,

> [T]he defendant should have been aware of a substantial and unjustifiable risk. . . . The risk must be of such a nature and degree that the defendant's failure to perceive it, considering the nature and purpose of his conduct and the circumstances known to him, involves a gross deviation from the standard of care that a reasonable person would observe in the defendant's situation.

[Proposed Instruction No. 1][13] A quite similar definition is set forth in the Proposed Federal Criminal Code § 302(d), Final Report of the National Commission on Reform of Federal Criminal Laws, 1971.

1. **A Criminal Conviction for Negligence Requires Proof of a Gross Deviation From a Reasonable Standard of Care**

There are two critical differences between the Model Penal Code definition and that provided by the court. First of all, the risk under the Model Penal Code must be more than just that which a reasonably careful person would avoid. It must be "a substantial and unjustifiable risk." The failure to perceive the risk must involve "a gross deviation from the standard of care that a reasonable person would observe. . ." The court's instruction criminalized any

---

[13] Defendants objected to the trial court's instruction and the refusal to give the proposed instruction [RT 453, 461].

deviation from that standard of care, rather than only gross deviations.

There is a dearth of federal case law regarding the meaning of "negligent" within criminal statutes. This is not surprising, because there are few federal statutes which criminalize negligent behavior. Nevertheless, there are several authorities throughout the law directly supporting our position.

Although not using the word "negligent," 18 U.S.C. § 1112(a) defines involuntary manslaughter in negligence terms, namely a killing "without due caution and circumspection." This has consistently been interpreted to require proof of gross negligence. United States v. Benally, 756 F.2d 773, 776 (10th Cir. 1985); United States v. Pardee, 368 F.2d 368, 375 (4th Cir. 1966). In Trexler v. Tug Raven, 290 F. Supp. 429, 446 (E.D. Va. 1968), rev'd on other grounds, 419 F.2d 536 (4th Cir. 1969), the court stated that criminal negligence is a higher standard even than gross negligence.

Given this sparse federal case law, this Court must seek other authority. When the Supreme Court has had difficulty in interpreting a *mens rea* requirement in a statute, it has frequently looked to the Model Penal Code for assistance. See, e.g., Liparota, 471 U.S. 419, 423 n. 5; United States Gypsum Co., 438 U.S. at 438; Leary v. United States, 395 U.S. 6, 46, n. 93, 90 S.Ct 642, 24 L.Ed.2d 610 (1970); Turner v. United States, 396 U.S. 398, 416, n. 29, 89 S.Ct. 1532, 23 L.Ed.2d 57 (1969). The circuit courts have also turned to the Model Penal Code for guidance on state of mind issues. See, e.g., United States v. Montoya, 739 F.2d 1437, 1438 (9th Cir. 1984); United States v. Barker, 546 F.2d 940, 948, n. 23 (D.C. Cir. 1976). In a similar

APPENDIX B

fashion, the Proposed Federal Criminal Code has served as a guide for the courts on intent issues. United States v. Maverick, 601 F.2d 921, 926, n. 3 (6th Cir. 1979); United States v. Mandujano, 499 F.2d 370, 377, n. 6 (5th Cir. 1974). Both of these authorities, the Model Penal Code and the Proposed Federal Criminal Code, directly support defendants' view of the term "negligently."

Yet another source of authority confirms defendants' reading of the statute. In resolving the meaning of statutory terms, the courts will look to the meaning of that term in the common law. "[W]here a federal criminal statute uses a common law term without defining it, the term is given its common law meaning." United States v. Guilbert, 692 F.2d 1340, 1343 (11th Cir. 1982), cert. denied, 460 U.S. 1016 (1983)

Most of the law on the meaning of "negligent" is set forth by statute. In such circumstances, the courts look also to the term as it has been used in the various legislatures. "We therefore look to similar statutes, the common law, and common sense to aid in the interpretation of these words..." United States v. Porter, 591 F.2d 1048, 1053 (5th Cir. 1979), cert. denied, Freedlander v. United States, 449 U.S. 952 (1980) (emphasis added) (holding that term "kickback" in 42 U.S.C. § 1395nn(b)(1) requires that payment be to an earlier possessor; reversing conviction). In Moragne v. States Marine Lines, Inc., 398 U.S. 375, 90 S.Ct. 1772, 26 L.Ed.2d 339 (1970) the Supreme Court confirmed that when discerning the common law the courts examine statutes as well as cases.

> As Professor Landis has said, "much of what is ordinarily regarded as 'common law' finds it source in legislative enactment." (citation omitted) It has always been the duty of the common-law court to perceive the impact of major

Published by The Bureau of National Affairs, Inc.

legislative innovations and to interweave the new legislative policies with the inherited body of common-law principles - many of them deriving from earlier legislative exertions. 398 U.S. at 392.

As discussed in 1 W. LaFave and A. Scott, <u>Substantive Criminal Law</u> (2d ed. 1986) § 3.7(b) at 329 - 333 and n. 26, the "major legislative innovations" and the "new legislative policies" are fully in accord with defendants' position. At least twenty-two states, in recent codifications, have defined negligence in line with defendants' approach and only one, South Dakota, applies a standard comparable to normal tort negligence. The common law of negligence in criminal statutes, a clear guide to Congress's intent, thus wholeheartedly rejects the standard applied by the trial court and embraces defendants' position.

One additional factor guiding this Court is the policy consideration underlying the criminalization of different levels of negligence. As suggested by several commentators, the threat of punishment for civil tort negligence cannot serve to deter people from negligent conduct; one who is unaware of the risk he is creating cannot be deterred from creating it by the thought of possible conviction. 1 LaFave and Scott, § 3.7(a)(2) at 329 and J. Hall, <u>General Principles of Criminal Law</u>, 137 (2d ed. 1960).

Finally, this Court should again consider the incredibly broad reach of the Act. Given the types of conduct prohibited, it is hardly likely that Congress intended to impose a lower standard of culpability than usually applied for convictions of negligence.

To the extent the government wishes to impose punishment on those whose culpability is below criminal negligence, the Act provides ample opportunity. Section 1319(d) allows fines of up to $10,000 per day for violations.[14] These penalties require no culpability at all. Insisting on criminal standards of negligence for criminal convictions will thus not hamper the government's enforcement efforts against those with lesser fault, or even no fault at all.

Given the law on criminal negligence, and the policies set forth above, the term "negligently" as used in the Act requires an instruction consistent with the Model Penal Code. The most that could be said for the prosecution's position is that the term is ambiguous. If so, principles of strict construction mandate interpretation in defendants' favor.

2. **Negligence Under Both Tort and Criminal Law May Be Judged Only By the Circumstances Known to the Defendant**

A second critical deficiency in the trial court's instruction relates to the factors which may be considered in determining if the prescribed standard of care has been violated. The court instructed the jury to consider "all of the surrounding circumstances, as shown by the evidence in the case." [Instruction No. 10, RT 471 (emphasis added)] The Model Penal Code and defendants' instruction make clear that in looking at the defendant's conduct, the jury must consider only the circumstances known to the defendant.

This requirement is no novelty with the Model Penal Code. It is a well-established standard of negligence. "[W]hether harm was legally foreseeable bears on what was apparent to the defendant at the time of his complained of conduct and not what may appear through the exercise of hindsight." Manning v. Ashland Oil Co., 721 F.2d 192, 196 (7th Cir.

---

[14] Those penalties are increased to $25,000 per day under the 1987 amendments. In addition, there is a new provision for administrative penalties, with fines up to $10,000 per day of violation.

1983) (applying Illinois law). Accord, State of La., ex rel. Guste v. M/V Testbank, 564 F. Supp. 729, 740 (E.D. La. 1983) (defendant not to be judged "by looking backward 'with the wisdom born of the event.'") (quoting W. Prosser, Handbook of the Law of Torts (4th ed. 1971) § 31 at 146).

The trial court's instruction on this element was thus a polar opposite to the correct state of the law. It improperly allowed conviction for negligence based on circumstances not known to defendants.

3. Conclusion

The trial court improperly instructed the jury on the essential elements of negligence, both as to what deviation from the standard of care is made criminal, and as to the factors the jury may consider. Each of these errors alone mandates reversal.

E. A CORPORATION IS NOT VICARIOUSLY LIABLE FOR THE ACTS OF INDEPENDENT CONTRACTORS WHO ARE NOT ITS AGENTS

The trial court instructed the jury that defendant Sea Gleaner Marine was criminally responsible for the acts of its agents performed in the course of their employment. The instruction defined "agents" as a corporation's "employees, officers or other authorized representatives." [Instruction No. 18, RT 472-73] Over objection by defendants, the court refused to define agents in terms of the legal relationship between an individual and the corporation. [Proposed Instruction No. 28, RT 463][15]

---

[15] Although only defendant Sea Gleaner was directly implicated in this instruction, the court's error in refusing defendants' proposed instruction invalidates defendant Schwitters' conviction also.

The problem was in the court's inclusion of the vague term "authorized representative" in defining "agents." It should be obvious that a corporation is not liable for all criminal acts committed by every person ever authorized to act in its behalf. When a corporation uses a courier service, for example, the courier is certainly an authorized representative of the corporation for some purposes. Yet if that courier were to commit vehicular homicide while delivering a package, the corporation would not be liable. As held in United States v. Georgetown University, 331 F. Supp. 69 (D.C. Cir. 1971), a corporation is not criminally liable for the acts of its independent contractors who are not agents of the corporation.

These results in both common sense example and case law conform to the policy behind corporate liability. The doctrine of corporate criminal liability is founded on principles of tort liability. One well-established doctrine in tort law is that "an independent contractor is responsible for both his torts and for those of his servants yet the one engaging the contractor to perform the services is not responsible." Dumansky v. United States, 486 F. Supp. 1078, 1091 (D.N.J. 1980); accord, Wilson v. Good Humor Corp., 757 F.2d 1293, 1301 (D.C. Cir. 1985). There are exceptions to this general rule, none of which are applicable here (e.g., ultrahazardous activities such as explosions).

In accordance with these clear principles of civil corporate liability, defendants submitted Proposed Instruction No. 28. That instruction defined the term "agent" in conformance with established

---

Defendant Schwitters was subject to conviction as a corporate officer, which theory required conviction of defendant Sea Gleaner. See Part IV.C. Thus, any error in defendant Sea Gleaner's conviction created error as to defendant Schwitters.

elements of agency, as established by this circuit and the <u>Restatement (Second) of Agency</u> (1958).

The most critical of these elements was the requirement that the corporation have the power to exercise control over the manner in which the person worked: without such power, there is no basis in law, policy, or reason for convicting the corporation. That portion of the instruction read:

> 3) the corporation had the power to exercise control over the manner in which the person works. If the corporation had control over the result to be obtained, but not over the exact methods to be used, the party is not an agent.

This clause was based on <u>Fenton v. Freedman</u>, 748 F.2d 1358 (9th Cir. 1984), which held that "if control may be exercised only as to the <u>result</u> of the service performed and not the means and methods by which it is accomplished, then the provider is an independent contractor, and not an agent." 748 F.2d at 1362 (emphasis in original). The Supreme Court has stated that "<u>the critical factor</u> in making this determination [as to liability of the contractor's hirer] is the authority of the principal to control the detailed physical performance of the contractor." <u>Logue v. United States</u>, 412 U.S. 521, 527-528, 93 S.Ct. 2215, 37 L.Ed.2d 121 (1973) (emphasis added). This attribute of agency is discussed in <u>Restatement (Second) of Agency</u> § 14.

The principles set forth in defendants' instruction are summed up in Comment b to <u>Restatement (Second) of Agency</u> § 2.

> Thus, one who contracts for a stipulated price to build a house for another and who reserves no direction over the conduct of the work is an independent contractor; but he is not an agent, since he is not a fiduciary, has no power to make the one employing him a party to a transaction, and is subject to no control over his conduct.

APPENDIX B   B-51

The deficiencies in the trial court's instruction were especially critical in this case. As to Count Two, the individual allegedly discharging pollutants was an independent contractor, G.W. Bateman. As to the Counts Three and Four, there was differing testimony as to whether any discharging was done by defendants' employees or instead by Chris Peterson, the son of the vessel's owner. The jury could certainly have concluded that, under the trial court's definition, Chris Peterson was an agent, since he was implicitly authorized to work on his father's vessel at Sea Gleaner's docks. As to any of these counts, then, the jury could have concluded that the person discharging was an authorized representative, given that term's extremely vague reach, where they would not have concluded that such person was an agent, as that term is properly defined in the law.

Doctrines of corporate criminal liability have been frequently criticized, especially when applied to a crime requiring mens rea committed by lower level employees. 1 LaFave and Scott, § 3.10(c) at 366; 1 K. Brickey, Corporate Criminal Liability (1984) § 3.04 at 56-57 (assumption behind liability, that corporation can effectively supervise agents, lacks reality when dealing with lower-level employees). With these considerations in mind, the Model Code and nearly all recent state enactments limit corporate liability in most circumstances to only those actions authorized or recklessly tolerated by the board of directors or a high managerial agent. Model Penal Code § 2.07 and statutes cited in 1 LaFave and Scott § 3.10(c) at 367, nn. 56 - 59.

Defendants do not suggest that firmly established federal case law, allowing corporate liability for the acts of all employees, should be reversed because of these criticisms or the modern trend in criminal statutes. But given these policy considerations, this Court should refuse to extend corporate liability even further, beyond employees and "agents," as defined by the law, to some vague concept of "authorized representatives."

The trial court's instruction thus made Sea Gleaner vicariously liable for individuals who were not its agents, as that term is defined in law. Because this element was incorrectly set forth, the convictions must be reversed.

F. PROOF OF "WILLFULNESS" REQUIRES THAT DEFENDANTS WERE AWARE THEY VIOLATED THE CLEAN WATER ACT

1. Introduction

Title 33 U.S.C. § 1319(c)(1) provides:

> Any person who willfully or negligently violates section 1311...shall be punished by a fine of not less than $2,500 nor more than $25,000 per day of violation, or by imprisonment for not more than one year, or both.

Section 1311(a) provides:

> Except as in compliance with this section and section...1342 [the NPDES permitting section]...of this title, the discharge of any pollutant by any person shall be unlawful.

The trial court instructed the jury that:

> A defendant does an act "willfully" if it is done voluntarily and deliberately, with knowledge of what he is doing. It is not necessary for the government to show that defendant actually knew the law or read the statute or has any actual familiarity with the rules themselves.

[Instruction No. 8, RT 469-470] Defendants proposed an instruction requiring proof that they knew their discharges were in violation of the Clean Water Act [Proposed Instruction No. 1]. Defendants also submitted instructions defining "willfully" and requiring proof of a

APPENDIX B B-53

specific intent to violate the law [Proposed Instruction Nos. 15, 16].[16] Defendants contend that the court wrongly defined "willfully," thus omitting an element of the crime.

It is important to understand from the outset just what this dispute involves. Defendants do _not_ contend that they had to know their behavior was criminal before they could be convicted. Defendants do contend that they had to know, as Section 1319(c)(1) requires, that they were violating Section 1311 of the Act.[17]

The layman is of course quite familiar with the adage that "ignorance of the law is no excuse." A very few courts have also relied on this maxim to readily dispose of intent issues. But the clear thrust of hundreds of cases, interpreting scores of statutes, is that ignorance of the law is indeed an excuse when knowledge of some aspect of the law is an element of the crime. Thus, such intent issues cannot be disposed of with the quick turn of a phrase, but instead require careful analysis of what elements a crime encompasses.

As stated in the commentary to the Model Penal Code, "[T]he general principal that ignorance or mistake of law is no excuse is usually greatly overstated; it has no application when the circumstances made material by the definition of the offense include a legal element." Model Penal Code § 2.02 comment 11 at p. 131 (Tent. Draft No. 4, 1955) (quoted in United States v. Golitschek, 808 F.2d

---

[16] Defendants objected to the court's failure to give their proposed instructions [RT 461,463].

[17] Nor is this appeal about the appropriateness of "bad purpose" language. Defendants acknowledge the numerous cases holding that such language generally need not be given. Although defendants did submit such an instruction, the issue raised here is the trial court's refusal to define the elements of the crime to include knowledge that their discharges were in violation of the Act.

Published by The Bureau of National Affairs, Inc.

195, 202 (2d Cir. 1986). This point is elaborated carefully in Liparota, 471 U.S. 419, 105 S.Ct 2084 (1985). Liparota held that 7 U.S.C. § 2024(b), which makes it a crime to knowingly use food stamps in a manner "not authorized" by statute or regulation, requires proof that the defendant know his conduct was unauthorized.

> Our holding today no more creates a "mistake of law" defense than does a statute making knowing receipt of stolen goods unlawful. In both cases, there is a legal element in the definition of the offense. In the case of a receipt of stolen goods statute, the legal element is that the goods were stolen; in this case, the legal element is that the "use, transfer, acquisition," etc. were in a manner not authorized by statute or regulations. It is not a defense to a charge of receipt of stolen goods that one did not know that such receipt was illegal, and it is not a defense to a charge of a § 2024(b) violation that one did not know that possessing food stamps in a manner unauthorized by statute or regulations was illegal. It *is*, however, a defense to a charge of knowing receipt of stolen goods that one did not know that the goods were stolen, just as it is a defense to a charge of a § 2024(b) violation that one did not know that one's possession was unauthorized.

471 U.S. at 425 n. 9 (emphasis in original) (citations omitted).

Similarly, it is not a defense to the present charge that defendants did not know that violating certain provisions of the Clean Water Act was criminal. It *is* a defense that they did not know that their actions violated those provisions.[18]

As the following sections will demonstrate, knowledge of some legal status is a quite common element of federal crimes. In most of those crimes, as in the Clean Water Act, the legal fact which must be known is that one is violating some provision of the law.

As stated in Spies v. United States, 317 U.S. 492, 497 (1943) "willful . . . is a word of many meanings, its construction often being

---

[18] An excellent explication of this distinction is set forth in Golitschek, 808 F.2d at 202-203.

APPENDIX B

influenced by its context." Both defendants and the prosecution can cite cases in which "willfully" has been defined consistent with their respective positions. The following sections will show, however, that the context in which the word "willfully" is used in the Clean Water Act, both as to the specific language in which it is set forth and as to the behavior it encompasses, clearly demonstrates that the trial court's instruction omitted an essential element of the crime.

2. The Legislative History of the Clean Water Act Demonstrates Congress's Intent to Require Awareness That a Violation Has Occurred

There is also clear legislative history on the meaning of the term "willfully" in the Clean Water Act.

> Assuming there was some discharge of pollutants contrary to this act and the Administrator notified the violating party as he is required under this act, and told him what he was doing was wrong, and told him where it was happening, and ordered the violator to stop, and if the polluter did not obey that order, then the polluter becomes a willful violator and can be charged under this Section as a willful violator.

A Legislative History of the Water Pollution Control Act Amendments of 1972, Congressional Research Service of the Library of Congress, Serial No. 93-1 (1973), Vol. 1 at 530 (statement of Representative William Harsha, floor manager of the bill). A more clear expression that violations become willful only when the violator knows he is committing violations cannot be imagined.

This evidence of congressional intent should be compared with that noted in United States v. Winston, 558 F.2d 105, 108 (2d Cir. 1977) in determining that willfulness under 45 U.S.C. § 152 requires an intentional violation of a known legal duty. The court relied on an observation that "it is a difficult matter to secure a conviction with that word [willful] in a statute and requires an array of most convincing evidence." The legislative history in this case, with its conclusion that one becomes a willful violator only _after_ one is informed of the law, is obviously far stronger.

Further evidence of Congress's intent in using the term "willfully" comes from the 1987 amendments to the Clean Water Act. The term "willfully" has been deleted and the word "knowingly" has been substituted.[19] This is the sort of "striking change of expression" that shows Congress was altering the level of intent. LaFave and Scott, § 2.2(g) at 116-117. The obvious implication of Congress's using "knowingly" at one time and "willfully" at another time is that "willfully" requires a higher level of awareness. For example, in United States v. $122,043 in U.S. Currency, 792 F.2d 1470 (9th Cir. 1986), the court pointed to the use of the term "knowingly" in 31 U.S.C. § 5316, the civil provision regarding transportation of currency, as compared with the use of "willfully" in 31 U.S.C. § 5317. Although criminal violations under the term "willfully" require awareness of the reporting requirements under the Act, a civil violation occurs whenever one knowingly transports the funds, regardless of one's awareness of the law. Accord, United States v. Allied Chemical Corp., 431 F. Supp. 361, 369 (W.D.N.Y. 1977) (discussing higher levels of _mens rea_ for "willfully" in 49 U.S.C. § 1809(b) than for "knowingly" in 49 U.S.C. § 1809(a)(1).

3. The Language "Willfully Violates" Has Consistently Been Used by Congress to Require Awareness That a Violation Has Occurred

---

[19] Because of this change, the decision in this case regarding the meaning of "willfully" will have no effect on prosecutions under the amended statute.

APPENDIX B

Further support for defendants' position comes from the specific wording of the statute. What is made criminal is not willfully doing certain acts, but willfully violating certain provisions of the law. This is a clear indication of Congress's intent that the mental state encompass the fact that a provision is being violated, not simply the fact that an act is occurring.

Where Congress has used similar language, the courts have almost universally interpreted "willfully" as defendants suggest. See, e.g.,

1) 50 U.S.C. App. § 16 (Trading with the Enemy Act) ("whoever shall willfully violate any of the provisions of this Act . . ."); United States v. Frade, 709 F.2d 1387, 1392 (11th Cir. 1983) (willfulness requires awareness that activities are regulated);

2) 2 U.S.C. § 437(g)(D)(1)(b) (disclosure of federal campaign funds); ("any person who knowingly and willfully commits a violation of any provision of this Act . . ."); American Federation of Labor and Congress of Industrial Organizations v. Federal Election Commission, 628 F.2d 97, 101 (D.C. Cir.), cert. denied, 449 U.S. 982 (1980) (interpreting this language in a civil action, holding "a 'willful' violation must necessarily connote 'defiance or such reckless disregard of the consequences as to be equivalent to a knowing, conscious, and deliberate flaunting of the Act.'");

3) 45 U.S.C. § 152 (railway labor) ("the willful failure or refusal . . . to comply with the terms of . . . this section. . ."); Winston, 558 F.2d at 108 (conduct must constitute a "voluntary, intentional violation of a known legal duty.");

4) 49 U.S.C. § 1472(a) (federal aviation regulations; "any person who knowingly and willfully violates any provision of this

chapter . . ."); United States v. Eastern Airlines, 192 F. Supp. 187, 192 (S.D. Fla. 1961) (requiring "conscious and deliberate intent to disobey");

    5) 31 U.S.C. § 5322 (reporting of monetary instruments transactions; "a person willfully violating this subchapter . . ."); United States v. Granda, 565 F.2d 922, 926 (5th Cir. 1978) (willfulness requires knowledge of the reporting requirement); Ivers v. United States, 581 F.2d 1362, 1366 (9th Cir. 1978);

    6) 22 U.S.C. 2778(c)[20] (exportation of ammunition; "any person who willfully violates any provision of this section. . ."); Golitschek, 808 F.2d at 203; United States v. Lizarraga-Lizarraga, 541 F.2d 826, 828 (9th Cir. 1976) (willfulness requires proof of defendant's "specific intent to do or fail to do what he knows is unlawful");

For other statutes with similar language, the courts have not always required absolute knowledge that one is violating the referenced provisions, but have required some state of mind with regard to the violation. See, e.g.,

    7) 29 U.S.C. § 439 (labor-management reporting and disclosure; "any person who willfully violates this subchapter . . ."); United States v. Otley, 509 F.2d 667, 672 (2nd Cir. 1975) (willfulness requires knowledge of law or action "in reckless disregard of the law's requirement.");

    8) 29 U.S.C. § 216(a) (fair labor standards; "any person who willfully violates any of the provisions . . ."); Nabob Oil Co. v. United States, 190 F.2d 478 (10th Cir.), cert. denied, 342 U.S. 876

---

[20] Section 2778(c) was formerly codified as 22 U.S.C. § 1934.

APPENDIX B

(1951) (defendant not guilty "unless he is either conscious of the fact that what he is doing constitutes a violation of the Act or unless he wholly disregards the law and pursues a course without making any reasonable effort to determine whether the plan he is following would constitute a violation of the law or not.") 190 F.2d at 479-80; accord, Marshall v. Root's Restaurant, 667 F.2d 559, 561 (6th Cir. 1982) (interpreting term in civil suit).

9) 29 U.S.C. § 666(e) (Occupational Safety and Health Act) ("Any employer who willfully violates any standard . . ."); United States v. Dye Construction Co., 510 F.2d 78, 82 (10th Cir. 1978) (defendant must intentionally disregard the standard or be plainly indifferent to its requirement); accord, Nat. Steel, Etc. v. Occupational Safety and Health Comm'n, 607 F.2d 311 (9th Cir. 1979) (interpreting identical language in Section 666(a), civil penalties).

It might be thought that the "willfully violates" Section 1311 language of Section 1319 is not evidence of Congress's intent regarding the scope of the term "willfully," but was simply an attempt to deal, in simple language, with the fact that many different types of acts were being prohibited. To the contrary, Congress has shown several times that it can clearly make the term "willfully" modify actions, rather than violations of provisions, even when several types of actions are involved. See, e.g., 47 U.S.C. § 501 ("any person who willfully and knowingly does . . . any act, matter, or thing, in this chapter prohibited or declared to be unlawful . . ."); 15 U.S.C. § 1990c ("any person who knowingly and willfully commits any act . . . that violates any provision . . ."); 49 U.S.C. § 1472(1)(2) ("whoever willfully . . . shall commit an act prohibited . . ."). That Congress chose the language it did for Section 1319 thus demonstrates its intent that one must be willful as to the fact that one is violating a section of the law, rather than that one be willful simply as to the act.

4. **Where a Statute Prohibits Conduct Which Would Not Alert Citizens To the Likelihood of Criminal Regulation, the Term "Willfully" Requires Awareness of the Regulation**

Numerous cases have discussed the situation where a particular statute encompasses at least some behavior which is relatively innocuous. In such situations, the courts have observed that the behavior would not put reasonable persons on notice of the likelihood of criminal regulation. As a result, the courts have found that the term "willfully" in such statutes requires proof of awareness of the criminal statute. This conclusion has been based both on an inference of congressional intent and at times on due process notice requirements.

For example, Frade, 709 F.2d at 1392, dealt with violations of the Trading With the Enemy Act, 50 U.S.C. App. 5(b). The statute, through its implementing regulations, criminalized "activities which laymen do not consider wrong . . . items not known generally to be controlled by the government." 709 F.2d at 1392.

> Since the purpose of all law, and the criminal law in particular, is to conform conduct to the norms expressed in that law, no useful end is served by prosecuting the "violators" when they have no knowledge of the law's provisions.

Id., quoting United States v. Granda, 565 F.2d at 926.[21] The court held that this interpretation was necessary to satisfy the notice

---

[21] The court in Granda applied this rationale in holding that "willfully" requires knowledge of the law's provisions under the currency transportation laws.

requirement of the due process clause. The _Frade_ court reversed for failure to grant a judgment of acquittal where the evidence did not establish knowledge of the violation.

The Ninth Circuit made similar observations in _Lizarraga-Lizarraga_, interpreting 22 U.S.C. § 1934. Pointing to the "exhaustive list" of items which could not be exported, the court observed

> Unlike those substances which are known generally to be controlled by government regulation, such as heroin or like drugs, these items might be exported or imported innocently. Under such circumstances, it appears likely that Congress would have wanted to require a voluntary, intentional violation of a known legal duty not to export such items before predicating criminal liability.

541 F.2d at 828. The court in _Lizarraga-Lizarraga_ reversed because the jury instructions did not adequately explain this requirement.

United States v. Simpson, 561 F.2d 53 (7th Cir. 1977) dealt with 47 U.S.C. § 501, which makes criminal willfully doing any act prohibited by the Federal Communications Act. This prohibition encompasses acts as innocent as operating a licensed CB station without an operator's license. "This is not a situation in which the actor should know from the nature of the prohibited act that it was likely to create danger or produce deleterious results, as in _United States v. International Minerals_." 561 F.2d at 62. As a result, the court found that willful violations required a voluntary, intentional violation of a known legal duty. Since the evidence was insufficient to support such a finding, the court reversed and entered a judgment of acquittal.

The result and rationale of these cases are consistent with the views expressed by the commentators that such proof is especially necessary when dealing with the "lesser regulatory crimes involving conduct not inherently immoral." 1 LaFave and Scott § 5.1(d) at 587-

588 and numerous authorities cited therein. As LaFave and Scott observe, "Cases recognizing some sort of ignorance of law defense typically are of this type." Id. at 588 n. 79.

The Clean Water Act does cover some conduct which seriously threatens the community and which by its inherent dangerousness would put individuals on notice of likely regulation. But as discussed in Part IV.A, it also reaches every stone thrown into a lake, any heat added to a pond, and any sea grass cut and redeposited. Such conduct is a far cry from "conduct that a reasonable person should know is subject to stringent public regulation and may seriously threaten the community's health and safety." For this latter category, the examples given by the Supreme Court have been limited to hand grenades, United States v. Freed, 401 U.S. 601, 91 S.Ct. 1112, 28 L.Ed.2d 356 (1971); corrosive liquids, United States v. International Minerals and Chemical Corp., 402 U.S. 558, 91 S.Ct. 1697, 29 L.Ed.2d 178 (1971); adulterated foods, Dotterweich, 320 U.S. at 264; and narcotics, United States v. Balint, 258 U.S. 250, 42 S.Ct. 301, 66 L.Ed.2d 604 (1922).

The Clean Water Act thus reaches behavior as innocent as that dealt with in Frade, Granda, Lizarraga-Lizarraga and Simpson. Under these circumstances, Congress clearly intended that persons would not be made criminals by virtue of their acts without some awareness that their conduct was regulated.

The issue is not whether the particular conduct of the defendants in this case would put one on notice of regulation. The issue is the entire range of conduct encompassed by the Clean Water Act. For example, in Liparota, the Court discussed at length examples of potentially innocent conduct covered by the Act, although the defendant had purchased food stamps at far below face value, clear evidence of a fraudulent intent. Since the court was determining the meaning of the statute for all cases, and not that particular defendant, the "innocence" or "non-innocence" of individual acts was irrelevant.

Similarly, in Lizarraga-Lizarraga, to determine congressional intent, the court looked to the full range of activities encompassed by the statute. Although the defendants themselves had been transporting ammunition, an item which would certainly put one on notice of likely regulation, the court noted that other items regulated by the statute included numerous seemingly innocent items. Frade and Simpson reached their conclusions about innocent conduct and the meaning of "willfully" when interpreting statutes which encompassed some conduct which would clearly put one on notice of its wrongfulness (e.g., extending credit to Communist China's banks during Korean war, United States v. China Daily News, 224 F.2d 670 (2d Cir. 1955); selling decoders to unauthorized recipients of subscription television, United States v. Westbrook, 502 F. Supp. 588 (E.D.Mi. 1980).

In this case, Paul Schwitters should not have been aware that his conduct required permits. Frequent visits by regulatory agencies resulted in assurances by Sea Gleaner's contractor that the sandblasting was in full compliance with the law. And despite Schwitters' years of exposure to the boat-building industry, he had never heard of NPDES permits. Defendants expect the prosecution to challenge these assertions. The debate need not be resolved by this Court, however, since it is this Court's task to interpret the intent requirements of the statute for all defendants. It is the jury's job, under proper instructions, to decide if the prosecution can establish that intent.

4. **The Cases Interpreting the Clean Water Act Do Not Support the Prosecution's Interpretation of "Willful"**

Only three cases decided under the Clean Water Act deal with the mens rea required for willful violations. In *Frezzo Bros. Inc.*, 602 F.2d at 1123, the court simply found that there had been sufficient evidence of willfulness, without elaborating on what that term meant. In doing so, the opinion noted that there was evidence of defendants' numerous confrontations with government authorities prior to the crimes charged. Id. at 1129, n. 9. If anything, this observation supports the conclusion that the court believed willfulness required knowledge that the discharge was prohibited.

United States v. Hamel, 551 F.2d 107 (6th Cir. 1977), also found that the evidence was sufficient to establish mens rea, without directly holding what level of mens rea was necessary. However, its discussion of the facts also supports defendants' position. The court emphasized Hamel's "deceptive responses" to investigators. If the only mens rea requirement were knowledge that he acted, and no knowledge that his actions were wrongful, Hamel's deceptiveness would be completely irrelevant.

One district court decision does conclude that no intent to violate the statute is required. *United States v. Frezzo Bros., Inc.*, 546 F. Supp. 713 (E.D. Pa. 1982). Its analysis is unpersuasive. The entirety of the discussion is devoted to establishing that Congress can constitutionally eliminate mens rea requirements. The opinion then states in a conclusory fashion that "by its terms, the statute does not require that a defendant intend a criminal act." Id. at 713. "In order to be convicted of a statutory violation, the Act requires only that the defendant have willfully or negligently committed the acts in question." Id. at 721. The opinion ignores the direct statutory language stating that violations, not acts, must be committed willfully, as discussed in Part IV.F.4. It ignores, too, the extensive case law establishing that Congress usually intends "willfully" to require knowledge that one is violating a provision of law.

Thus, instead of actually analyzing Congress's intent, the opinion relies on a most amazing syllogism: Congress could constitutionally exclude a specific intent requirement from the Clean Water Act, therefore Congress must have intended to exclude such a requirement, despite its use of the term "willfully." This flawed reasoning is of no value to this Court in discerning Congress's intent.[22]

6. This Circuit Requires an Instruction on Willfulness When Congress Makes Willfulness an Element of the Crime

The Ninth Circuit has repeatedly reaffirmed the meaning of "willfully" as proposed by defendants. "[T]he willfulness requirement is satisfied if the defendant's act or failure to act is voluntary and purposeful, and if committed with the specific intent to do or fail to do what he knows is unlawful." Lizarraga-Lizarraga, 541 F.2d at 828. In United States v. Sirhan, 504 F.2d 818 (9th Cir. 1974), the requirement was further explicated:

---

[22] The discussion in Frezzo Bros. as to the constitutional issue is also deficient. Relying primarily on decisions from the first few decades of this century, the opinion totally ignores the recent discussion in International Minerals, 402 U.S. at 564-565 (see discussion in Part IV.G), suggesting that due process may place significant constraints on when a statute may eliminate mens rea.

> A "willfulness" instruction talks about bad purpose either to disobey or to disregard the law, while a "knowingly" instruction talks about defendant's knowingly doing an act which the law forbids purposely intending to violate the act. It appears that a "willful" violation of the law requires more of a specific intent, though the difference may be more one of semantics than actual substance. This is not to say that one or the other instruction may be given. <u>If the statute requires a willful intent for conviction, then an instruction on willfulness must be given</u>, and vice versa.

504 F.2d at 820, n. 3 (emphasis added).

Further support is found in <u>United States v. Flores</u>, 753 F.2d 1499, 1505 (9th Cir. 1985). In declining to read a specific intent requirement into 18 U.S.C. § 922(e), the court observed,

> the absence of words such as "intent" and "willfully," which traditionally accompany specific intent crimes, supports our conclusion. "Congress would have included similar language...had it intended to require proof of willful conduct." (quoting <u>United States v. Launder</u>, 743 F.2d at 692 (Choy, dissenting)).

In Section 1319, Congress did include such language, and did intend to require such proof. Refusal of the proposed instructions was error.

7. Conclusion

Paul Schwitters did everything possible to comply with the law, given the facts known to him and the facts he reasonably should have known. He simply did not know he was violating the Clean Water Act. Every factor available for this Court's consideration demonstrates that Congress did not intend to make criminals out of individuals such as Schwitters, that the term "willfully violates" requires knowledge of a violation: the plain language of the statute, the clear statement in the legislative history, the implications of the recent amendments, the potentially draconian reach the law would have if there were no such element.

APPENDIX B   B-67

If there were any ambiguity on this question, that ambiguity should be resolved in the favor of lenity. As made clear in Liparota, 471 U.S. at 427, that principle certainly applies when it is unclear which elements of a crime are modified by the mens rea requirement.

The trial court's instruction to the jury thus omitted an essential element, mandating reversal.

G. WHERE THE CLEAN WATER ACT PROHIBITS "NEGLIGENTLY VIOLAT[ING]" PROVISIONS OF THE ACT, CONVICTION REQUIRES PROOF OF A NEGLIGENT STATE OF MIND AS TO THE FACT THAT A VIOLATION IS OCCURRING

As discussed in Part IV.D, one question in criminalizing negligent conduct is what level of negligence must be proven. The second question, to which this section is addressed, is which elements must be covered by that state of mind. Must one only be negligent in performing the act, or must one also be negligent as to the fact that one is violating a section of the Clean Water Act? Defendants submit that the latter, more restrictive requirement, was intended by Congress.[23]

Several factors support this conclusion. First, as with "willfully," the plain reading of the statute reveals that "negligently" modifies "violates," rather than any particular act.[24] This is not a statute where several different elements of the crime are

---

[23] Defendants submitted an instruction reflecting this position [Proposed Instruction No. 1] and made proper objections [RT 461].

[24] If this Court rejects defendants' argument in Part IV.F, and holds that willfulness requires no awareness as to the fact that a violation is occurring, then defendants would expect this Court to also reject our position that one must be negligent as to the existence of a violation. However, this conclusion would have no bearing on the question of whether a conviction may be based on simple tort negligence or if it instead requires a higher standard, as discussed in Part IV.D.

Published by The Bureau of National Affairs, Inc.

mentioned after the mental element, creating ambiguity about what portions of the statute the mental element is supposed to modify. Liparota, 471 U.S. at 424-425 n. 7, discusses this question of "how far down the sentence the word . . . is supposed to travel." In this case, the statute is clear. There is only one place for "negligently" to travel. Congress did not criminalize negligently performing acts which constitute violations,[25] but rather negligently violating such provisions.

Secondly, the linkage of "willfully" and "negligently" supports defendants' position. In Section 1319(c), Congress created one crime, with one penalty. It would be anomolous to conclude that for this single crime Congress set forth one method of violation which requires proof of specific intent, but included another method which requires no intent at all. It makes far more sense to conclude that Congress, in adding the term "negligently," simply wanted to foreclose arguments about proof of absolute knowledge, to reach those who can reasonably close their eyes to the requirements of the law.

Counsel is unaware of any criminal statute in which Congress has criminalized two levels of mens rea as different as "willfully" and "negligently" (as the government and the court interpreted that latter term), while providing the same penalty and same level of offense. In fact, even in the Clean Water Act, where Congress has reached behavior at two different of levels of mens rea, it has provided different penalties. For example, in Sections 1321(f)(1) - (3), the Act establishes civil penalties for the discharge of oil and hazardous

---

[25] Congress has frequently used such language with other levels of mens rea and could easily have done so here, had it intended "negligently" to modify "acts." See discussion at p. 46.

APPENDIX B

substances. Two levels of violation are provided, one requiring willful violation and one under strict liability. Much higher penalties were provided for willful violations.

Defendants' position follows, too, from the broad reach of the Act. As discussed in Part IV.A, the Act reaches such potentially innocent behavior as skipping rocks on a lake, brushing sand off one's body at the shore, being lax in securing one's paper plate while picnicking at the beach, or even putting one's warm body into the water. Defendants submit that it was hardly Congress's intent to make such actions subject to a year in jail and a $25,000 fine, unless the individual should have been aware his act was prohibited.

Up to this point, defendants have been referring to negligence as a level of *mens rea*. Negligence, however, is truly a non-"*mens rea*" offense, because it requires no actual subjective state of mind.[26] J. Hall, General Principals of Criminal Law at 135-141. In *International Minerals*, the Supreme Court discussed the constitutional limitations in omitting a *mens rea* requirement.

> In *Balint* the court was dealing with drugs, in *Freed* with hand grenades, in this case with sulfuric and other dangerous acids. Pencils, dental floss, paper clips may also be regulated. But they may be the type of products which might raise substantial due process questions if Congress did not require, as in *Murdock*, "*mens rea*" as to each ingredient of the offense.

402 U.S. at 564-565.

Statutes such as those referred to in *International Minerals* regulate items which by their inherently dangerous nature provide the

---

[26] As negligence is defined in some statutes, it does require a subjective awareness of the risk. See 1 LaFave and Scott § 3.7(b) at 331-32. Neither the definition provided by the court, nor that requested by defendants, required such subjective awareness.

possessor with warning of likely regulation. The Clean Water Act governs objects which provide no such warning, by its extremely broad definition of pollutants that include almost any item. In essence, its reach encompasses "pencils, dental floss, [and] paper clips."

A person who deliberately discharges pollutants might be held to have notice of potential regulation, so perhaps Congress could constitutionally prohibit knowing discharges, without requiring that they be willful. But one who negligently causes a discharge of some (by itself) innocuous item may not be presumed to have such knowledge, and substantial due process questions would be raised by criminalizing such acts without proof of some *mens rea*.

Even if this Court felt Congress could constitutionally enact such a statute, it should be quite loath to attribute to Congress the intent to eliminate *mens rea*, without a far more explicit directive in the statute.

> Of course, Congress could have intended that this broad range of conduct be made illegal, perhaps with the understanding that prosecutors would exercise their discretion to avoid such harsh results. However, given the paucity of materials suggesting that Congress did so intend, we are reluctant to adopt such a sweeping interpretation. [Emphasis in the original]

Liparota, 471 U.S. at 427.

This is especially so given the significant penalties attendant upon a conviction for negligence. Imprisonment of up to a year in jail, and $25,000 in fines (with a minimum of $2,500) may be imposed for each day of violation. Adhering to defendants' interpretation of "negligently" does not interfere with the government's ability to stringently enforce the Act. The government may always, without the opprobrium or imprisonment which may accompany criminal conviction,

APPENDIX B

seek civil penalties. As with most of the issues addressed in this brief, if the statute is not clearly in defendants' favor, it is at most ambiguous. This Court must resolve any ambiguity through lenity.

The trial court thus omitted an element of the offense by not requiring a negligent state of mind as to the fact of violation. This error mandates reversal.

H. THE TRIAL COURT'S REFUSAL TO ADMIT ANY DEFENSE EVIDENCE ON AN ESSENTIAL ELEMENT WAS ERROR

Consistent with its interpretation of the terms "willfully" and "negligently," the trial court excluded all evidence that defendants lacked awareness that they were violating provisions of the Act [8/11/86 RT 31,37]. Defendants made an offer of proof regarding that evidence [CR 68, 10/6/86 RT 8-9].

Although a trial court normally has broad discretion regarding the admissibility of evidence, exclusion of all evidence relating to an essential element of the crime is reversible error. The court's discretion is abused if the exclusion "prejudicially deprived [the defendant] of material evidence critical to his defense." United States v. Ives, 609 F.2d 930, 933 (9th Cir. 1979), cert. denied, 445 U.S. 919 (1980).

As demonstrated in Parts IV.F and G, it is an essential element of willfulness that one know a violation has occurred and it is an essential element of "negligently violating" that one be negligent as to the fact of violation. The exclusion of all defense evidence on these issues mandates reversal.

I. THE COURT'S REFUSAL TO DEFINE THE MENTAL ELEMENT REQUIRED FOR CONVICTION AS AN AIDER AND ABETTOR WAS ERROR

The trial court instructed the jury that the defendants could be convicted as aiders and abettors [Instruction No. 21; RT 474-75]. That instruction properly set forth the acts which would constitute aiding and abetting, namely 1) counseling, commanding, inducing or procuring the commission of an offense or 2) causing an act to be done. However, as to the first clause, the court gave no instructions on what mental elements were necessary.[27] As to the second clause, the court simply stated that such acts must be done "willfully," without ever explaining that term. Defendants submitted instructions [Proposed Instruction No.

---

[27] The court's instruction stated:

> The term "vicarious responsibility" refers to a person's criminal liability for the acts of his associates. Under certain circumstances you may find a defendant guilty of an offense charged in an information without finding that he personally committed each of the acts constituting the offense or that he was personally present at the commission of the offenses.
>
> Whoever commits an offense against the United States, or counsels, commands, induces, or procures its commission, or willfully causes an act to be done which if directly performed by him or another would be an offense against the United States is punishable as a principal. That is, he is as guilty of the offense as if he had personally committed each of the acts constituting the offense.
>
> Mere physical presence by a defendant at the time and place of the commission of an offense is not by itself sufficient to establish his guilt. Some conduct by the defendant of an affirmative character in furtherance of a common criminal design or purpose is necessary. [Instruction No. 21, RT 474-75]

APPENDIX B

14] which defined those mental elements in accordance with consistent case law.[28]

As set forth in United States v. Avila-Macias, 577 F.2d 1384, 1390 n. 5 (9th Cir. 1978),

> In order to aid and abet another to commit a crime it is necessary that the accused aider and abettor willfully associate himself in some way with the criminal venture and willfully participate in it as he would in something he wants to bring about; that is to say, he willfully seeks by some act of his to make the criminal venture succeed.

Through this formulation, and similar ones, aiding and abetting has consistently been held to be a crime requiring proof of "willfulness." See, e.g., United States v. Zemek, 634 F.2d 1159 (9th Cir. 1980), cert. denied, 450 U.S. 916 (1981); United States v. Andreen, 628 F.2d 1236 (9th Cir. 1980); United States v. Indelicato, 611 F.2d 376 (1st Cir. 1979); United States v. Freeze, 707 F.2d 132

---

[28] Defendant's instruction stated:

> In order to aid and abet another to commit a crime it is necessary that the accused willfully associate himself in some way with the criminal venture, and willfully participate in it as he would in something he wishes to bring about; that is to say, that he willfully seek by some act or omission of his to make the criminal venture succeed.
>
> An act or omission is "willfully" done, if done voluntarily and intentionally and with the specific intent to do something the law forbids, or with the specific intent to fail to do something the law requires to be done; that is to say, with bad purpose either to disobey or to disregard the law.
>
> You of course may not find any defendant guilty unless you find beyond reasonable doubt that every element of the offense as defined in these instructions was committed by some person or persons, and that the defendant participated in its commission.

Defendants also submitted Proposed Instruction No. 2 defining the elements of "willfully causing" another to act. Defendants made proper objection to the failure to give these instructions [RT 461, 463].

(5th Cir. 1983); United States v. Wilford, 710 F.2d 439 (8th Cir. 1983), cert. denied, 464 U.S. 1039 (1984); United States v. Barker, 735 F.2d 1280 (11th Cir. 1980), cert. denied, 105 S.Ct. 329 (1984)[AZ: trial brief has lower court date as 1984]; United States v. Austin, 462 F.2d 724 (10th Cir.), cert. denied, 409 U.S. 1048 (1972); United States v. Harris, 713 F.2d 623 (11th Cir. 1983); United States v. Newman, 490 F.2d 139 (3rd Cir. 1974), cert. denied, DeLetelier v. Republic of Chile, 471 U.S. 1125 (1985).

In Newman, 490 F.2d at 142-143, the court reversed for failure to instruct the jury that conviction of aiding and abetting requires a finding of willfulness. Although the instructions listed and defined willfulness as an element of the substantive offense, the omission of this element from the aiding and abetting instruction mandated a new trial.

Although the Model Jury Instruction for the Ninth Circuit, § 5.03, Aiding and Abetting (Manual of Model Jury Instructions, 1985), contains no mention of "willfulness," the comment to this instruction cites to Avila-Macias, 577 F.2d at 1390, n. 5 as approving "substantially the same language." The instruction defined as "accurate" in Avila-Macias, however, included the element of "willfulness" which the trial court excluded.

The 11th Circuit Pattern Jury Instructions (Basic Instruction 9.1, Special Instruction 6) require proof of "willfulness" for aiding and abetting, and define that term in a nearly identical fashion to defendants' proposed instruction. Accord, 5th Circuit Pattern Jury Instructions. Defendants' proposed instruction "is entirely proper and '[has] been approved many times.'" United States v. Marshall, 532 F.2d

APPENDIX B

1279, 1287 (9th Cir. 1976) (quoting Sewell v. United States, 406 F.2d 1289, 1293 (8th Cir. 1969)).[29]

Other cases have been even more forceful in their insistence on specific intent as an element of aiding and abetting. In United States v. Barnett, 507 F. Supp. 670 (E.D. Ca. 1981) rev'd on other grounds, 667 F.2d 835 (9th Cir. 1982) this issue was discussed in far fuller detail than usual. The court concluded that:

> the government must prove that the person allegedly aiding and abetting the transaction must intend that an activity succeed which the accused knows is of a criminal nature.

507 F. Supp. at 674.

Other authorities have used similar language. See, e.g., Benchwick v. United States, 297 F.2d 330, 332 (9th Cir. 1961) ("An aider and abettor must, of course, know that a wrong is to be committed."). Several cases hold than an element of aiding and abetting is "specific intent to facilitate the commission of a crime by another." United States v. Prince, 529 F.2d 1108, 1112 (6th Cir.), cert. denied, 429 U.S. 838 (1976); United States v. Raper, 676 F.2d 841, 849 (D.C. Cir. 1981); United States v. Talbot, 460 F. Supp. 253, 265 (S.D. Oh. 1978). As discussed in 1 Wharton, Criminal Law (1978) § 29 at 158 "[a]n 'abettor' by definition knows that a crime is about to be committed." (Emphasis added)

Even beyond the failure to require willfulness, the court's instruction was error. The instruction requires no mental elements at all, only acts. This is in sharp contrast to Model Jury Instruction

---

[29] Marshall approved Devitt and Blackmar, Federal Jury Practice and Instructions §§ 11.07 and 11.08, which are now numbered as §§ 12.03 and 12.04.

for the Ninth Circuit, § 5.03, which requires proof "that the defendant acted with the knowledge and intention of helping [principals] violate the law." No such knowledge or intention are required by the court's instruction.

By omitting any <u>mens rea</u> requirement, and in particular by refusing to define "willfully," the court denied defendants the right to have the jury consider all elements of the crime. Accordingly, the convictions must be reversed.

APPENDIX B

V.

CONCLUSION

The acts encompassed by the Clean Water Act are extremely broad. As a result, the *mens rea* required by Congress for criminal violations imposes important limits. Defendants attempted to present the defenses envisioned by Congress, by showing that they lacked the requisite *mens rea*. They sought to show that they believed they were in full compliance with the law, and reasonably so, because of lax enforcement by the government, the universal acceptance of permit-less sandblasting throughout the industry, and the specific discussions held with environmental agencies.

Virtually every ruling of the trial court denied defendants the right to have the jury consider the true elements of the crime. Where Congress required proof of an awareness of a violation, the instructions eliminated this defense. Schwitters was even denied the protection of any *mens rea* elements and was convicted under strict liability. Criminal negligence standards were replaced with tort doctrines, and important requirements of tort liability were even eliminated. Defendants were made liable for the actions of those who were not its agents. The *mens rea* required for aiding and abetting was never explained.

In short, not only were the requirements of the Act eviscerated, but long-standing doctrines of criminal responsibility were ignored. The convictions must be reversed.

DATED this 2nd day of March, 1987.

LAW OFFICES OF DAN R. DUBITZKY

By _____
Alan Zarky

By _____
Dan R. Dubitzky
Attorneys for Defendant-Appellants

APPENDIX B

BRIEF OF APPELLEE IN
UNITED STATES OF AMERICA v. PAUL D. SCHWITTERS
AND SEA GLEANER MARINE, INC.
**(No. CR86-129S, U.S. District Court,
Western District of Washington, at Seattle.)**

TABLE OF CONTENTS

TABLE OF AUTHORITIES

    A. CASES

    B. STATUTES

    C. RULES

    D. OTHER

I. STATEMENT OF THE CASE

II. STATEMENT OF FACTS

    A. Overview

    B. Specific Charges

        1. Count I: COASTAL TRADER

        2. Count II: MARK I

        3. Counts III and IV: PAT SAN MARIE.

III. ARGUMENT

    A. Introduction

    B. Standard of Review

    C. The Court's Responsible Corporate Officer Instruction Was Proper

        1. The Responsible Corporate Officer Doctrine Is Available For Public Welfare Offenses Generally, And Is Not Limited To Strict Liability Offenses

        2. The Jury Instructions Taken as a Whole Required a Finding of Willfulness or Negligence Prior to a Conviction Under a Responsible Corporate Officer Theory

APPENDIX B

TABLE OF CONTENTS

III. ARGUMENT, Cont'd.

    D. The Criminal Provisions Of The Clean Water Act Do Not Require Knowledge That The Defendant Is Violating The Law (Or Neglience With Respect To That Fact)..

        1. Proof of Knowledge of the Law is Not Required to Establish a Willful Violation of the Clean Water Act

        2. Ignorance of the Law is Not a Defense to a Clean Water Act Prosecution

        3. Conclusion.

    E. The Instructions Given by the Court Concerning the Term "Negligently" Were Proper

    F. The Magistrate's Instruction Concerning the Responsibility of a Corporation for the Acts of its Agents Was Proper

IV. CONCLUSION

TABLE OF AUTHORITIES

A. CASES

American Federation of Labor and Congress of Industrial Organizations v. Federal Election Commission, 628 F.2d 97 (D.C. Cir. 1980)

Blum v. Stenson, 465 U.S. 886 (1984)

Fenton v. Freedman, 748 F.2d 1358 (9th Cir. 1984)

Lambert v. California, 355 U.S. 225 (1957)

Liporata v. United States, ___ U.S. ___, 105 S. Ct. 2084 (1985)

Moorhead v. United States, 774 F.2d 936 (9th Cir. 1985)

Morrisette v. United States, 342 U.S. 246 (1952)

New York Central and Hudson River Railroad v. United States, 212 U.S. 481 (1909)

The President Coolidge, 101 F.2d 638 (9th Cir. 1939)

Riss & Company, Inc. v. United States, 262 F.2d 245 (8th Cir. 1958)

Sandstrom v. Montana, 422 U.S. 510 (1979)

Scow No. 36, 144 F. 932 (1st Cir. 1906)

Smith v. California, 361 U.S. 147 (1959)

Spies v. United States, 317 U.S. 492 (1943)

Standard Oil Company of Texas v. United States, 307 F.2d 120 (5th Cir. 1962)

Trailer Train Co. v. State Board of Equalization, 697 F.2d 860 (9th Cir.), cert. denied, 464 U.S. 846 (1983)

APPENDIX B

TABLE OF AUTHORITIES

A. CASES, Cont'd.

Travestad v. United States, 418 F.2d 1043
(8th Cir. 1969), cert. denied,
397 U.S. 935 (1970)

United States v. American Cyanamid Co.,
354 F. Supp. 1202 (S.D. N.Y. 1973),
aff'd, 480 F.2d 1132 (1973)

United States v. Balint, 258 U.S. 250 (1922)

United States v. Barker, 546 F.2d 940
(D.C. Cir. 1976)

United States v. Beusch, 596 F.2d 871
(9th Cir. 1979)

United States v. E. Brooke Matlack, Inc.,
149 F. Supp. 814 (D. Md. 1957)

United States v. Brown, 578 F.2d 1280
(9th Cir. 1978)

United States v. Candelaria, 704 F.2d 1129
(9th Cir. 1983)

United States v. Cattle King Packing Co., Inc.,
793 F.2d 232 (10th Cir. 1986).......

United States v. Charney, 537 F.2d 341
(9th Cir. 1976)

United States v. Coin, 753 F.2d 1510
(9th Cir. 1985)

United States v. Corbin Farm Service,
444 F. Supp. 510 (E.D. Cal.), aff'd,
578 F.2d 259 (9th Cir. 1978)

United States v. Dotterweich, 320 U.S.
277 (1943)

United States v. Eastern Airlines, Inc., 192 F.
Supp. 187 (S.D. Fla. 1961)

TABLE OF AUTHORITIES

A. CASES, Cont'd.

United States v. Fierros, 692 F.2d 1291
(9th Cir. 1982), cert. denied,
462 U.S. 1120 (1983)

United States v. Frade, 709 F.2d 1387
(11th Cir. 1983)

United States v. Freed, 401 U.S. 601 (1971)

United States v. Frezzo Brothers,
461 F. Supp. 266 (E.D. Pa. 1978),
aff'd, 602 F.2d 1123 (3d Cir. 1979)

United States v. Frezzo Brothers, Inc.,
546 F. Supp 713 (E.D. Pa. 1982),
aff'd, 703 F.2d 62 (3d Cir.),
cert. denied, 464 U.S. 829 (1983)

United States v. Frezzo Brothers, Inc.,
602 F.2d 1123 (3d Cir. 1979),
cert. denied, 444 U.S. 1074 (1980)

United States v. Golitschiek, 808 F.2d 195 (2d
Cir. 1986)

United States v. Granda, 565 F.2d 922
(5th Cir. 1978)

United States v. Gris, 247 F.2d 860 (1957)

United States v. Hamel, 551 F.2d 107
(6th Cir. 1977)

United States v. Hayes, 794 F.2d 1348
(9th Cir. 1986)

United States v. Hayes International Corp.,
786 F.2d 1499 (11th Cir. 1986)

United States v. Hoflin, No. 85-82T,
U.S.D.C. (W.D. Wa. 1986)

United States v. Illinois Central Railroad Co.,
303 U.S. 239 (1938)

APPENDIX B

TABLE OF AUTHORITIES

A. **CASES**, Cont'd.

United States v. Interlake Steel Corp., 297 F. Supp. 912 (N.D. Ill. 1969)

United States v. International Minerals & Chemical Corp., 402 U.S. 558 (1971)

United States v. Johnson and Towers, 741 F.2d 662 (3d Cir. 1984)

United States v. Kenny, 645 F.2d 1323 (9th Cir.), cert. denied, 452 U.S. 920 (1981)

United States v. Lizarraga-Lizarraga, 541 F.2d 826 (9th Cir. 1976)

United States v. Launder, 743 F.2d 686 (9th Cir. 1984)

United States v. M.C.C. of Florida, 772 F.2d 1501 (11th Cir. 1985)

United States v. Moore, 586 F.2d 1029 (4th Cir. 1978)

United States v. Murdock, 290 U.S. 389 (1933)

United States v. Outboard Marine Corp., 549 F. Supp. 1032 (D.C. Ill. 1982)

United States v. Park, 421 U.S. 658 (1975)

United States v. Peltz, 433 F.2d 48 (2d Cir. 1970)

United States v. Pennsylvania Industrial Chemical Corporation, 411 U.S. 655 (1973)

United States v. Petersen, 513 F.2d 1133 (9th Cir. 1975)

United States v. Polizzi, 801 F.2d 1543 (9th Cir. 1986)

TABLE OF AUTHORITIES

A. **CASES**, Cont'd.

United States v. Republic Steel Corp.,
362 U.S. 482 (1960)

United States v. Robinson, 523 F. Supp. 1006
(E.D.N.Y. 1981), aff'd, 685 F.2d 427 (1982)

United States v. Simpson, 561 F.2d 53
(7th Cir. 1977)

United States v. Standard Oil Co.,
384 U.S. 224 (1966)

United States v. United States Steel Corp.,
328 F. Supp. 354 (N.D. Ind. 1970),
aff'd, 482 F.2d 439 (7th Cir.),
cert. denied, 414 U.S. 909 (1973)

United Statesv. Wellington, 754 F.2d 1457
(9th Cir.), cert. denied,
___ U.S. ___, 106 S. Ct. 593 (1985)

United States v. White, et al.,
No. CR 86-20015 (W.D. Ark. 1987)

United States v. White Fuel Corp., 498 F.2d 619
(1st Cir. 1974)

United States v. Winston, 558 F.2d 105
(2d Cir. 1977)

Whisper Soft Mills, Inc. v. NLRB,
754 F.2d 1381 (9th Cir. 1984)

Wilson v. Good Humor Corp., 757 F.2d 1293
(D.C. Cir. 1985)

B. **STATUTES**

7 U.S.C. § 136

15 U.S.C. § 77x

18 U.S.C. § 834(f)

APPENDIX B

TABLE OF AUTHORITIES

B. **STATUTES**, Cont'd.

   21 U.S.C. § 601-24

   21 U.S.C. § 661-80

   21 U.S.C. § 676(a)

   21 U.S.C. § 841(a)(1)

   22 U.S.C. § 1934

   22 U.S.C. § 2778(b)(2)

   33 U.S.C. § 407

   33 U.S.C. § 411

   33 U.S.C. § 1251

   33 U.S.C. § 1251(a)

   33 U.S.C. § 1311

   33 U.S.C. § 1311(a)

   33 U.S.C. § 1319(c)(1)

   33 U.S.C. § 1319(c)(3)

   33 U.S.C. § 1362(6)

   33 U.S.C. § 1371(a)

   42 U.S.C. § 6928(d)(1)

   49 U.S.C. § 301

   Pub. L. 100-4

C. **RULES**

   Rule 7 of the Rules of Procedure for the Trial of Misdemeanors before United States Magistrates

   Fed. R. Crim. P. 30

Published by The Bureau of National Affairs, Inc.

TABLE OF AUTHORITIES

D. OTHER

Federal Meat Inspection Act, 21 U.S.C. §§ 601 to 624 and 661 to 680

Birkey, "Corporate Criminal Liability: A Primer for Corporate Counsel," 40 Bus. L. 129, (1984)

McMurry and Ramsey, "Environmental Crime: The Use of Criminal Sanctions in Enforcing Environmental Laws," 19 Loy. of L.A. L. Rev. 1133 (1986)

A Legislative History of the Water Pollution Control Act Amendments of 1972, Congressional Research Service of the Library of Congress, Serial No. 93-1 (1973)

Prosser & Keeton, Torts § 70 at 501 (5th ed.)

APPENDIX B

B-89

I

STATEMENT OF THE CASE

This case is before this Court after judgments of conviction were entered by a United States Magistrate following a jury trial.

On May 8, 1986, defendants Paul D. Schwitters and Sea Gleaner Marine, Inc. (hereinafter "Sea Gleaner") were charged in a four-count information with violations of the Clean Water Act (hereinafter, the "Act"), 33 U.S.C. §§ 1311 and 1319(c)(1). [CR 1.][1/] Both defendants entered pleas of not guilty on May 15, 1986.

Trial in this matter was held before Magistrate Philip K. Sweigert beginning on August 11, 1986, and concluding on August 14, 1986. [CR 41, 42, 43, 49.] At the close of trial, the jury returned a verdict of guilty as to each defendant on Counts II, III, and IV. The jury acquitted both defendants as to Count I. At sentencing on October 6, 1986, defendant Sea Gleaner was fined $60,000, of which $30,000 was suspended, and placed on probation for five years. Defendant Schwitters was fined $10,000, of which $5,000 was suspended, and placed on probation for one year. Timely notices of appeal were filed; through an oversight the appeals were taken to the United States Court of

---

1/ Hereafter, references to the Clerk's Docket entries shall be "CR __"; to the Reporter's Trial Transcript as "TR __"; and to Plaintiff's Exhibits as "Ex. __".

Published by The Bureau of National Affairs, Inc.

Appeals for the Ninth Circuit--by stipulation of the parties, the matter was remanded to this Court. This Court has jurisdiction pursuant to the Rules of Procedure for the Trial of Misdemeanors before United States Magistrates, Rule 7(b).

II

STATEMENT OF FACTS

A. Overview

This case involves activities which occurred on the premises of defendant Sea Gleaner, a ship repair facility which was located on the north shore of Lake Union in Seattle, Washington. [TR 29.] The business included (1) offices on the first floor of a two-story building and, approximately 130 feet from this office building, (2) a dock which extended south into Lake Union. [Exs. 1.1, 2; TR 28, 122, 130, 155, 222.] Defendant Paul D. Schwitters was the president and co-owner of Sea Gleaner. [Exs. 8.1-8.3; TR 220, 314, 326.] During the time period at issue, he generally ran the business of the company and often performed work on vessels himself. [TR 220-221, 226, 280, 433.] The work done by defendant Sea Gleaner included the repair and refitting of vessels and the cleaning and painting of parts of the hulls of vessels. Pollutants discharged from this cleaning and painting activity were the basis of the convictions herein.

APPENDIX B

The Sea Gleaner premises did not include a drydock. [Exs. 1.1, 2, 7.1-7.5; TR 341.] Any work, including work on the outside hull of a vessel, had to be done while the vessel was in the water. [Exs. 1.1, 2; TR 312, 341.] The cleaning and preparation of the vessel hull before painting generally included the blasting of the outer surface of the hull with an abrasive blast material or some similar activity, such as grinding, for removal of old paint and marine growth. [TR 434.] Spent grit and paint chips from these processes were allowed to enter the waters of Lake Union without any efforts to eliminate or even minimize this consequence. [TR 119, 270, 345.] Indeed, during the execution of a search warrant in March 1985, Paul D. Schwitters specifically admitted to Special Agent Gerd Hattwig, with the United States Environmental Protection Agency (hereinafter "EPA"), that no such precautions were taken. [TR 345.]

After cleaning, the outside of a vessel hull was generally spray painted. Spray painting was also done directly over the water, causing paint overspray to enter the water. [TR 118-119.] Defendants did not obtain a National Pollutant Discharge Elimination System (NPDES) permit, as required by the Clean Water Act, 33 U.S.C. § 1251, *et seq.*, before causing these pollutant discharges. [TR 72, 78.]

Present and former employees of Sea Gleaner, and members of the Seattle Yacht Club, whose small dock is located immediately adjacent to the Sea Gleaner dock, testified at trial concerning the Sea Gleaner practices. The evidence produced at trial included the following:

Vessels generally were blasted with an abrasive grit made from a metal slag. It was shiny black in color and very heavy. [Ex. 20; TR 116, 196-97.] The grit commonly contained the heavy metals arsenic and lead [TR 100, 116], which was probably partly responsible for the heavy weight. Sacks of blast grit usually were yellow in color, weighed about 100 pounds, and were delivered to the facility on wooden pallets. [TR 125, 437.] A fork lift was required to move the pallets loaded with grit. [TR 172.]

Blasting of a vessel generally required use of certain equipment at Sea Gleaner, including a fork lift, a raft or small barge used by employees to stand on while blasting the water side of a ship, scaffolding used to reach the upper part of the hull (hung from the vessel rails), and a compressor to provide power to propel the grit against the side of the vessel. [TR 103.] The compressor was extremely loud [TR 103, 210], and could be heard inside the boats at the Seattle Yacht Club dock, as well as inside the Seattle Yacht Club building adjacent to the Sea Gleaner offices. [TR 105, 157.] Because of the nature of the Sea Gleaner dock, vessels being repaired were turned around in order to reach the side of the vessel which had been next to the dock. A smaller vessel, called the LITTLE PUP, which belonged to

APPENDIX B

Sea Gleaner and was operated only by Sea Gleaner employees, was used for this purpose. [TR 240.]

Until late February 1985, blasting of vessels at the Sea Gleaner facility was done by J.W. Bateman, a subcontractor. [TR 223, 428.] Eugene Kelly, a Sea Gleaner employee, testified that Bateman would bring to the Sea Gleaner facility only some of the equipment necessary to complete a blast job: a compressor, a blasting pot, and bags of blast grit. Bateman did not bring a fork lift, rafts, barges, scaffolding, or a skiff. [TR 285.] He used the equipment at the Sea Gleaner facility, which was essential for the work. [TR 338, 346.]

In late February 1985, Sea Gleaner obtained its own blasting equipment. [TR 341.] Paul Schwitters taught two of his employees, Gus Holman and Eugene Kelly, how to use this equipment. [TR 242, 290.] He also did some of the blasting himself. [TR 288.]

As previously noted, the blasting of the sides of vessels was done directly over the water, with the use of rafts and barges. Paul Schwitters stated so during his interview with Special Agent Hattwig. [TR 346.] No efforts were made to prevent the blast material and paint chips from entering the water. The debris caused a highly visible film on the surface of the water which floated on the surface for quite some time. [TR 100, 440.] On calm days, this material floated up against the bulkhead on the Sea Gleaner property line, thus remaining visible to Sea Gleaner personnel and Paul Schwitters. [TR 440.]

Airborne debris from the blasting operations commonly covered the boats moored at the Seattle Yacht Club dock. [TR 99.] Yacht Club members complained to Mr. Schwitters and to other agencies, including the Seattle Police Department. [TR 65, 108, 160.] Mr. Schwitters was well aware of these complaints by the Yacht Club--he discussed them with Agent Hattwig during his interview. [TR 343.]

On one occasion, the debris entering Lake Union from blasting operations at the Sea Gleaner facility led to a complaint to the Washington State Department of Ecology (DOE), on October 24, 1984. [TR 77.] Barbara Smith, an employee of DOE, telephoned Sea Gleaner and asked to speak to the person in charge. [TR 79.] She informed the gentleman who responded--whom she believed to be Paul Schwitters--that the discharges of blasting wastes could cause water quality problems. She mentioned that the abrasive slag generally contained arsenic and lead, and emphasized the need to use controls to prevent this material from entering the waters of Lake Union. [TR 82.] She was told that efforts would be made to prevent any further materials from entering the lake. [TR 82.] Although Ms. Smith did not remember whether she had advised this individual of the need to get an NPDES permit, such a permit would not have been necessary if all pollutant discharges had ceased, consistent with Sea Gleaner's promise. [TR 88.]

APPENDIX B

EPA employees Michael Matta and Charles Morgan testified concerning their observations of the bottom of Lake Union near the Sea Gleaner dock, made during dives on March 15, 1985. They observed piles of blast grit, which appeared to be 18 inches thick, immediately adjacent to the north end of the Sea Gleaner pier. [TR 385, 398.] The grit was intermixed with paint chips. [Ex. 21; TR 386, 390.] Blasting grit and paint chips appeared all over the lake bottom in the general area adjacent to the Sea Gleaner dock. [TR 390-91, 398.]

B. **Specific Charges**

The information herein charged each defendant with four separate counts under the Clean Water Act, for negligently or willfully discharging pollutants, from a point source, to a water of the United States, without an NPDES permit in violation of 33 U.S.C. §§ 1311 and 1319(c)(1). Count I related to discharges on May 30, 1984, from work on the vessel COASTAL TRADER. Count II involved discharges on October 19, 1984, from work on the vessel MARK I. Counts III and IV involved discharges related to the vessel PAT SAN MARIE on March 2, 1985, and March 10, 1985, respectively. The evidence adduced at trial specific to these charges follows:

1. Count I: COASTAL TRADER

The COASTAL TRADER was owned by Peter Strong, who had leased office space on the second floor of the Sea Gleaner office building. [TR 223, 332.] During the months of May and June 1984, Sea Gleaner performed extensive work on the COASTAL TRADER. [TR 332, 441.] Invoices prepared regarding this work list the amount $300,000. [Exs. 9, 10, 11, 13.] This was a large contract and Paul Schwitters took an active interest in the work that was being done. [TR 442.]

Blasting work was done on the COASTAL TRADER [TR 101, 341-42] by J.W. Bateman under contract with Peter Strong. [TR 342.] Bateman used a raft which was the property of Sea Gleaner. [TR 102.] The work caused blasting grit to enter the water. On May 30, 1984, two individuals shoveled spent blast material from the deck of the COASTAL TRADER directly into Lake Union. [TR 92-98, 188-89.] Defendants were charged with negligently permitting these discharges by failing to control work at their dock done with their obvious knowledge. The jury acquitted both defendants on this count.

2. Count II: MARK I

The MARK I was a vessel owned by Einar Peterson. [TR 342.] Paul Schwitters provided Mr. Peterson with a written quote for the work to be performed on the MARK I in the amount of $260,000. [Ex. 15; TR 333.] Paul Schwitters hired J.W. Bateman to blast the vessel. Bateman billed Schwitters $11,873.00 for this work. [Ex. 19.] Schwitters admitted to Agent Hattwig that he was aware of the blasting work which had been performed on the MARK I. [TR 342.] Blasting work performed on this vessel on October 19, 1984, led to a complaint by members of the Seattle Yacht Club to the Seattle Police Department. The club members complained about damage to vessels moored at the club dock from airborne blasting grit. [TR 65-67, 166-67.] As previously noted, Barbara Smith of DOE responded to a complaint about this activity on October 24, 1984.

3. Counts III and IV: PAT SAN MARIE

The PAT SAN MARIE was a second vessel owned by Einar Peterson. Sea Gleaner agreed to perform modifications to this vessel at an approximate cost of $100,000. [Ex. 17; TR 334-335.] The work included blasting by Sea Gleaner employees. [TR 285, 287.] Mr. Schwitters admitted to Agent Hattwig that his employees had performed this work. [TR 346.] An electric grinder was also used on the PAT SAN MARIE. [TR 431-32.]

On March 2, 1985, work on the hull of the PAT SAN MARIE caused a large red slick on the surface of the lake. [Exs. 6.1-6.5; TR 169, 203-04, 209.] The hull of the vessel was painted red. Photographs taken by Seattle Yacht Club members of the slick remaining following certain work included an individual standing on a raft working on the rub rail of the vessel using a grinder. The rub rail was painted white. [Ex. 6.1.] Further blasting work was done on the vessel on March 10, 1985. [TR 119,

179.] This work was done by Eugene Kelly and Paul Schwitters.
[TR 288.]

III
ARGUMENT

A. Introduction

The arguments raised by the defendants generally concern the nature of the intent standard to be applied to sustain a conviction for a violation of the Clean Water Act. Defendants have challenged the jury instructions given by Magistrate Sweigert concerning the meaning of the terms "willfully," "negligently," and "responsible corporate officer," as those terms are used in the Act.

The Clean Water Act was enacted in its present form in 1972, with the declared objective of restoring and maintaining the chemical, physical, and biological integrity of our nation's waters, and the elimination of the discharge of all pollutants into navigable waters by the year 1985. The statute further calls for a goal of achieving, by 1983, sufficient water quality in all of the nation's waters to allow for fishing and swimming. 33 U.S.C. § 1251. To meet these objectives, the Act specifically prohibits the discharge of any pollutant, from a point source,[2/] to a water of the United States, except in compliance

---

[2/] "Point source" is defined as "any discernible, confined, and discrete conveyance, including but not limited to any pipe, ditch, channel . . . or vessel or other floating craft from which pollutants are or may be discharged." 33 U.S.C. § 1362(6). [Instruction No. 15, TR 472.]

APPENDIX B

with enumerated sections of the Act, including that section specifying the necessity for obtaining a permit under the National Pollutant Discharge Elimination System (NPDES) prior to discharge. 33 U.S.C. § 1311(a).[3/] The goals and objectives of the Act clearly bring it within the ambit of those statutes designed to protect the public health and welfare, important to analysis of its intent standard.

Defendants' arguments consistently ignore the public welfare nature of the Clean Water Act and the rules of construction applicable to such statutes. They urge this Court to adopt an interpretation of the Act which would require a showing of specific intent in order to sustain a conviction. Courts interpreting the Clean Water Act and other similar public welfare offenses have repeatedly refused to impose such burdens. See, e.g., United States v. Frezzo Brothers, Inc., 546 F. Supp 713 (E.D. Pa. 1982) (Clean Water Act), aff'd, 703 F.2d 62 (3d Cir.), cert. denied, 464 U.S. 829 (1983); United States v. International Minerals & Chemical Corp., 402 U.S. 558 (1971) (transportation of corrosive liquids); United States v. Balint, 258 U.S. 250 (1922) (sale of narcotic drugs); United States v. Hayes International Corp., 786 F.2d 1499 (11th Cir. 1986) (the Resource Conservation and Recovery Act--"RCRA"--regulating the

---

[3/] The NPDES system responsibilities are generally delegated to state environmental agencies, when state programs are adequate; thus, permits under the system are usually issued by states.

handling of hazardous wastes); and *United States v. Corbin Farm Service*, 444 F. Supp. 510 (E.D. Cal.) (Federal Insecticide, Fungicide, and Rodenticide Act regulating the manufacture, sale, distribution, and use of pesticides), aff'd, 578 F.2d 259 (9th Cir. 1978). Further, defendants ignore the maxim that jury instructions are not to be viewed in isolation, but rather are to be judged as a group. In this way, they seek to find a flaw in a single instruction which is easily resolved by reading the instructions as a whole. All of these arguments must fail.

With one exception, the issues raised in this appeal involve the propriety of the instructions given to the jury by the Magistrate in this case. In general, a defendant cannot challenge a jury instruction on appeal unless he has made a specific objection to the instruction at trial. See Fed. R. Crim. P. 30. Further, the adequacy of jury instructions are to be determined by examining the instructions as a whole. *United States v. Polizzi*, 801 F.2d 1543, 1549 (9th Cir. 1986); *United States v. Hayes*, 794 F.2d 1348, 1351 (9th Cir. 1986); *United States v. Wellington*, 754 F.2d 1457, 1463 (9th Cir.), cert. denied, ___ U.S. ___, 106 S. Ct. 593 (1985); *United States v. Kenny*, 645 F.2d 1323, 1337 (9th Cir.), cert. denied, 452 U.S. 920 (1981). "It is axiomatic that jury instructions are not to be read in isolation, but rather are to be considered as a whole." *United States v. Cattle King Packing Co., Inc.*, 793 F.2d 232, 241 (10th Cir. 1986) [citing *United States v. Park*, 421 U.S. 658, 674 (1975).]

APPENDIX B

B. **Standard of Review**

This appeal is before this Court pursuant to Rule 7 of the Rules of Procedure for the Trial of Misdemeanors before United States Magistrates. That rule provides:

> (e) Scope of Appeal. The defendant shall not be entitled to a trial de novo by a judge of the district court. The scope of appeal shall be the same as on appeal from a judgment of a district court to a court of appeals.

Thus, the Court must apply the same basis for review as used by the Courts of Appeal in these matters. See United States v. Robinson, 523 F. Supp. 1006, 1012 (E.D.N.Y. 1981), aff'd, 685 F.2d 427 (1982); United States v. Moore, 586 F.2d 1029, 1032 (4th Cir. 1978). Where the question raised addresses an interpretation of the statute or regulations, the appellate Court provides de novo review. United States v. Launder, 743 F.2d 686, 688-89 (9th Cir. 1984).

C. **The Court's Responsible Corporate Officer Instruction Was Proper**

Defendants argue both: (i) that the responsible corporate officer doctrine does not apply to Clean Water Act offenses, claiming that it is limited to strict liability crimes; and (ii) that the responsible corporate officer charge given was flawed because that instruction did not reference the necessity for a finding of negligence or willfulness before conviction under this theory. The first of these two arguments is plainly wrong.

Courts that have considered the issue have held that the responsible corporate officer doctrine applies to public welfare offenses generally, and is not limited to strict liability offenses. Defendants' second argument is equally without merit. The instructions, fairly read as a whole, as they must be, clearly required the jury to find negligence or willfulness before they could convict, even under a responsible corporate officer theory.

1. **The Responsible Corporate Officer Doctrine is Available for Public Welfare Offenses Generally, and is Not Limited to Strict Liability Offenses**

Defendants repeatedly assert that "[t]he responsible corporate officers' doctrine is applicable only to strict liability offenses." Appellants' Brief, at 21-23. The law, however, is to the contrary. The responsible corporate officer doctrine has been held to apply to public welfare offenses generally, including those requiring a mens rea element.

In *United States v. Cattle King Products Co., Inc.*, 793 F.2d at 232, the Tenth Circuit considered the propriety of a responsible corporate officer instruction given in a case involving charges under the Federal Meat Inspection Act, 21 U.S.C. §§ 601-24 and 661-80. This statute provides felony penalties where the violative acts are done with an intent to defraud. 21 U.S.C. § 676(a). Defendants in that case argued that a responsible corporate officer instruction, based upon *United States v. Park*, 421 U.S. at 658, was only appropriate in a misdemeanor case involving a strict liability offense. The

APPENDIX B   B-103

Circuit Court refused to limit the scope of *Park* in this way, and indicated that a responsible corporate officer instruction is appropriate in any case where the defendant is a corporate officer and the crime involves a violation of a statute designed to protect the public health and welfare. *Cattle King*, 793 F.2d at 240.

Similarly, in *United States v. Frezzo Brothers, Inc.*, 602 F.2d 1123 (3d Cir. 1979), the Third Circuit, in a Clean Water Act case, approved use of a responsible corporate officer charge similar to that given here. *Id.* at 1130 n.11. Although defendants seek to discount *Frezzo Brothers* by asserting that the specifics of the responsible corporate officer instruction were not at issue, *see* Appellants' Brief at 24, the true fact of the matter is that the Third Circuit specifically approved the use of a responsible corporate officer charge in a non-strict liability Clean Water Act case:

> The Government argued the case on the "responsible corporate officer doctrine" recognized by the United States Supreme Court in *United States v. Park*, 421 U.S. 658 (1975) and *United States v. Dotterweich*, 320 U.S. 277 (1943). We have examined the judge's charge and we perceive no error in the instruction to the jury on this theory.

Id. at 1130 n.11 (parallel citations omitted).

The reason for applying the responsible corporate officer doctrine in Clean Water Act cases (and other environmental cases) is obvious. The doctrine, as developed in *Park* and *Dotterweich*, is designed to effectuate Congress' intent to protect the public through enactment of such public welfare statutes, by holding responsible corporate officers to a duty to prevent, detect, and correct statutory violations. See Park, 421 U.S. at 672; Dotterweich, 320 U.S. at 284-85; see also Morrisette v. United States, 342 U.S. 246, 256 (1952).

The Clean Water Act, like other environmental statutes, clearly is a public welfare statute. See, e.g., 33 U.S.C. § 1251(a); United States v. Hamel, 551 F.2d 107, 112-113 (6th Cir. 1977); United States v. Frezzo Brothers, Inc., 546 F. Supp. at 720-21. Cf. United States v. Hayes International Corp., 786 F.2d at 1503 (RCRA); United States v. Johnson & Towers, Inc., 741 F.2d 622, 667 (3d Cir. 1984) (RCRA); United States v. Republic Steel Corp., 362 U.S. 482, 491 (1960) (Rivers and Harbors Act). See generally, Birkey, "Corporate Criminal Liability: A Primer for Corporate Counsel," 40 Bus. L. 129, 142-43 & nn. 52-56 (1984); McMurry and Ramsey, "Environmental Crime: The Use of Criminal Sanctions in Enforcing Environmental Laws," 19 Loy. of L.A. L. Rev. 1133, 1153 (1986). Thus, a responsible corporate officer instruction is appropriate in prosecutions under this statute.

Finally, the fact that Congress intended the responsible corporate officer doctrine to apply to the Clean Water Act is clearly set forth in the statute. Title 33, U.S.C. § 1319(c)(3) specifically provides that the term "person," as it is used in the criminal provisions of the Act, includes "any

APPENDIX B

responsible corporate officer." A more direct expression of Congressional intent is difficult to imagine.

2. **The Jury Instructions Taken as a Whole Required a Finding of Willfulness or Negligence Prior to a Conviction Under a Responsible Corporate Officer Theory**

Defendants seek to have this Court review the responsible corporate officer instruction in the abstract and thus find error in the fact that this specific instruction, the Magistrate's instruction number 20, made no use of the terms negligently or willfully.[4/] However, as noted above, jury instructions are not to be read in isolation but must be considered as a whole. United States v. Hayes, 794 F.2d at 1351. In this case, the jury instructions as a group clearly required a finding of the requisite intent by the jury prior to conviction.

[4/] Although there was much discussion by defendants of their objections in general to a responsible corporate officer instruction prior to the start of trial [pages 13-16 of the transcript of proceedings before Honorable Philip K. Sweigert, August 11, 1986], defendants failed to raise the specific objection to instruction 20 now raised for the first time on appeal--that is, the lack of a requirement of willfulness or negligence within the text of instruction 20--during the trial conference on jury instructions. [TR 457.] Defendants merely objected generally to the use of a responsible corporate officer instruction in other than a strict liability offense. As argued above, that objection is plainly unfounded.

First, at the start of the trial, the Court instructed the jury that:

> The Government must prove that on or about the date set forth <u>in each count the defendants willfully or negligently</u>, one, two, discharged pollutants, three, from a point source, four, into navigable waters in the Western District of Washington, five, without a permit.

[TR 3] (Emphasis added). At the close of the case, in Instruction No. Two, the Court read the Information to the jury. Each count of the Information specifically alleged that defendants acted "negligently," "willfully and negligently," or "willfully or negligently." [TR 466-67.] In Instruction No. Three, the Court again informed the jury that the charge was that defendants "willfully or negligently" discharged pollutants by paraphrasing the language of the Information.

Instruction No. Five set forth for the jury the elements of the offenses charged. The Court stated that:

> the government must prove beyond a reasonable doubt each and every one of the of the [sic] following elements:
>
> (1) that on or about the date set forth the defendant <u>willfully or negligently</u>
>
> (2) discharged pollutants
>
> (3) from a point source
>
> (4) into a navigable water of the United States
>
> (5) without a permit.

[TR 470-71] (Emphasis added).

In Instruction No. 11, the Court again instructed the jury as to the Government's burden to show intent.[5/] The Court stated:

> [t]o establish the Clean Water Act offenses charged in the information, the government must prove the defendants acted willfully or negligently. You need not find both.

[TR 471.]

Finally, the Court instructed that all instructions must be considered together, with no one instruction singled out [TR 465], and that defendants could not be convicted of any of the offenses unless all elements were proven beyond a reasonable doubt, which included the requirement of willfulness or negligence. [Instruction No. Three, TR 467-68; Instruction No. Four, TR 468; Instruction No. Five, TR 468-69.]

Under these circumstances, the jury clearly was intructed to find that the defendants acted willfully or negligently before it could convict, even though those terms were not specifically included within the responsible corporate officer instruction. The fact that jury instructions could have been written differently is not grounds for reversal. Where, as here, the jury instructions taken as a whole clearly inform the

---

[5/] Moreover, the Government's closing argument clearly acknowledged the need to establish negligence or willfulness, and did not argue a strict liability theory. See, e.g., [TR 488] ("It's agreed by the Government that the only way he [Schwitters] could be found responsible for count I is he was negligent in allowing it to happen. That's what the count says.").

jury of the Government's burden, failure to repeat a concept in one of the instructions does not require reversal. See United States v. Hayes, 794 F.2d at 1352.

Indeed, the precise issue raised in this appeal was considered by the Tenth Circuit in United States v. Cattle King Packing Corp., Inc., 793 F.2d at 232. In that case, although the statute required an intent to defraud as an element of the offense, the responsible corporate officer charge did not include a reference to an intent requirement. Rather, as was the case here, the intent requirement was included elsewhere in the instructions. The Court held that these instructions were proper:

> Instruction No. 42 [the responsible corporate officer charge] . . . without more, would not be sufficient to find [defendant] guilty of a felony.
>
> Instruction No. 42, nevertheless, is sufficient to put to the jury the issue of [defendant's] criminal responsibility for Cattle King's meat inspection violations. So long as the jury was instructed that it must also find that [defendant] had the "intent to defraud," the jury instructions were proper and [defendant's] challenge on this basis must fail.
>
> It is axiomatic that jury instructions are not to be read in isolation, but rather are to be considered as a whole. Park, 421 U.S. at 674. Instruction No. 45 specifically charges that for all counts except count 9, "the crimes charged in this indictment require proof of specific intent before the defendants can be convicted." Contrary to [defendant's] arguments, Instruction 45 complements Instruction No. 42 rather than contradicts it. Moreover, each jury instruction of each

APPENDIX B

> .substantive count except count 9 contains the
> charge that the jury must find that "the
> defendant acted with the intent to defraud."
> Each such instruction also charges that the
> jury is to evaluate "[t]he question [of guilt]
> as to each defendant considered
> separately."6/ . . . It is fair to conclude
> that a reasonable juror, so instructed, would
> believe that he or she must find that
> [defendant] had the "intent to defraud" before
> finding him guilty of the felony charges. See
> Sandstrom v. Montana, 422 U.S. 510, 514 (1979).

793 F.2d at 241 (parallel citations and footnote omitted).

Similarly, in United States v. Hayes, 794 F.2d at 1348, the Ninth Circuit considered a challenge to an instruction on an element of the offense. The defendant in that case had been convicted of prescribing Schedule II drugs to patients in violation of the Controlled Substances Act, 21 U.S.C. § 841(a)(1). On appeal, he claimed as misleading the instruction given by the district court concerning the meaning of the phrase "prescriptions issued other than in good faith for a legitimate medical purpose." He argued that the instruction given impermissibly allowed the jury to convict him based upon negligence. The Court concluded that while the specific instruction viewed alone might permit this interpretation, the instructions viewed in the entirety clearly required a finding of the requisite intent. Id. at 1352.

6/ A similar instruction was given here. Instruction No. Four, TR 468.

The jury instructions taken as a whole here did not impermissibly dispense with the need to prove that the defendants acted negligently or willfully.

D. **The Criminal Provisions of the Clean Water Act do not Require Knowledge that the Defendant is Violating the Law (or Negligence with Respect to that Fact)**

Three of defendants' arguments (Points F, G, and H) involve essentially the same issue: the assertion that the criminal provisions of the Clean Water Act require that the defendant know (or be negligent with respect to the fact) that he is violating the law.[7/] Defendants seek to establish ignorance of the law as a defense to a Clean Water Act prosecution. Their arguments also seek to draw a distinction between knowledge of the regulatory requirements and knowledge that the behavior which violates the regulatory requirements is criminal. This fine line distinction, if it in fact exists, ignores the overwhelming authority with respect to public welfare offenses, like the Clean Water Act, that knowledge of the law--whether of the statutory requirements or the criminality of behavior--is not an element of

---

[7/] Defendants argue that the Magistrate improperly defined willfully by not requiring knowledge that the defendant was violating the law (Point F); that the Court improperly defined negligently by not requiring negligence with respect to the fact that the defendant was violating the law (Point G); and that the Court improperly excluded evidence that defendants lacked awareness that they were violating the law (Point H).

APPENDIX B

the offense. Violations of the Clean Water Act do not fall within those categories of offenses for which ignorance of the law is an excuse. Thus, any evidence on this point was clearly irrelevant and was properly excluded.

1. Proof of Knowledge of the Law is Not Required to Establish a Willful Violation of the Clean Water Act

"Willfully" is a word of many meanings. United States v. Murdock, 290 U.S. 389, 394-95 (1933). Its construction and meaning must be drawn from its context. Murdock, 290 U.S. at 395; United States v. Illinois Central Railroad Co., 303 U.S. 239, 242 (1938); Spies v. United States, 317 U.S. 492, 497 (1943).

As the Supreme Court has explained:

> In statutes denouncing offenses involving turpitude, "willfully" is generally used to mean with evil purpose, criminal intent or the like. But in those denouncing acts not in themselves wrong, the word is often used without any such implication.

United States v. Illinois Central Railroad Co., 303 U.S. at 242.

As Mr. Justice Douglas stated in Lambert v. California, 355 U.S. 225 (1957), "[w]e do not go with Blackstone in saying that 'a vicious will' is necessary to constitute a crime, . . . for conduct alone without regard to the intent of the doer is often sufficient. . . . [such as] the commission of acts, or the failure to act under circumstances that should alert the doer to the consequences of his deed." Lambert, 355 U.S. at 228. Such is the case with public welfare offenses.

As previously noted, the Clean Water Act is clearly a public welfare offense. Its purposes, like those of the Food and Drug Act, ". . . touch phases of the lives and health of people which, in the circumstances of modern industrialism, are largely beyond self protection." United States v. Dotterweich, 320 U.S. at 280. There is no question that unpolluted water is a necessity.

Contrary to defendants' assertion, the public welfare nature of this statute is in no way diminished by the potential extent of its regulatory reach. The need to preserve and protect our nation's water resources is fundamental. In order to accomplish its stated goals of unpolluted waters, Congress wisely chose to broaden the reach of the statute to include the point source discharge of virtually any material which may have an effect on water quality and, thus, the uses to which a body of water may be put. See 33 U.S.C. § 1362(6). Like other public welfare offenses, the likelihood of regulation of activities resulting in water pollution is so great that a person who performs such activities proceeds at his peril. See, United States v. International Minerals, 402 U.S. at 565. This is particularly true where, as here, the discharge results from industrial activity and creates obvious, highly visible pollution effects.

Analysis of the criminal statutes cited in defendants' brief, see pp. 44-46, does little to assist the resolution of this case. Unlike here, those cited statutes are not of the

APPENDIX B   B-113

public health and welfare nature. Courts have consistently avoided the necessity for a finding of knowledge of the law prior to conviction when interpreting public welfare statutes. For example, in United States v. International Minerals Corporation, 402 U.S. at 588, the Supreme Court defined the term "knowingly" when used in the context of public welfare statutes. The defendant in International Minerals was charged with a violation of 18 U.S.C. § 834(f), the Explosives and Dangerous Articles Act. The language of that criminal provision--similar to that at issue here--states that whoever "knowingly violates any regulation" promulgated by the Interstate Commerce Commission, and related to safe transport of corrosive liquids, is guilty of a crime. The regulation at issue required that shipping papers accompanying corrosive liquids be marked corrosive liquids. The Court held that "knowingly" referred to the acts made criminal, not to knowledge of the regulation. The Court found

> no reason why the word "regulations" should not be construed as a shorthand designation for specific acts or omissions which violate the Act. The Act, so viewed, does not signal an exception to the rule that ignorance of the law is no excuse . . . .
>
> . . . . .
>
> The principle that ignorance of the law is no defense applies whether the law be a statute or a duly promulgated and published regulation.

United States v. International Minerals Corporation, 402 U.S. at 562-63. International Minerals followed earlier decisions, involving public welfare offenses, which consistently held that ignorance of the law is no defense and proof of the defendant's knowledge of the law is not required. See, e.g., United States v. Freed, 401 U.S. 601 (1971); and United States v. Balint, 258 U.S. 250 (1922).

Other cases involving environmental statutes have produced similar results. In United States v. Hayes International Corp., 786 F.2d at 1499, the Eleventh Circuit addressed the issue of the degree of knowledge necessary to sustain a conviction under the Resource Conservation and Recovery Act (hereafter "RCRA") for the knowing transportation of a hazardous waste to an unpermitted facility, in violation of 42 U.S.C. § 6928(d)(1). That Court specifically concluded that knowledge of the regulations and the law are not necessary for a conviction under this felony statute. The Court stated that:

> section 6928(d)(1) is not drafted in a manner which makes knowledge of illegality an element of the offense . . . . In addition, section 6928(d)(1) is undeniably a public welfare statute, involving a heavily regulated area with great ramifications for public health and safety. As the Supreme Court has explained, it is completely fair and reasonable to charge those who choose to operate in such areas with knowledge of the regulatory provisions . . . . Accordingly, in a prosecution under 42 U.S. § 6928(d)(1) it would be no defense to claim no knowledge that the paint waste was a hazardous waste within the meaning of the regulations; nor would it be a defense to argue ignorance of the permit requirement.

Hayes International, 786 F.2d at 1503.

APPENDIX B

In <u>United States v. Corbin Farm Service</u>, 444 F. Supp. at 510, the defendant was charged with criminal violations under the Federal Insecticide, Fungicide, and Rodenticide Act (hereinafter "FIFRA"), 7 U.S.C. § 136, <u>et seq.</u>, an environmental statute regulating the manufacture, distribution, and use of pesticides. Similar to the Clean Water Act, FIFRA makes it a crime to "knowingly violate any provision of this subchapter." The Court held that the use of the word "knowingly" in the penalty section of FIFRA required only proof that defendants, whose spraying activities resulted in the death of protected waterfowl, knew they were dealing with a pesticide when they sprayed the field or caused it to be sprayed.

> The penalty provisions . . . were drafted in general fashion to encompass the wide variety of possible violations of FIFRA . . . . Congress was enacting a general provision, using the word "knowingly" as it had in the context of other statutes creating <u>malum prohibitum</u> crimes. The word was used to reflect the requirement that general intent be proved in order to establish a violation.

<u>United States v. Corbin Farm Service</u>, 444 F. Supp. at 519.

Although no relevant case law existed under FIFRA, the <u>Corbin Farm Service</u> Court cited <u>International Minerals</u>, 402 U.S. at 558, stating that knowledge of the facts is required in the sense of a general intent to do the actions constituting the violation, but a specific intent to violate the law or a knowledge of the regulation is not a necessary element of the crime. See also United States v. Dotterweich, 320 U.S. 277, 281 (1943).

Although the public welfare offenses discussed above use the term "knowingly" to specify the scienter requirement, a similar interpretation has been given to the term "willfully" in the context of public welfare offenses. For example, in Riss & Company, Inc. v. United States, 262 F.2d 245 (8th Cir. 1958), the Court interpreted "willfully" in the context of the Interstate Commerce Act, 49 U.S.C. § 301, et seq., which limited the number of hours in any twenty-four hour period that a driver could operate motor vehicles. The statute provided criminal penalties for "knowingly and willfully violating any provision of this [chapter], or any rule, [or] regulation . . . thereunder . . . ." The Court stated, "[t]he meaning of [willful] rested upon the character of the offense charged," 262 F.2d at 248, and held "[i]n the context of the criminal statute involved in this case the word does not connote the existence of an evil motive . . . as, for instance, in an attempt to willfully evade the payment of income taxes and thus to cheat the government." 262 F.2d at 249, quoting United States v. E. Brooke Matlack, Inc., 149 F. Supp. 814, 819 (D. Md. 1957).

In United States v. Moore, 586 F.2d 1029 (4th Cir. 1978), the Court reviewed the term "knowingly and willfully" in the context of gun regulations for airport security. The Court stated, "the requirement that it be done willfully, in its

APPENDIX B

ordinary connotation, means no more than the act be done voluntarily." Moore, 586 F.2d at 1032. The Court found the proscribed conduct to be a simple act, without any necessary proof of purpose. Moore, 586 F.2d at 1033. Thus, case law regarding public welfare offenses demonstrates that courts have been unwilling to impose a burden of proof of knowledge of the law prior to a conviction for such an offense.

Further, contrary to defendants' assertion, even in the context of statutes other than public welfare offenses, courts have concluded that the term "willfully" does not require proof of knowledge of the law. For example, in United States v. Fierros, 692 F.2d 1291, 1294-95 (9th Cir. 1982), cert. denied, 462 U.S. 1120 (1983), the Court concluded that where the subject matter of the offense--such as transporting and harboring illegal aliens--is one highly likely to be subject to governmental regulation, despite use of the term "willful" the Court would "attribute to Congress no intent to depart from the traditional rule" that ignorance of the law is no excuse.

In United States v. Gris, 247 F.2d 860 (1957), the Second Circuit dispatched with the defendant's claim, in a prosecution for unauthorized tapping of a telephone line, that he could not have acted willfully because he did not know he was violating a federal law. "It matters not whether appellant realized his conduct was unlawful. He knew exactly what he was doing; and what he did was a violation of the Federal

Communications Act. He intended to do what he did and that is sufficient." Id. at 864.

Likewise, cases involving willful violations of the securities laws have been upheld where juries were instructed that an act is done "willfully" if done knowingly and deliberately, and that the defendant need not know he is breaking a particular law. United States v. Brown, 578 F.2d 1280, 1284 (9th Cir. 1978); United States v. Charney, 537 F.2d 341, 352 (9th Cir. 1976); United States v. Peltz, 433 F.2d 48, 54-55 (2d Cir. 1970), Travestad v. United States, 418 F.2d 1043, 1047 (8th Cir. 1969), cert. denied, 397 U.S. 935 (1970).

For example, in United States v. Brown, 578 F.2d at 1284, the Ninth Circuit addressed the question of whether the term "willfully violates any provisions of this subchapter, or the rules and regulations promulgated . . . under authority thereof," as used in 15 U.S.C. § 77x, required evidence that a defendant was aware that the instruments sold were "securities" within the meaning of the Act. The Court rejected this burden, following opinions which established the scienter requirement as intent to commit the act prohibited, not knowledge of the law. United States v. Brown, 578 F.2d at 1284-85.

The Legislative History of the Clean Water Act does not demand an opposite result. The legislative history as a whole is devoid of any true discussion on the meaning of the term "willfully." Indeed, the one reference in the Legislative

APPENDIX B

History, which is quoted at page 42 of Appellants' brief, has been taken totally out of context. The language appears as part of the floor debate in the House of Representatives on a proposed amendment to the legislation, which amendment would have added language specifically stating that it is a crime to negligently or willfully violate "any order issued by the Administrator under subsection (a) of this section." Representative Harsha's statement, made in opposition to this amendment, illustrates the fact that the subject sought to be covered by the amendment, that is, a deliberate violation of an administrative order, was already covered in the proposed criminal provision. Indeed, the sentence immediately following the language quoted in defendants' brief, which sentence was conveniently omitted, states: "[t]hus, the amendment of the gentleman from Ohio is not needed." A Legislative History of the Water Pollution Control Act Amendments of 1972, Congressional Research Service of the Library of Congress, Serial No. 93-1 (1973) (hereinafter, Legislative History), Vol. 1, at 530.

Even if one were to assume for the moment that Rep. Harsha's statement was made as an illustration of what constitutes a willful violation of the Clean Water Act, this by no means is sufficient to set the parameters of the definition of the term willfully as requiring knowledge of the law in all cases. The language of the statement in no way implies such a result. It is simply an example of one type of behavior which constitutes a violation. Indeed, in this same discussion, Rep.

Harsha indicates that "in this legislation we already can charge a man for simple negligence." *Legislative History*, Vol. 1, at 530. His example then must be viewed as one type of conduct, out of a myriad, which would violate the act.

Defendants also seek to use the recent amendments to the Clean Water Act to support their theory.[8/] They focus on the fact that these amendments have deleted reference to the term "willfully" from the criminal provisions and substituted the term "knowingly." They argue that this action somehow implies a higher standard of intent existed for the term "willfully."

What defendants have blatantly failed to mention is the fact that these amendments have created felony penalties for "knowing" violations of the Act and retained the misdemeanor penalties for negligent violations. Under the criminal provisions applicable prior to these amendments, and applicable to this case, willful violations were also misdemeanors. Thus, defendants' argument, in effect, would have this Court require a higher standard of <u>mens rea</u> for a misdemeanor penalty under the old criminal provision than a felony penalty under the current provision. It is highly unlikely that Congress intended such a result.

[8/] These amendments, known as the Water Quality Act of 1987, Pub. L. 100-4, became effective on February 5, 1987. Offenses occurring prior to that date are still subject to the standards at issue in this case.

APPENDIX B

·Nor does the language of the statute demand a different result. As noted in the cases cited above, use of a phrase such as "knowingly or willfully violates a provision of the act" does not necessarily dictate a requirement of knowledge of the law as an element of the offense. Such phrases have been viewed by the courts, particularly in the context of public welfare offenses, ζ simply as a means of denoting the conduct which is a violation of the statute. See United States v. International Minerals Corporation, supra, 402 U.S. at 562-63; United States v. Hayes International Corporation, supra, 786 F.2d at 1503; United States v. Fierros, 692 F.2d at 1294-95; United States v. Brown, 578 F.2d at 1284-85. As discussed in detail below, the cases cited by defendants do not require a different result. They are distinguishable both factually and as other than public welfare offenses. In conclusion, because the Clean Water Act is a public welfare offense, a finding of knowledge of the law is not required for conviction.

2. Ignorance of the Law is Not a Defense to a Clean Water Act Prosecution

Defendants' arguments posit that a defense of ignorance of the law is appropriate to a Clean Water Act prosecution. That is simply not the case. There are only two categories of cases where such a defense has been found to be applicable. See discussion in United States v. Fierros, 692 F.2d at 1294-95. The first is a situation where an independently determined legal status or condition is an operative fact of the crime. Ignorance of this *status* may be a defense. An example is embezzlement or theft of government property. If the defendant is ignorant of the true legal status of the property, he cannot commit the crime. "[T]he mistake of the law is for practical purposes the mistake of fact." *Fierros*, 692 F.2d at 1294. See also *United States v. Petersen*, 513 F.2d 1133 (9th Cir. 1975); *United States v. Barker*, 546 F.2d 940 (D.C. Cir. 1976).

The second category of cases is that involving violations of truly complex regulatory schemes that have the potential for snaring "unwitting violators." *Fierros*, supra, 692 F.2d at 1295. For example, a case cited by the defendants, *United States v. Lizarraga-Lizarraga*, 541 F.2d 826 (9th Cir. 1976), falls within this category. *Lizarraga* involved a conviction for the exportation of a prohibited substance, in violation of 22 U.S.C. § 1934. The Court concluded that the list of substances included many items not known to be within government control, which items might be innocently exported. The Ninth Circuit in *Fierros* distinguished the statute in *Lizarraga* from those in cases, such as this one, where ignorance of the law would not be a defense. *Id.* at 1295.

The case at hand does not fall within either category. The crime--negligently or willfully discharging pollutants from a point source to a navigable water without a permit--does not involve ignorance of a legal status which is an element of the offense. There are no plausible claims that defendants were unaware of the status of the material discharged as pollutants or the status of Lake Union as a navigable water of the United States. Both were obvious. Discharges that create large surface scums on the water, remaining for hours, can hardly be argued not to be a pollutant; any rational citizen would assume such wrongful. The navigability of Lake Union is equally self evident. The Clean Water Act clearly does not fall within the first class of cases where a defense of ignorance of the law is appropriate.

Nor does the Clean Water Act involve a truly complex scheme which has the unjust potential for snaring innocent violators. It is remarkable that defendants would even attempt to argue that a business man whose industrial practices result in highly visible water pollution can honestly believe that this activity is not subject to some type of regulation.[9/] Indeed, discharges of "refuse" (broadly defined) have been illegal for almost 90 years. See 33 U.S.C. §§ 407 and 411 (Rivers and Harbors Act of 1899).

[9/] Defendants have cited examples of what they claim to be innocent conduct which would violate the Clean Water Act and, thus, create a "trap for the unwary." Among the conduct cited was a paper cup which blows into the water and a swimmer who brushes off sand. As to the swimmer, this conduct constitutes a recreational use of water which is, after all, a primary goal of the Clean Water Act. As to the paper cup, although the government in no way seeks to suggest that it would prosecute such conduct as a crime under the Clean Water Act, it is worth noting that, in light of anti-littering campaigns and ordinances,

(Footnote cont'd on next page)

In at least one opinion, the Supreme Court has deliberately distinguished public welfare offenses from those offenses where a defense of legal ignorance is appropriate. In Liporata v. United States, ___ U.S. ___, 105 S. Ct. 2084 (1985), a prosecution for illegal possession of food stamps, the Court held that the Government must prove a defendant knew his possession of food stamps was in a manner not authorized by the statute.[10] The Court stated to hold "otherwise would be to

---

[9] (Cont'd. from previous page)
it is difficult to imagine that a person would conclude that a non-accidental discharge of this nature could have no legal consequences.

Finally, defendants cite United States v. M.C.C. of Florida, 772 F.2d 1501 (11th Cir. 1985), as minor conduct made punishable by the Act, that is, the cutting of sea grass by propellers of a tug boat. That case involved a civil, not a criminal enforcement action. The propellers of the tugs had caused extensive damage to the bottom vegetation of two Wildlife Refuges. At one site, the bottom sediment had been completely denuded of vegetation. Much of the conduct continued to occur after specific instructions by the Court to confine tug trips to high tide. The conduct involved was not insignificant.

[10] The Liporata Court, however, made clear that even this burden is not unduly heavy:

> the Government need not show that [the defendant] had knowledge of specific regulations governing food stamp acquisition or possession. Nor must the Government introduce any extraordinary evidence that would conclusively demonstrate petitioner's state of mind. Rather, as in any other criminal prosecution requiring mens rea, the Government may prove by reference to facts and circumstances surrounding the case that [the defendant] knew that his conduct was unauthorized or illegal.

105 S. Ct. at 2092-93. This, the Court noted, could be done through evidence that stamps were sold at a discount in a backroom. 105 S. Ct. at 2093 n.17.

criminalize a broad range of apparently innocent conduct." 105 S. Ct. at 2088. The Court said, however, that the distinction between the statute at issue in Liporata and "public welfare" offenses is clear, and affirmed the Court's earlier decisions in Freed and International Minerals by expressly noting that Liporata did not involve "a type of conduct that a reasonable person should know is subject to stringent public regulation and may seriously threaten the community's health and safety." 105 S. Ct. at 2092.

Defendants have cited numerous cases where courts have interpreted the terms "willfully" or "willful" to require proof of knowledge of the law. These cases are clearly distinguishable. Most involve prosecutions under regulatory schemes which do not equate with the case at hand. They do not involve prosecutions under the public welfare offenses so deliberately distinguished by the Supreme Court. Rather, they involve the type of facts or regulatory schemes where a defense of legal ignorance is appropriate. For example, United States v. Frade, 709 F.2d 1387 (11th Cir. 1983), involved a prosecution for a violation of a regulation promulgated under the Trading with the Enemy Act. The defendants in Frade were two priests who assisted their Cuban-American parishioners to arrange for a boat to bring relatives to the United States from Cuba during the Mariel boatlift. Efforts by these defendants to arrange for a rescue mission had begun almost two weeks before the regulations which they were charged with violating were promulgated, though not published. The actions which they had taken prior to the change in regulations had already placed numerous individuals in Cuba in serious danger if the rescue effort was discontinued. Further, this regulation criminalized behavior which had previously been expressly authorized by published regulation. The facts and circumstances of Frade can hardly be analogized to those involved here.

American Federation of Labor and Congress of Industrial Organizations v. Federal Election Commission, 628 F.2d 97 (D.C. Cir. 1980), involved the interpretation of the term "willfully" in the civil context. The case was an enforcement action brought by the Federal Election Commission seeking a prohibition against future transfers from the union's education fund to their political contributions committee. A civil penalty had been assessed pursuant to a provision of the statute, which required "knowing and willful" violations, despite the fact that the Government conceded that there was no intentional wrongdoing and that there was a separate civil penalty provision which required no finding of intent. The violation at issue involved transfers of funds which had previously been permitted by the Government.

In summary, this was a civil case involving a complex regulatory scheme which did not involve the protection of the public health and welfare. The decision clearly should not be used as precedent for defining the scienter requirement in a case involving a public welfare offense.

APPENDIX B

United States v. Winston, 558 F.2d 105 (2nd Cir. 1977), involved a violation of the Railway Labor Act provision which makes it a crime for an employer to willfully influence or coerce employees in matters involving unionization or employee representation. The Court in that case distinguished that statute from malum prohibitum offenses [such as the Clean Water Act] which do not require an awareness of the law and, therefore, where a defense of ignorance of the law would not be appropriate. Id. at 108. Similarly, United States v. Eastern Airlines, Inc., 192 F. Supp. 187 (S.D. Fla. 1961), involved a willful violation of an order of the Civil Aeronautics Board (not, as suggested by defendants, of a section of the statute). The Court concluded, based upon the facts, that no willful violation of a technical requirement had occurred. This case did not involve a public welfare offense--it involved the alleged contempt of an administrative order relating to advertising practices of an airline.

United States v. Golitschiek, 808 F.2d 195 (2d Cir. 1986), cited several times throughout defendants' brief, involved an appeal from a conviction for offenses related to the planned shipment of helicopters from the United States to Iran. The offenses included conspiracy to violate 22 U.S.C. § 2778(b)(2) and conspiracy to defraud the United States. The defendant was an Austrian citizen who had never set foot in the United States. During the trial, the Government conceded that it was required to prove that the defendant violated a known legal duty. The appeal concerned a set of instructions which, despite an instruction that the defendant must have specific intent to violate the law, included a statement that every person is presumed to know that which the law forbids. *Id.* at 202. The Court concluded in light of the facts of the case, the nature of the charges (conspiracy), and the regulatory complexity, such an instruction was in error. We have not conceded such a *mens rea* is required here. Nor is such a concession in one case, where the Government may have chosen to avoid an argument in that specific case, of great precedential value. The unique facts of the case, and the rarely enforced provisions of the statute at issue, hardly assist analysis in an environmental context, where Congress obviously contemplated prosecutions even where conduct was merely negligent.

In *United States v. Granda*, 565 F.2d 922 (1978), the Fifth Circuit addressed the significance of the terms "knowingly" and "willfully" in the context of a prosecution for transporting monetary instruments in an amount exceeding $5,000 into the United States without filing the necessary reports. Currency reporting violations are clearly not public welfare offenses—they are technical regulatory offenses. Further, this is a case which the Ninth Circuit specifically cited in *Fierros* as the type of offense for which a defense of ignorance of the law is appropriate. It distinguished the offense involved in *Granda* from those offenses where "the subject matter . . . is one highly likely to be subject to government regulation" and thus ignorance of the law would be no excuse. *Fierros*, 692 F.2d at 1295.

APPENDIX B

United States v. Simpson, 561 F.2d 53 (7th Cir. 1977), is equally inapplicable to the case at bar. The defendant in that case had been convicted of "willfully and knowingly" doing an act prohibited by the Federal Communications Act, that is, operating a CB radio transmitter without a license. This transmitter had been licensed by the defendant's former wife at their then joint home; there was no evidence that, after his wife's departure, the defendant had ever been informed that he no longer had permission to broadcast. Further, the licensing requirement was contained in the regulations promulgated by the Federal Communications Commission (FCC). According to the Simpson Court, the regulations applicable, to all but the last of the transmissions for which the defendant was convicted, provided that "no operator license was required for the operation of a CB radio, except for stations manually transmitting Morse Code." Simpson, id. at 61. This language was later deleted because it might mislead one into believing that no broadcast license was required. Is it any wonder that the conviction was reversed? Does the case help here? Of course not.

In summary, the Clean Water Act offenses are not crimes for which a defense of ignorance of the law is appropriate. This statute does not fall within those categories of complex offenses which create traps for the unwary. The conduct at issue, discharging pollutants into our nation's lakes and rivers, is obviously conduct which the citizenry is well aware is regulated. Indeed, most children hear the catch phrase "Give a hoot, don't pollute." It strains credulity to suggest a sophisticated businessman should be able to claim ignorance. The broad reach of the statute does not change this fact, particularly at a time when public sentiments and concerns about pollution surely put everyone on notice that activities resulting in pollution may be regulated.

3. Conclusion

The Clean Water Act is a statute designed to protect the public health and welfare. Courts interpreting such statutes have consistently refused to impose a scienter requirement which would require a showing of knowledge of the law or, by logical extension to negligence, a showing of negligence as to the law. Public welfare cases have reached this conclusion despite language, like that in the Clean Water Act, which defines the crime in terms of violation of the statute or regulations. The Clean Water Act neither involves a complex regulatory scheme nor involves circumstances where a mistake of fact becomes a mistake of law. The Act's subject matter, prevention of water pollution, is of the nature where one would expect government regulation. Thus, a defense of ignorance of law was inappropriate here and any evidence as to this defense was irrelevant and properly excluded.

E. The Instructions Given by the Court Concerning the Term "Negligently" Were Proper

Defendants assign error to the instructions given by Magistrate Sweigert regarding the meaning of the term

APPENDIX B

"negligently" as used in the criminal provisions of the Clean Water Act. They seek to require a greater burden of proof than that imposed by the Magistrate, whose instruction required a finding of a "failure to use reasonable care." As throughout the rest of their brief, defendants' arguments ignore the public welfare nature of the Clean Water Act and the appropriate reluctance of courts in interpreting such statutes to impose higher burdens of proof.

As discussed at length infra, the Clean Water Act is a public welfare offense. It is well settled law that criminal penalties in regulatory statutes designed to protect public health are to be construed to effectuate a regulatory purpose. United States v. Park, 421 U.S. at 672-73; Smith v. California, 361 U.S. 147, 152-53 (1959); United States v. Balint, 258 U.S. at 251-52; United States v. Johnson and Towers, 741 F.2d at 666. This is particularly true with respect to statutes regulating water pollution. See United States v. Pennsylvania Industrial Chemical Corporation, 411 U.S. 655, 670 (1973) (Rivers and Harbors Act of 1899, 33 U.S.C. §§ 407 and 411); United States v. Standard Oil Co., 384 U.S. 224, 226 (1966) (Rivers and Harbors Act of 1899); and United States v. Frezzo Brothers, Inc., 602 F.2d 1123, 1128 (3rd Cir. 1979), cert. denied, 444 U.S. 1074 (1980)(Clean Water Act).

Long prior to the enactment of the Clean Water Act, Congress passed controls over the discharge of materials into navigable waters. See Rivers and Harbors Appropriations Act of 1899 (also known as the "Refuse Act"), 33 U.S.C. §§ 407 and 411. This statute prohibits the discharge of "refuse," a term which has been as broadly defined by the courts as "pollutants" under the Clean Water Act, to navigable waters. The Refuse Act history of enforcement is relevant background to the Clean Water Act criminal provisions which were first enacted in 1972. The Refuse Act codified pre-existing statutes dating from 1886, which related both to impediments to navigation and to pollution. <u>United States v. Standard Oil Co.</u>, 384 U.S. 224, 226-29 (1966). The Refuse Act imposed misdemeanor penalties (a minimum of thirty days imprisonment and a maximum of one year, and a fine of up to $2,500) for discharges regardless of whether <u>any</u> criminal intent existed at all. Over the course of its eighty-eight years of continued enforcement, the Refuse Act has repeatedly been held to be a strict liability <u>malum prohibitum</u> offense of the type designed to protect public health and welfare. E.g. <u>United States v. White Fuel Corp.</u>, 498 F. 2d 619, 622-23 (1st Cir. 1974); <u>The President Coolidge</u>, 101 F.2d 638, 640 (9th Cir. 1939); <u>Scow No. 36</u>, 144 F. 932, 936 (1st Cir. 1906); <u>United States v. American Cyanamid Co.</u>, 354 F. Supp. 1202, 1205 (S.D. N.Y. 1973), <u>aff'd</u>, 480 F.2d 1132 (1973); <u>United States v. United States Steel Corp.</u>, 328 F.Supp. 354 (N.D. Ind. 1970), <u>aff'd</u>, 482 F.2d 439 (7th Cir.), <u>cert. denied</u>, 414 U.S. 909 (1973); <u>United States v. Interlake Steel Corp.</u>, 297 F. Supp. 912, 915 (N.D. Ill. 1969).

The cases cited emphasized the purpose of the Refuse Act, to protect public health and welfare, and the fact that effectuating that purpose required that the statute be read broadly, even in criminal prosecutions (contrary to the general rule). Standard Oil, 384 U.S. at 226; United States v. Republic Steel, 362 U.S. 482, 491 (1960); American Cyanamid Company, 480 F.2d at 1133-34. The District Court in United States Steel Corporation, 328 F. Supp. at 356, remarked

> the offense of depositing refuse in navigable waters is a malum prohibitum, not a malum in se, and falls squarely within the category of "public welfare offenses" described in Morrisette [v. United States, 342 U.S. 246]. As such, it could properly have been made the subject of strict criminal lability, and in the opinion of this Court, it was. The public is injured just as much by unintentional pollution as it is by deliberate pollution, and it would have been entirely reasonable for Congress to attack both.

The Refuse Act was not repealed by the Clean Water Act. Indeed, it was the express subject of a "savings clause." 33 U.S.C. § 1371(a); United States v. Outboard Marine Corp., 549 F. Supp. 1032 (N.D. Ill. 1982). It continues to be used by Federal prosecutors.

The fact that a strict liability water pollution offense very similar to the Clean Water Act remains on the federal statute books is relevant to what Congress intended when it enacted the Clean Water Act. The Clean Water Act, with its procedures to delegate permit issuing authority to the states, and to establish nationwide standards of performance based on technology, may be more sophisticated than the Refuse Act's simple prohibitions. However, it expressly retained the Refuse Act's vitality as an enforcement statute, which is found in the same title of the United States Code. In light of the continued validity of the Refuse Act, it can hardly be said that Congress intended in the enactment of the Clean Water Act to prevent the imposition of any standard of liability short of gross negligence or willful violation of a known legal requirement, as defendants would have this Court rule. Perhaps if the Clean Water Act had repealed the Refuse Act's strict liability one could so argue. It did not. The more consistent interpretation is that Congress imposed a somewhat higher *mens rea* in the Clean Water Act in recognition of the enhanced financial penalties ($25,000 per day instead of $2,500 per discharge). That new *mens rea*, however, retained its basis in public welfare, *malum prohibitum* type principles of criminal liability. These same principles support the Magistrate's express conclusion below that the crimes here charged were indeed *malum prohibitum*, and required the intent level described in the jury instructions.

In light of the Clean Water Act's stated Congressional purpose to eliminate the discharge of *all* pollutants to waters of the United States by 1985, 33 U.S.C. § 1251, it is reasonable to conclude that Congress intended for ordinary concepts of negligence to apply. This standard is the most appropriate to effectuate the Congressional purpose, since it properly reflects the seriousness with which Congress approached the elimination of water pollution.

"When interpreting a statute, the court's objective is to ascertain the intent of Congress and to give effect to legislative will." Moorhead v. United States, 774 F.2d 936, 940 (9th Cir. 1985); Trailer Train Co. v. State Board of Equalization, 697 F. 2d 860, 865 (9th Cir.), cert. denied, 464 U.S. 846 (1983); American Cyanamid, 480 F.2d at 1135 ("[W]e are not unmindful of Learned Hand's eloquent guide to statutory construction, that we must always 'remember that statutes always have some purpose or object to accomplish, whose sympathetic and imaginative discovery is the surest guide to their meaning'"). To ascertain this intent, one must review the statutory language and, where this leaves questions, the legislative history. Blum v. Stenson, 465 U.S. 886, 896-97 (1984). The word "negligently" is not defined in the Clean Water Act. Thus, resort to a review of legislative history, including the past well-established history of enforcement of the Refuse Act, its predecessor statute, is appropriate.

The legislative history of the Clean Water Act does contain a reference to the standard of negligence to be employed. During debate in the House of Representatives concerning a floor amendment to the proposed criminal provisions, Representative William Harsha, floor manager of the bill, indicated that simple negligence concepts were to be applied. He stated: "I would like to call to the attention of my colleagues the fact that in this legislation we already can charge a man for simple negligence . . . ." Legislative History, Vol. 1, at p. 530. There was no dissenting discussion on this point nor contrary viewpoint voiced prior to the vote approving this legislation.

This then surely indicates the Congressional intent on the matter, particularly in light of the objectives of the statute. The courts called upon to decide this issue so far have given simple negligence instructions. See e.g., United States v. Frezzo Brothers, 461 F. Supp. 266 (E.D. Pa. 1978), aff'd, 602 F.2d 1123 (3d Cir. 1979); United States v. Hoflin, No. CR85-82T, U.S.D.C. W.D. Wa. 1986; United States v. White, et al., No. CR 86-20015, U.S.D.C. (W.D. Ark. 1987) (copies attached as Appendix A).

Defendants seek to have this Court use the interpretation given to the term "negligently" under other statutes, common law, and the model penal code, as guidance in its use under the Clean Water Act. Reference to other statutes and hypothetical model statutes is inappropriate where, as here, there is an expression of the Congressional intent on the issue. Furthermore, the statutory examples cited by the defendants are not public welfare statutes. For example, negligent homocide statutes, with substantial felony penalties, are hardly apposite. The precedents relied on are inapplicable to the case at hand.

The defendants also seek to assign error to the instruction given by Magistrate Sweigert concerning the term "reasonable care." First, defendants failed to specifically object to this instruction at trial. [See TR 453.] Second, this instruction, which required the jury to consider "all of the surrounding circumstances, as shown by the evidence in the case" did not improperly require the conduct to be viewed from hindsight (emphasis added). [Instruction No. Ten, TR 471.] The phrase "as shown by the evidence of the case" restricts the jury's consideration only to the evidence, properly adduced at trial, concerning circumstances known to the defendant. It does not conflict with the general law of negligence.

F. The Magistrate's Instruction Concerning the Responsibility of a Corporation for the Acts of its Agents Was Proper

The jury instruction given by the Magistrate concerning corporate responsibility was the Ninth Circuit Model Instruction on the question. That instruction was consistent with the Ninth Circuit's decision in United States v. Beusch, 596 F.2d 871, 877-78 (1979). The Magistrate's general corporate responsibility instruction was not objected to by the defendants. [TR 457.] Instead, defendants objected to, and now claim as error, the Magistrate's refusal to give a proposed instruction based upon agency law specifically defining what constitutes an agency relationship. Defendant's Proposed Instruction No. 28 (see n.10, infra). The defendants sought this instruction to support their theory regarding the liability of a corporation for the acts of an independent contractor. The proposed instruction, however, did not properly define the term agency as that term is used in the criminal context. Thus, the Magistrate appropriately refused the instruction.

A defendant is entitled to an instruction which reflects his theory of the case if this instruction has a basis in law. United States v. Hayes, 794 F.2d at 1351; United States v. Coin,

753 F.2d 1510, 1511 (9th Cir. 1985); and *United States v. Candelaria*, 704 F. 2d 1129, 1132 (9th Cir. 1983). The instruction proposed by defendants did not reflect the law applicable to this case. It reflected contractual and fiduciary concepts which were inappropriate in this criminal matter.

The issue which the defendants seek to address through their proposed instruction is the liability of an employee for the criminal acts of an independent contractor. *See* Appellants' Brief pp. 35-36, and Memorandum of Points and Authorities in Support of Defendant's Proposed Jury Instruction No. 28. The criminal liablity of a corporation for acts of independent contractors, like that for its employees, is grounded on principles of tort liability. *See* *New York Central and Hudson River Railroad v. United States*, 212 U.S. 481 (1909); and *Standard Oil Company of Texas v. United States*, 307 F.2d 120, 127 (5th Cir. 1962). Even defendants agree with this fact. *See* Appellants' Brief, p. 36. Thus, a review of tort concepts on this point is appropriate.

Employers will be held liable for the torts committed by their employees when committed during the course of employment. *See* Prosser & Keeton, *Torts* § 70 at 501 (5th ed.) (hereafter, *Prosser*), and the cases cited therein. In many circumstances, employers will be held responsible for the torts comitted by independent contractors. *Wilson v. Good Humor Corp.*, 757 F. 2d 1293 (D.C. Cir. 1985). Liability for the acts of independent contractors generally exists found in situations where "the employer is in the best position to identify, minimize, and administer the risks involved in the contractors activities." Id. at 1301. For example, where there is a forseeable risk of harm to others unless precautions are taken, the employer has an obligation to exercise reasonable care to insure that the harm does not occur during the contractor's work. This is particularly true where he retains control over the work or furnishes equipment, which was the case here. See Prosser at 510. This duty applies regardless of the independent contractor's ability to bind the corporation financially--that question is irrelevant to tort or criminal liability.

The instruction sought by defendants defines "agent" (thus, one for whom a corporation can be liable), in terms of the ability to commit the corporation to business relationships and fiduciary relationships. 10/ Defendants' proposed instruction

---

10/ The full instruction sought by defendants states:

A person, other than an employee or officer, may be hired by a corporation without being an agent of the corporation. To conclude that a person was an agent of a corporation, you must find beyond a reasonable doubt that all three of the following apply:

1) the person had the power to commit the corporation to business relationships with third parties;

2) the person was a fiduciary of the corporation. This means that he had a duty of loyalty to the corporation, such as to account for profits arising out of the employment, and the duty not to work for adverse parties without the corporation's consent; and

3) the corporation had the power to exercise control over the manner in which the person worked. If the corporation had control over the result obtained, but not over the exact method to be used, the party is not an agent.

cited a labor dispute case and a contract case. These concepts have no place in the context of a criminal matter. They are appropriate only to issues involving contractual-type relationships. The cases cited by the defendants as authority illustrate the point. Whisper Soft Mills, Inc. v. NLRB, 754 F.2d 1381 (9th Cir. 1984), involves the question of whether a local union had consented to act as the agent of an international union, thus imposing on the empoyer a duty to bargain with the local union. Fenton v. Freedman, 748 F.2d 1358 (9th Cir. 1984), involved claims that an art consultant breached her fiduciary duty of full disclosure to her clients.

The issue in this case was not whether J.W. Bateman or the grinder operator (we note there was a factual dispute over the identity of the operator) could enter into a business relationship on behalf of Sea Gleaner Marine. No such action was alleged. Further, there was no question that Sea Gleaner could be liable for the acts of J. W. Bateman without first demonstrating that Mr. Bateman had a duty to account to Sea Gleaner for any profits which he may have received from his employment. Rather, the issue was whether Sea Gleaner was liable for the discharge of pollutants caused by acts of these individuals occurring at the Sea Gleaner facility. No requirement of an agency relationship, as that term was defined in defendants' proposed instruction, was essential to establish this liability. The only issue was the extent to which Sea Gleaner was able to control the violative acts of these so-called

APPENDIX B

independent contractors. Because the defendants' proposed instruction failed to properly state the law, the instruction was properly refused.

IV
CONCLUSION

For the reasons stated above, the judgments of conviction and sentence entered by the Magistrate should be affirmed.

DATED this 24th day of June, 1987.

Respectfully submitted,

GENE S. ANDERSON
United States Attorney

DAVID V. MARSHALL
Assistant United States Attorney

HELEN J. BRUNNER
Environmental Crimes Section
Land and Natural Resources Division
United States Department of Justice

APPENDIX TO BRIEF

Published by The Bureau of National Affairs, Inc.

APPENDIX B

IN THE UNITED STATES DISTRICT COURT

FOR THE EASTERN DISTRICT OF PENNSYLVANIA

UNITED STATES OF AMERICA   :   CRIMINAL NO. 78-218
                              :
vs.   :   CHARGE
                              :   Volume IVb
FREZZO BROTHERS, INC.,   :
GUIDO FREZZO and   :
JAMES L. FREZZO,   :
     Defendants   :

Philadelphia, Pennsylvania
October 19, 1978

BEFORE HON. RAYMOND J. BRODERICK, U.S.D.J.

APPEARANCES:

　　　　　PETER J. VAIRA, ESQ.,
　　　　　United States Attorney,
　　　　　for the Government
　　　　　By: BRUCE J. CHASAN, A.U.S.A.
　　　　　　　and
　　　　　　　MICHAEL P. CARLTON,
　　　　　　　Special Attorney,
　　　　　　　Department of Justice,
　　　　　　　Washington, D. C.

　　　　　WILLIAM J. GALLAGHER,
　　　　　for the Defendants

Published by The Bureau of National Affairs, Inc.

Charge

Now, I am going to talk to you about negligence, or negligently. I just want to say, again, that that second element -- yes, the second element that I am on now is the defendant's discharge of the pollutant was done willfully or negligently.

Now, I have defined what willfully means, and now I am going to tell you what negligently means.

Negligence is the doing of some act which a reasonably prudent person would not do; or it is the failure to do something which a reasonably prudent person would do when prompted by considerations which ordinarily regulate the conduct of human affairs.

Now, that is a time-honored definition of negligence. In other words, my way of explaining it is: The failure to use ordinary care under the circumstances. And what is ordinary care? Ordinary care, that's a relative term, and it is not an absolute one. That is to say, in deciding whether ordinary care was exercised in a given case, the conduct in question must be viewed in the light of all the surrounding circumstances, as shown by the evidence in the case.

APPENDIX B

Instructions given by
Judge Jack E. Tanner

United States v. Hoflin
CR85-82T
United States District Court
Western District of Washington

INSTRUCTION NO. 21

The term "negligence" means failure to use reasonable care. Reasonable care is the care which a reasonably careful person would use under similar circumstances. Negligence may consist of doing something that a reasonably careful person would not do under similar circumstances or failing to do something that a reasonable person would do under similar circumstances.

INSTRUCTION NO. 22

A negligent act is distinguished from one which is intentional or willful. Negligence does not require awareness on the part of the actor. A person acts "negligently" when he acts with a careless disregard of the consequences of his acts that would not be shown by a careful person under the circumstances. A willful act, however, is a knowing act by a person who intends the natural and probable consequences of his acts.

The term "reasonable care" is a relative one. In deciding whether reasonable care was exercised in a given case, the conduct in question must be viewed in the light of all the surrounding circumstances, as shown by the evidence in the case.

Instruction given in

United States v. White, et al.,
CR86-20015
United States District Court
Western District of Arkansas

COURT'S INSTRUCTION NO. 60

NEGLIGENCE --
DEFINITION   Black's Law Dictionary 931 (5th ed. 1979)

With respect to the crime of discharge of pollutants without a permit, the term "negligence" means the omission on the part of a person to do some act which an ordinarily careful and prudent person would do under the circumstances, or the doing of some act which an ordinarily careful and prudent person under like circumstances would not do.

COURT'S INSTRUCTION NO. 61

ORDINARY CARE

D&B 80.05,
D&B 80.06 modified

The term "ordinary care" is not an absolute one but a relative one. In deciding whether ordinary care was exercised in a given case, the conduct in question must be viewed in the light of all the surrounding circumstances, as shown by the evidence in the case. The more foreseeable the harm is in a given situation, the more care is required.

COURT'S INSTRUCTION NO. 61 A

**KNOWLEDGE OF LAW
PRESUMED IN CIRCUMSTANCES
AS TO NEGLIGENCE** D&B 80.13 modified

Since everyone is required to act with knowledge of what the law forbids and what the law requires, the provisions of federal law as to the discharge of pollutants without a permit are to be considered by you as one of the circumstances in evidence in this case.

UNITED STATES DISTRICT COURT
FOR THE WESTERN DISTRICT OF WASHINGTON AT SEATTLE

UNITED STATES OF AMERICA,)
    Plaintiff-Appellee,)
)
v.)
)
PAUL D. SCHWITTERS and)
SEA GLEANER MARINE, INC.,)
)
    Defendant-Appellants.)
_____)
	NO. CR 86-129 D

APPELLANTS' REPLY BRIEF

APPENDIX B

B-153

TABLE OF AUTHORITIES

    Cases Cited
    Statutes Cited
    Rules Cited
    Other Authorities Cited

I. DEFENDANT SCHWITTERS WAS IMPERMISSIBLY CONVICTED ON A THEORY ELIMINATING ANY REQUIREMENT OF MENS REA

    A. INSTRUCTION 20 ALLOWED CONVICTION OF CORPORATE OFFICERS WITHOUT PROOF OF MENS REA

    B. CONVICTION UNDER THE CLEAN WATER ACT REQUIRES PROOF OF WILLFULNESS OR NEGLIGENCE FOR ALL PERSONS, INCLUDING CORPORATE OFFICERS. ....

II. CONVICTION UNDER THE CLEAN WATER ACT REQUIRES PROOF OF GROSS NEGLIGENCE

    A. THE MEANING OF THE TERM "NEGLIGENTLY"

    B. THE PRINCIPLE OF LENITY

III. THE COURT IMPROPERLY ALLOWED CONVICTION FOR NEGLIGENCE BASED ON CIRCUMSTANCES NOT KNOWN TO DEFENDANTS

IV. THE COURT ERRED IN REFUSING TO DEFINE WHICH "AUTHORIZED AGENTS" OF CORPORATIONS COULD MAKE THE CORPORATION VICARIOUSLY LIABLE

V. THE COURT'S REFUSAL TO DEFINE THE MENTAL ELEMENT REQUIRED FOR CONVICTION AS AN AIDER AND ABETTOR WAS ERROR

VI. A WILLFUL VIOLATION OF A PROVISION OF THE CLEAN WATER ACT RQUIRES KNOWLEDGE THAT THE PROVISION IS BEING VIOLATED

    A. WILLFULNESS VERSUS AN IGNORANCE OF LAW DEFENSE

    B. WILLFULNESS IN PUBLIC WELFARE STATUTES

Published by The Bureau of National Affairs, Inc.

C. WILLFULNESS AS A PROTECTION FOR THE UNWARY

D. LEGISLATIVE HISTORY OF THE ACT

E. THE TERM "WILLFULLY VIOLATES"

APPENDIX

APPENDIX B

TABLE OF AUTHORITIES

Cases Cited

Bollenbach v. United States, 326 U.S. 607 (1946)

Boone v. United States, 109 F.2d 560 (6th Cir. 1940)

Francis v. Franklin, 471 U.S. 307, 105 S.Ct. 1975 (1985)

Liparota v. United States, 471 U.S. 419 (1985)

Logue v. United States, 412 U.S. 521 (1973)

McNally v. United States, ___ U.S. ___, 107 S.Ct. 2875 (1987)

Morrisette v. United States, 342 U.S. 246 (1952)

People of Territory of Guam v. Alvarez, 763 F.2d 1036 (9th Cir. 1985)

Riss & Company v. United States, 262 F.2d 245 (8th Cir. 1958)

St. Louis-San Francisco Ry. Co. v. United States, 169 F. 69 (8th Cir. 1909)

Stromberg v. California, 283 U.S. 359 (1931)

Tarvestad v. United States, 418 F.2d 1043 (8th Cir. 1969), cert. denied, 397 U.S. 935 (1970)

United States v. Aitken, 755 F.2d 188 (1st Cir. 1985)

United States v. Anton, 683 F.2d 1011 (7th Cir. 1982)

United States v. Balint, 258 U.S. 250 (1922)

United States v. Beusch, 596 F.2d 871 (9th Cir. 1979)

United States v. Brown, 578 F.2d 1280 (9th Cir. 1978)

United States v. Cattle King Packing Co., Inc., 793 F.2d 232 (10th Cir.), cert. denied, 107 S.Ct. 573 (1986)

United States v. Charney, 537 F.2d 341 (9th Cir.), cert. denied, 429 U.S. 1000 (1976)

United States v. Corbin Farm Service, 444 F. Supp. 510 (E.D. Cal. 1978)

United States v. Dotterweich, 320 U.S. 277 (1943)

United States v. Dye Construction Co., 510 F.2d 78 (10th Cir. 1975)...........................

United States v. English, 409 F.2d 200 (3d Cir. 1969)

United States v. Fierros, 692 F.2d 1291 (9th Cir. 1982), cert. denied, 462 U.S. 1120 (1983)

United States v. Flores, 753 F.2d 1499 (9th Cir. 1985)

United States v. Frade, 709 F.2d 1387 (11th Cir. 1983)

United States v. Freed, 401 U.S. 601 (1971)

United States v. Frezzo Bros., 461 F. Supp. 266 (E.D. Pa. 1978)

United States v. Frezzo Bros., Inc., 602 F.2d 1123 (3rd Cir. 1979), cert. denied, 444 U.S. 1074 (1980)

United States v. Garza, 426 F.2d 949 (5th Cir. 1970)

United States v. Georgetown University, 331 F. Supp. 69 (D.C. Cir. 1971)

United States v. Golitschek, 808 F.2d 195 (2d Cir. 1986)

United States v. Gris, 247 F.2d 860 (1957)

United States v. Hayes, 794 F.2d 1348 (9th Cir. 1986)

APPENDIX B

United States v. Hayes International Corp., 786 F.2d 1499 (11th Cir. 1986)

United States v. Hudson, 564 F2d 1377 (9th Cir. 1977)

United States v. Illinois Central Railroad Co., 303 U.S. 239 (1938)

United States v. International Minerals & Chemical Corp., 402 U.S. 558 (1971)

United States v. Johnson & Towers, Inc., 741 F.2d 662 (3rd Cir. 1984), cert. denied, 469 U.S. 1208 (1985)

United States v. Lizarraga-Lizarraga, 541 F.2d 826 (9th Cir. 1976)

United States v. Moore, 586 F.2d 1029 (4th Cir. 1978)

United States v. Ohio Barge Lines, Inc., 607 F.2d 624 (3rd Cir. 1979)

United States v. Park, 421 U.S. 658 (1975)

United States v. Peltz, 433 F.2d 48 (2d Cir. 1970), cert. denied, 401 U.S. 955 (1971)

United States v. Prujansky, 415 F.2d 1045 (6th Cir. 1969)

United States v. Republic Steel, 362 U.S. 482 (1960)

United States v. Schwartz, 464 F.2d 499 (2nd Cir.), cert. denied, 409 U.S. 1009 (1972)

United States v. Simpson, 561 F.2d 53 (7th Cir. 1977)

United States v. Sirhan, 504 F.2d 818 (9th Cir. 1974)

United States v. Smeaton, 762 F.2d 796 (9th Cir. 1985)

United States v. Standard Oil, 384 U.S. 224 (1966)

United States v. Walker, 677 F.2d 1014 (4th Cir. 1982)

United States v. Wolf, 787 F.2d 1094 (7th Cir. 1986)

Statutes Cited

8 U.S.C. § 1324

15 U.S.C. § 77

18 U.S.C. § 834

29 U.S.C. § 666

33 U.S.C. § 403

33 U.S.C. § 407

33 U.S.C. § 1319

42 U.S.C. § 6928

47 U.S.C. § 401

50 U.S.C. § App. 16

Rules Cited

Ninth Circuit Rule 21

Other Authorities Cited

A Legislative History of the Water Pollution Control Act Amendments of 1972, Congressional Research Service of the Library of Congress, Serial No. 93-1 (1973)

Model Penal Code

Proposed Federal Criminal Code.

APPENDIX B

I.

DEFENDANT SCHWITTERS WAS IMPERMISSIBLY CONVICTED ON A THEORY ELIMINATING ANY REQUIREMENT OF MENS REA

A. INSTRUCTION 20 ALLOWED CONVICTION OF CORPORATE OFFICERS WITHOUT PROOF OF MENS REA

We are frankly at a loss to understand the government's position regarding the responsible corporate officer doctrine. This is because the government never defines what it means by the term. The term has traditionally meant a doctrine whereby corporate officers are legally responsible for crimes committed by their corporation, even if the officer had no personal involvement in the crime or even any knowledge of it. United States v. Park, 421 U.S. 658 (1975). This is the position taken by the government in its trial brief (CR 30 at 7, "the government need only show that an individual has a responsibility for the acts or transactions which the statute forbids . . ."), and urged upon the jury as a basis for conviction (RT 528-30). As we demonstrated in our opening brief, this doctrine simply does not apply to the Clean Water Act, a statute requiring proof of willfulness or negligence.

On appeal, the government has switched gears. It now appears to acknowledge that for corporate officers to be convicted, they have to act, and do so with willfulness or negligence. This is precisely the position we asserted at trial. In short, the government's new interpretation of the responsible corporate officer doctrine is the unremarkable conclusion that when corporate officers are proven to commit every element of the crime, they are guilty, just as any other person would be.[1] The government's new position is that Instruction 20, clearly allowing conviction without such proof, can be rescued by looking to other instructions.

The government's position is extremely disingenuous. Having fought vociferously for the right to convict Paul Schwitters on a alternative theory to Instruction 5, having won that right and having argued that alternative theory, the government now claims that the only theory before the jury was that under Instruction 5. This position cannot withstand scrutiny.

Instruction 20 was unambiguous. It began by making clear that corporate officers can be held responsible for the acts of their corporation. It then told the jury that if it made three specific findings, it could find defendant Schwitters guilty. Those three elements were 1) that Sea Gleaner was guilty, 2) that Schwitters had the power to prevent the violations, and 3) that he failed to prevent the violations. This definitively sets forth an alternative theory of liability, requiring no proof of personal involvement or mens rea. The government's purported interpretation of the instructions would render Instruction 20 a nullity. If Schwitters could only be convicted if he satisfied each element of the crime, what in the world does Instruction 20 add? His corporate position would be totally irrelevant. Why did

---

[1] The government's refusal to state what it understands the corporate officer doctrine to mean is striking. Our opening brief is clearly directed to establishing that corporate officers, like others, can be convicted only upon proof of willfulness or negligence. Had this been the government's position at trial, surely the government's brief would have contended that we were debating an undisputed point.

APPENDIX B

the government submit, brief, and argue for this instruction except to escape the requirements of Instruction 5 in convicting Schwitters?

Government counsel clearly argued that Schwitters' liability as a corporate officer was an alternate theory to conviction as an individual. How now can the government contend that Schwitters could only be convicted if he satisfied all elements of Instruction 5? If Instruction 5 controlled, and a defendant could be convicted only if he discharged pollutants, how could the government argue that Paul Schwitters could be convicted on a "kind of vicarious liability concept and it's a liability that basically says a person who doesn't have anything to do with the actual act itself . . . can be responsible for the crime committed by others." RT 529-30. Government counsel argued further, "The law allows him to be held liable for the acts of others if those acts are ones he could have stopped." RT 530 Mere ability to stop acts does not satisfy the requisites of Instruction 5. Clearly the government interpreted Instruction 20, just as the court and jury did, as allowing a basis for conviction <u>independent of</u> the requirements in Instruction 5.

The fallaciousness of the government's reasoning can be seen by looking at a different theory of alternate liability, that for corporations. Although Instruction 5 says that each defendant cannot be convicted unless it acted willfully or negligently, a corporation obviously cannot act at all, let alone with a particular mental state. Under the government's brand new interpretation of the instructions, in which Instruction 5 controls all other instructions, the corporation could not be convicted at all. This quandry is resolved because

Instruction 5 does not control; Instruction 18 provides an alternate theory of liability, in which the corporation is made responsible for the acts of its agents. Similarly, Instruction 20 provides an alternate theory of liability, in which the corporate officer is made responsible for the acts of the corporation.[2]

United States v. Hayes, 794 F.2d 1348 (9th Cir. 1986) is not instructive. The challenged language was a portion of the instruction listing the elements of the offense. The language relating to good faith left unresolved whether conviction could be had on an objective standard. But the instruction which defined good faith made clear that a subjective standard applied. This clear definition augmented the unresolved language in the other instruction. In this case, however, Instruction 20 unambiguously allows conviction on a strict liability basis. It cannot be rescued by instructions which set forth the requirements for an alternative basis for conviction.

---

[2] The government contends that we have not preserved this error. Our position that corporate officers could not be convicted without proof of mens rea was clearly presented. It was briefed at length in our trial brief [CR 5], our supplemental trial brief [CR 35] and in extended argument to the court [8/11/86 RT 10-16, 20-21, 24-28]. In objecting to Instruction 20, we specifically referred to the language making Schwitters liable for the actions of others [RT 457]. The trial judge made clear that he did not wish a rehashing of these positions during the instruction conference [RT 451] and even cut defense counsel off as we tried to make objections to other instructions on the issue of intent [RT 463]. The government contends that we should have objected to Instruction 20 on the grounds that, in supplementing Instruction 5, it should have included the mens rea language. Since Instruction 20 was never intended to supplement Instruction 5, we of course did not phrase our objection this way. The instruction provided an alternate theory of liability; we consistently and strenuously objected to its providing that theory of liability and thereby preserved the court's error. Even if it had not been objected to, the error, by eliminating elements of the crime, affected substantial rights of defendant and could be heard on appeal. See note 8, p. 18, infra.

The decision in <u>United States v. Cattle King Packing Co., Inc.</u>, 793 F.2d 232 (10th Cir.), <u>cert. denied</u>, 107 S.Ct. 573 (1986) does appear to support the government's position. The opinion does not set forth the language of the instruction given in that case, or whether, as in the present case, it made liability as a corporate officer an alternative theory of liability to that set forth in the other instructions. On the assumption that it did, and that <u>Cattle King</u> is not distinguishable, we submit that this decision, not binding on this court, is simply flawed. How could the instruction complement the other elements instruction, rather than contradict it? 793 F.2d at 241. If a corporate officer must satisfy all elements of the crime, what is there to supplement? And if a corporate officer must satisfy all elements of the crime, what does it mean to give the jury the opportunity to decide if he was responsible for the corporation's violations? 793 F.2d at 240. With all due respect, this opinion makes no sense. It perhaps can be understood from the facts of that case, in which the corporate officer "set in motion the very acts which were carried out, pursuant to direction, by his employees, clearly a form of aiding, abetting, ordering commanding, or inducing." 793 F.2d at 241. But this factor cannot rescue Instruction 20 in the present case. While there may have been sufficient evidence to convict Paul Schwitters on an aiding and abetting theory, we cannot know that the jury did so, given the impermissible corporate officer instruction.

The government's proposed resolution of Instruction 5, with its general instruction on the elements, and Instruction 20, with its specific directive on conviction of Paul Schwitters as a corporate officer, flies in the face of Francis v. Franklin, 471 U.S. 307, 105 S.Ct. 1975 (1985). Although that case deals with Sandstrom error, it is directly applicable. Sandstrom error involves a conclusive presumption on an intent element; this case involves the complete elimination of that element. Francis is instructive on two issues: 1) what standard to apply in determining if Instruction 20 allowed conviction on an impermissible basis and 2) what standard to apply in determining if the instructions as a whole eliminated any error in Instruction 20.

Even if Instruction 20, standing alone, were ambiguous as to whether it establishes impermissible vicarious liability, the conviction must be reversed. "A conviction ought not to rest on an equivocal direction to the jury on a basic issue." Bollenbach v. United States, 326 U.S. 607, 613 (1946). In Francis, the government contended that the challenged instruction was not in violation of Sandstrom, but instead was a constitutionally valid permissive inference instruction. The Court recognized that both interpretations were plausible, but found the instruction invalid because a reasonable juror "could" have understood the instruction to present a mandatory presumption. 105 S.Ct. at 1972. In this case, a reasonable juror could indeed have understood Instruction 20 to allow conviction on a vicarious liability theory.

In Francis, the state contended that even if the one instruction, standing alone, involved Sandstrom error, that error was cured by other instructions on the burden of proof and the lack of a presumption of criminal intent. In rejecting this contention, the Court made clear that the jury instructions, taken as a whole, were erroneous, unless this other language "explain[ed] the particular infirm language to the extent that a reasonable juror could not have considered the charge to have created an unconstitutional presumption." 105 S.Ct. at 1971. In this case, despite the presence of Instruction 5, a reasonable juror could have understood the charge to allow conviction of corporate officers without proof of mens rea.

As in the present case, the government in Francis pointed to language in another instruction, correctly requiring proof as to each element. Francis held that this instruction did not cure the error, because a juror could have thought that the presumption instruction meant that intent could be proven by way of the presumption. 105 S.Ct. at 174. Similarly, in this case, a juror could have thought that the intent required by Instruction 5 could be satisfied by the elements set forth in Instruction 20.

Even if juror did not reach this conclusion, he or she could well have understood Instructions 5 and 20 to be inconsistent. Francis held that, if the instructions could be seen as inconsistent, reversal was mandated.

> Language that merely contradicts and does not explain a constitutionally infirm instruction will not suffice to absolve the infirmity. A reviewing court has no way of knowing which of the two irreconcilable instructions the jurors applied in reaching their verdict.

105 S.Ct. at 1975. This principle is well-established. "The fact that an instruction is correct does not cure the error in giving another that is inconsistent with it." United States v. Garza, 426 F.2d 949, 955 (5th Cir. 1970) (correct instruction that overt act is insufficient for conspiracy conviction does not cure instruction that phone

phone conversation sufficient in itself to establish guilt); accord, United States v. Walker, 677 F.2d 1014 (4th Cir. 1982) (instruction that jury must resolve issue of defendant's sole access to funds does not cure ambiguous instruction, interpretable as stating that defendant had such access).

The mandate of Francis extends far beyond Sandstrom errors:

> [I]t has been settled law since Stromberg v. California, 283 U.S. 359 (1931), that when there exists a reasonable possibility that the jury relied on an unconstitutional understanding of the law in reaching a verdict, that verdict must be set aside.

105 S.Ct. at 1976, n. 8. Because a reasonable juror could have understood Instruction 20 as allowing conviction simply on the basis of Paul Schwitters' corporate position, his conviction must be reversed.

B. CONVICTION UNDER THE CLEAN WATER ACT REQUIRES PROOF OF WILLFULNESS OR NEGLIGENCE FOR ALL PERSONS, INCLUDING CORPORATE OFFICERS

Although the government appears to concede that proof of willfulness or negligence was necessary, it devotes a few pages to asserting that the Clean Water Act does indeed incorporate the responsible corporate officer doctrine. Since the government doesn't define that term, we don't know if this position is inconsistent with the rest of its brief, or not. If the government is claiming that the traditional doctrine does apply, its argument utterly fails to establish that point.

Cattle King, 793 F.2d at 241, does not endorse conviction of corporate officers in non-strict liability offenses, without proof that they personally satisfy the elements of the crime. Exactly to the contrary. The decision squarely holds that conviction for a scienter crime cannot be based on a responsible corporate officer theory alone but instead demands proof of the intent required under the particular statute. 793 F.2d at 241. The court found that the instructions in that case did not make a corporate officer theory a separate basis of liability, a finding we discuss in Part I.A. But that conclusion does not undercut the clear holding that corporate officers, like everyone else, must satisfy the elements of a crime to be convicted.

The government also looks to United States v. Frezzo Bros., Inc., 602 F.2d 1123, 1130 n. 11 (3rd Cir. 1979), cert. denied, 444 U.S. 1074 (1980). As we carefully explained in our opening brief, the sole issue before the court was whether the defendants could be convicted under a primary liability theory, although they were charged only under a vicarious responsible officer theory. This is made even more clear by the trial transcript, showing objections to the charge. [CR 83, p. 32] and the discussion of post-trial motions, United States v. Frezzo Bros., 461 F. Supp. 266, 272-73 (E.D. Pa. 1978). Nor did defendants challenge the corporate officer instructions on appeal (Brief in Frezzo Bros., currently the subject of a motion to supplement the record on appeal). The Court of Appeals rejected defendants' position, saying it saw no error in the instructions on "this theory," i.e. the challenged theory, the non-corporate officer theory. To read the reference to "this theory" as a broad pronouncement on the propriety of the corporate officer instruction would mean that the court had reached out to approve, without any briefing, an unchallenged jury instruction. We do not assume, as the government does, that the Tenth Circuit would so readily and unnecessarily violate the principle against deciding issues not on appeal.

Finally, the government's reference to the statutory language in no way demonstrates a Congressional intent to eliminate proof of willfulness or negligence for corporate officers. It only establishes that corporate officers are liable if they act as other persons do, which is exactly our position.

II.

CONVICTION UNDER THE CLEAN WATER ACT REQUIRES PROOF OF GROSS NEGLIGENCE

A. THE MEANING OF THE TERM "NEGLIGENTLY"

In our Opening Brief, we discussed the meaning of the term "negligently," as it is used in the Clean Water Act. Since the word is undefined in federal law, we discussed the clear guidance provided by the terms's regular use throughout common law, other statutes, the Model Penal Code, and Proposed Federal Criminal Code. The government's response is a talismanic reliance on the phrase "public welfare offense."[3] Because the government sees the Clean Water Act as a public welfare offense, it concludes that Congress must have intended a far different meaning for the term "negligence" than its normal meaning in criminal statutes.[4]

---

[3] The government uses the phrase "public welfare offense," or its equivalent, at least once a page throughout its argument, as if the mere recitation of this expression can dispose of all the complex mens rea issues raised by this appeal.

[4] We fully agree with the government that negligent homicide is not the best analogy for discerning the meaning of "negligent" in pollution statutes (Government's Brief, p. 48). It is for that very reason our opening brief looked beyond the sparse federal law. The definition of negligence throughout the Model Penal Code, common law, and state statutes is not restricted to felonies or other serious crimes.

APPENDIX B

There are two flaws with this analysis. First of all, the government's conception of a public welfare offense is very different from the Supreme Court's. As defined in *Liparota v. United States*, 471 U.S. 419, 105 S.Ct. 2084, 85 L.Ed.2d 434 (1985), such statutes "depend on no mental element but consist only of forbidden acts or omissions." 105 S.Ct. at 2092. Rather obviously, by limiting the criminal application of the Clean Water Act to those who act willfully or negligently, Congress made a determination that the Act would *not* be a public welfare offense.[5] As discussed in our opening brief, this is quite appropriate, given the incredibly broad reach of the law. Thus, the major premise of the government's analysis is false.

Furthermore, the government's reasoning, that application of the normal criminal meaning of negligence would frustrate the purpose of the Act, is circular.

> Of course, the purpose of every statute would be "obstructed" by requiring a finding of [a particular level of] intent, if we assume that it had a purpose to convict without it. Therefore, the obstruction rationale does not help us to learn the purpose [of Congress].

Morrisette v. United States, 342 U.S. 246, 259 (1952).

Congress's purpose in enacting the Clean Water Act was indeed the elimination of all water pollution. But Congress approached the issue of water pollution in several ways, including grants, civil penalties, and administrative penalties. These penalties can be imposed on a strict liability basis. Thus, criminal enforcement is only one piece of a wide-ranging attack on the problem. Congress decided that the

---

[5] Obviously the Act is devoted to protecting health and welfare. But it is not a member of that unique genre of "public health and welfare" offenses in which normal *mens rea* principles are altered.

more encompassing enforcement, which would reach those who did not act with criminal intent, would be based on the civil and administrative penalties.[6] Rather obviously, Congress concluded that it did not have to impose the extreme sanction of criminal penalties on all polluters, only the more egregious ones. The government's assertion that Congress, in restricting criminal penalties, intended a very low threshold of _mens rea_ is only that, an assertion, not a conclusion.

In attempting to infer Congress's intent on the meaning of "negligently" under the Clean Water Act, the government devotes several pages to establishing that the Rivers and Harbor Act imposes a strict liability standard. The government acknowledges that Congress imposed a more restrictive _mens rea_ requirement under the Clean Water Act. But then the government insists that the only possible conclusion is that "negligently" was intended to be a tiny bit more restrictive than strict liability, but not as restrictive as it has been used almost uniformly throughout criminal laws. This is a leap of faith, not a logical conclusion. When Congress authorized fines ten times those in the Rivers and Harbors Act, it demanded a higher level of proof, and there is no reason to believe the language Congress used should deviate from its normal meaning. Our position is again reinforced by the fact that the Clean Water Act authorizes strong enforcement action at the same quantum of proof as the Rivers and Harbor Act, i.e., strict

---

[6] In _United States v. Anton_, 683 F.2d 1011, 1015 (7th Cir. 1982), the existence of "a non-penal alternative to remedy the same harm" was an important factor in concluding that Congress intended a higher, rather than lower, level of _mens rea_ in the corresponding criminal statute. There was no need for the criminal statute to have an unfairly broad reach when it was not the sole method of addressing the problem.

liability, albeit at the civil rather than criminal level. Congress frequently has statutes covering similar behavior, with comparable penalties, but with one statute requiring a far higher level of proof.

The legislative history on this issue does not support the government's position at all. Rep. Harsha's reference to "negligence" was to contrast it with willful violations. It was not an attempt to define precisely what meaning should be given to the term "negligently," or to contrast civil tort negligence with gross or criminal negligence. A Legislative History of the Water Pollution Control Act Amendments of 1972, Congressional Research Service of the Library of Congress, Serial No. 93-1 (1973) ("Legislative History"), Vol. 1 at 530.

Finally, the government cites to the fact that three district courts have given the challenged instruction. Only published opinions may be cited to the district court. Ninth Circuit Rule 21(c). These citations are not only improper authority, they are totally unpersuasive. There is no record indicating that these instructions were objected to or that the definition of negligence was fully briefed or even raised. In fact, in each of these cases, the meaning of negligence was not an issue and was not addressed by trial counsel (see Appendix). Thus, none of these particular definitions was endorsed by the different trial courts; these were instructions submitted without challenge, of no concern to the party involved.

B. THE PRINCIPLE OF LENITY

As we discussed in our Opening Brief, an ambiguity in the meaning of the term "negligence" must be resolved in favor of defendants, applying the principle of lenity. The government, in an almost off-hand manner, makes the incredible suggestion that this well-entrenched principle does not apply to the Rivers and Harbors Act or (by implication) to the Clean Water Act and that the opposite principle of construction applies (Government's Brief at 44-45). Contrary to the government's assertion, the principle of lenity is alive and well in all phases of criminal law, including the Clean Water Act.

United States v. Republic Steel, 362 U.S. 482 (1960), interpreted two provisions of the Rivers and Harbors Act, 33 U.S.C. § 403 and 33 U.S.C. § 407. The Court found that the explicitly broad language of one provision, banning "the creation of any obstruction . . . to the navigable capacity of any of the waters of the United States . . ." (emphasis in Republic Steel) included obstructing a channel with industrial waste. Similarly, language barring the discharge of "any refuse matter of any kind or description whatever . . ." applied to discharging industrial solids in suspension which ultimately settled out and formed an obstruction. These decisions were grounded on the explicit language of the clauses, a long-standing history of administrative construction consistent with the court's interpretation, and the legislative history showing that, in enacting this law, Congress was directly responding to case law which limited enforcement actions against obstruction of navigability. The Court thus refused to give "a narrow, cramped reading" to either provision. 362 U.S. at 491.

The decision in United States v. Standard Oil, 384 U.S. 224 (1966) again involved 33 U.S.C. § 407. The issue was whether the phrase "any refuse matter of any kind or description" encompassed commercially valuable oil or gasoline. The court held that it did, observing, "More comprehensive language would be difficult to select." 384 U.S. at 229. In addition to this clear language, the court looked to the predecessor statutes, which had banned the discharge of "other waste of any kind" and "any other matter of any kind" and the clear intent of Section 403 simply to consolidate these prior Acts without substantive change. Lastly, the court looked to the intent of the law, which was to prevent the discharge of material which might obstruct navigation. The court recognized that commercially valuable matter has just as great a potential for obstruction as does worthless material.

In so holding, the court reiterated that this legislative purpose in history "forbids a narrow, cramped reading" of the Act. In this context, the court observed, "But whatever may be said of the rule of strict construction, it cannot provide a substitute for common sense, precedent, and legislative history." 384 U.S. at 225.

Neither of these decisions, then, in any way undoes the well-established principle of lenity. They simply reassert the flip-side of that principle: unambiguous language, clear legislative history, or unassailable Congressional purpose control over a strained, albeit lenient, reading of a statute. Since there is nothing inherently broad about the term "negligently" to indicate it refers to simple negligence, rather than its usual criminal meaning, nor is there explicit legislative history or Congressional purpose mandating the government's interpretation, the principle of lenity supports defendants' position.

United States v. Ohio Barge Lines, Inc., 607 F.2d 624 (3rd Cir. 1979) explicitly considers whether the language in Republic Steel and Standard Oil upsets the normal strict construction of criminal statutes is. That decision recognizes that those cases did not make any changes in rules of interpretation, but instead are fully consistent "with the application of accepted principles of statutory construction." 607 F.2d at 629. Accordingly, in interpreting the mens rea requirements of Section 10 of the Rivers and Harbors Act, the court applied the doctrine of strict construction.[7]

The principle of lenity has been reaffirmed in forceful language as recently as this last Supreme Court term. "The Court has often stated that when there are two rational readings of a criminal statute, one harsher than the other, we are to choose the harsher only when Congress has spoken in clear and definite language." McNally v. United States, ___ U.S. ___, 107 S.Ct. 2875, 2881 (1987). That principle cannot be undone by stretching the language of Standard Oil or Republic Steel far beyond the intended meaning.

III.

THE COURT IMPROPERLY ALLOWED CONVICTION FOR NEGLIGENCE BASED ON CIRCUMSTANCES NOT KNOWN TO DEFENDANTS

The government (Brief at 48-49) does not dispute defendants' analysis of the law of negligence: negligence may be judged only on the

---

[7] Ohio Barge is actually a civil case but, recognizing that Section 403 exposes one to criminal sanctions under Section 406, the court applied criminal principles of statutory construction.

APPENDIX B

basis of what was known to the defendant at the time. Instead, the government contends that the jury was so instructed.

The jury was told:

> In deciding whether reasonable care was exercised in a given case, the conduct in question must be viewed in the light of all the surrounding circumstances, as shown by the evidence in the case.

RT 471. We simply do not understand how the government reads this instruction to require that the jury look only to the circumstances shown to be known by the defendants at that time. The instruction clearly directs the jury to consider all of the circumstances shown by the evidence to exist. Circumstances which were shown to exist, but which were unknown to the defendants, are in no way excluded by this instruction.

The government contends that we did not object to the failure to include language instructing the jury to consider only circumstances known to the defendants. This is not true. In discussing the court's negligence definition, we stated that the Model Penal Code definition was the proper one [RT 453]. We took specific exception to the court's failure to give our Proposed Instruction No. 1 [RT 461]. That instruction, in defining negligence, included the language which the law requires:

> The risk must be of such a nature and degree that the defendant's failure to perceive it, considering the nature and purpose of his conduct <u>and the circumstances known to him</u>, involved a gross deviation from the standard of care that a reasonable person would observe <u>in the defendant's situation</u>.

Published by The Bureau of National Affairs, Inc.

[CR 32]. The error was properly preserved.[8]

IV.

THE COURT ERRED IN REFUSING TO DEFINE WHICH "AUTHORIZED AGENTS" OF CORPORATIONS COULD MAKE THE CORPORATION VICARIOUSLY LIABLE

As discussed in our Opening Brief, the court's instructions allowed conviction of defendant Sea Gleaner based on the acts of the corporation's "authorized agents." The court refused to explicate just what this term means and we predicated error on that refusal.

The government does not contend that the court's instruction was an adequate statement of the law.[9] In fact, the government agrees that employers are not always criminally liable for the acts of independent contractors and it does not suggest that the term "authorized representative" properly defines the circumstances when such liability may attach. Instead, the government relies solely on its claim that our proposed instruction was not completely correct.

---

[8] Even if the error had not been preserved, it may be considered by this Court if it involves "plain errors or defects affecting substantial rights." F. R. Crim. P. 52(b). Instructions which incorrectly define the elements of the offense affect substantial rights. See, e.g., United States v. Wolf, 787 F.2d 1094, 1098 (7nd Cir. 1986); People of Territory of Guam v. Alvarez, 763 F.2d 1036 (9th Cir. 1985); United States v. Smeaton, 762 F.2d 796, 799 (9th Cir. 1985); United States v. Aitken, 755 F.2d 188, 194 (1st Cir. 1985); United States v. Hudson, 564 F.2d 1377, 1380 n.3 (9th Cir. 1977).

[9] The government states that the instruction was "consistent with" United States v. Beusch, 596 F.2d 871 (9th Cir. 1979). That case dealt with whether a corporation could be held liable for an employee who acted contrary to corporate directives. The issue of when a corporation would be liable for the crimes of non-employee individuals was never even discussed in Beusch. In fact, it appears that the ambiguous language at issue here, "authorized representatives," was not even used in Beusch.

We agree with the government that corporate criminal liability is predicated on tort principles and that some of the criteria which we suggested in Proposed Instruction No. 28 would be more appropriate to a contract issue than a tort issue. This is an unlitigated area of criminal law and, just as the government is "learning to some degree" as it goes along [8/11/86 RT 25], so are we. But the third criteria we proposed, the ability to control the manner of work, is undeniably an essential element of tort liability for the acts of independent contractors. Logue v. United States, 412 U.S. 521, 527-28 (1973). The lack of this element was the basis for the judgment of acquittal in United States v. Georgetown University, 331 F. Supp. 69 (D.C. Cir. 1971). The refusal to give an instruction along these lines was error.

Even if this part of defendants' proposed instruction had not been the proper statement of the law, defendants preserved the court's error in not properly defining "authorized representatives." We made clear that our problem with Instruction 18 was its failure to define this term. RT 457, 463. Had we simply objected on this basis, the issue would be preserved. United States v. English, 409 F.2d 200 (3d Cir. 1969) (exception to inadequate charge preserves error, despite failure to submit instructions). But the error could also have been corrected by keeping Instruction 18 intact and adding a supplemental instruction defining the term. That was our approach. Even if our proposed supplement were erroneous, it was the court's obligation to correct its own error once the basis for our position was made known. In fact, we specifically stated that if the court had objections to Proposed Instruction 28, the court should supplement Instruction 18 with a proper definition. RT 463. To contend that the issue was not preserved, because we formulated our position through a supplemental instruction, rather than an objection to Instruction 18, is to exalt form over substance.[10] The purpose of Rule 30 is to "give the trial court an opportunity to correct errors of omission or commission." United States v. Prujansky, 415 F.2d 1045, 1048 (6th Cir. 1969). That is exactly what we did.[11]

The issue then becomes whether the court's inclusion of the term "authorized representatives," without further explication, was error. We fully agree with the government that employers can, in certain circumstances, be liable for the acts of their independent contractors. The problem is that the jury was never told what those circumstances might be. The government does not even contend that Instruction 18 allowed the jury to determine whether those circumstances were present in this case, it simply asserts that those circumstances were present. The government cannot rescue a faulty instruction because, in its view, the jury *could* have made the necessary finding under a proper instruction. By use of the vague term "authorized representative," the court denied defendants' their right to a jury determination on this issue. The error requires reversal.

---

[10] Looked at another way, had we submitted Proposed Instruction 28, with its three different portions, as three different instructions, the court's failure to give the instruction based on Logue would clearly have been a properly preserved error. The form in which we submitted this instruction does not affect preservation of the error.

[11] Even if not preserved, the error, establishing vicarious liability for the acts of the wrong agents, affected defendants' substantial rights and may be noticed on appeal. See note 8, p. 18, supra.

APPENDIX B

V.

THE COURT'S REFUSAL TO DEFINE THE MENTAL ELEMENT REQUIRED FOR CONVICTION AS AN AIDER AND ABETTOR WAS ERROR

In Part IV.I of our Opening Brief, we demonstrated that the court's refusal to define the mental element required for conviction as an aider and abettor was error. The government has not responded to our contentions. No valid response would be possible. The clear case law is that the failure to instruct on the requirement of willfulness, and the failure to require an intention to help others violate the law, is reversible error.

VI.

A WILLFUL VIOLATION OF A PROVISION OF THE CLEAN WATER ACT REQUIRES KNOWLEDGE THAT THE PROVISION IS BEING VIOLATED

A. WILLFULNESS VERSUS AN IGNORANCE OF LAW DEFENSE

As we made quite clear in our opening brief, the issue in this case is whether defendants charged with willfully violating provisions of the Clean Water Act must know that they are violating such a provision, not whether they must know such violation is criminal. The government considers this a "fine line distinction, if it in fact exists . . ." [Brief at 22]. Unlike the government, the courts and commentators have been able to understand the distinction.

> [A] defendant normally need not be shown to know that there is a law that penalizes the offense he is charged with committing. However, he must be proven to have whatever state of mind is required to establish that offense, and sometimes that state of mind includes knowledge of a legal requirement. The most familiar example of this principle occurs in prosecutions for tax offenses. The state of mind

> required for conviction under those statutes proscribing "willful" tax misconduct includes knowledge of a legal duty to comply with statutory tax obligations...Knowledge of this legal duty must be proved. However, it is not necessary for the prosecution to go further and prove that the defendant knew there was a law punishing willful non-payment of taxes.

United States v. Golitschek, 808 F.2d 195, 202 (2d Cir. 1986).

Similarly, defendants under the Clean Water Act must be proved to know that some provision of the Act creates a duty which they violated (in this case to have a permit before discharging pollutants). They need not be proven to know that Section 1319 makes such violations criminal.

As the opinion in Golitschek continues:

> When we say that ignorance of the law is no excuse...we mean only the law that makes the offense punishable, not the law that in some circumstances sets out legal requirements that must be known in order to have committed the offense. The distinction is not the less vital because it is subtle.

808 F.2d at 203.

B. WILLFULNESS IN PUBLIC WELFARE STATUTES

We agree with the government that the term "willfully" is a word of many meanings. Where we disagree is the methods the government uses to discern the meaning for the Clean Water Act. Essentially, the government's approach is to create its own definition of "public welfare statutes," classify the Act as such, and use that classification as the source of all wisdom. In reliance on that classification, the government discerns the meaning of "willfully" by looking to statutes that use a totally different *mens rea* requirement or that lack any *mens rea* requirement at all! The government also classifies the Act with statutes that involve radically different types of harm.

APPENDIX B   B-181

As we discuss in Part II.A, by definition the Act is not a public welfare offense, because such offenses "depend on no mental element." Liparota, 105 S.Ct. at 2092. Regardless of how the Act is classified, there is simply no comparison between the wide range of pollution covered by the Act and those items which are governed by public welfare statutes. Although the Act is certainly designed to address potential harm to health, it does so by reaching all items which, regardless of their individual impact, may combine to contribute to the pollution problem. It thus is far different from those statutes which deal only with inherently dangerous items, such as adulterated food (United States v. Dotterweich, 320 U.S. 277 (1943)), hand grenades (United States v. Freed, 401 U.S. 601 (1971)) or narcotics (United States v. Balint, 258 U.S. 250 (1922)). See, Liparota, 105 S.Ct. at 2092 and note 5, p. 11, supra.

Just as in its discussion of negligence, the government tries to bootstrap its conclusion from the important goal of limiting pollution. (See pp. 11, supra.) Given the broad range of tools available in the Clean Water Act to counteract pollution, including stringent fines imposed on a strict liability basis, applying the term "willfully" consistent with the case law we discuss does not undermine the purposes of the Act at all.

The government cites only two cases involving a "public welfare" statute which supposedly define the term "willfully" consistent with the government's position. Riss & Company v. United States, 262 F.2d 245 (8th Cir. 1958) does indeed hold that willfully does not require

Published by The Bureau of National Affairs, Inc.

"evil motive."[12] But in resolving the meaning of "willfully," the decision supports our position, not the government's. In contrast to the meaning of "willfully" under statutes which do require "evil motive," Riss looked to other "public welfare" decisions. It quoted first from St. Louis-San Francisco Ry. Co. v. United States, 169 F. 69, 70 (8th Cir. 1909), "[W]illfully is designed to describe one who either intentionally disregards the statute or is plainly indifferent to its consequences." (emphasis in Riss). Similar language was quoted from Boone v. United States, 109 F.2d 560, 563 (6th Cir. 1940), "[Penalties for willfulness are imposed] for intentionally, carelessly, knowingly or voluntarily disregarding the provisions of the Act." Contrary to the government's assertions, these cases, and Riss, explicitly define willfulness to require a state of mind regarding the prohibitions of the statute.[13]

United States v. Moore, 586 F.2d 1029 (4th Cir. 1978) does in fact hold as the government claims. The case is extremely distinguishable, because it involves armaments, which have been generally held to give notice of the likelihood of regulation. Freed, 401 U.S. at 601. Some of the discussion in Moore, however, reflects a misunderstanding of modern principles of mens rea. The observation that "willfully" ordinarily means only "voluntarily" is rebutted by scores of cases,

---

[12] We specifically stated in our opening brief that the lack of an evil motive instruction was not at issue.

[13] Similarly, United States v. Illinois Central Railroad Co., 303 U.S. 239 (1938) states that willfulness in regulatory statutes does not require evil motive. It does require awareness of the prohibition, i.e., intentional disregard of, or plain indifference to the statute. 303 U.S. at 243.

APPENDIX B

many cited in our opening brief. The opinion also demonstrates confusion regarding the term "ignorance of the law" as modern jurisprudence interprets it (compare Moore, 586 F.2d at 1031 with Liparota, 105 S.Ct. at 3088 n.9 and Golitschek, 308 F.2d at 202-203).

The government seeks succor in two other environmental statutes. United States v. Hayes International Corp., 786 F.2d 1499 (11th Cir. 1986), is distinguishable on several critical grounds. It involves transportation of hazardous waste, an item which would reasonably put one on notice of likely regulation, unlike many of the items covered by the Clean Water Act. The statute prohibits knowing conduct, a far different level from willfulness. United States v. Flores, 753 F.2d 1499, 1505 (9th Cir. 1985); United States v. Sirhan, 504 F.2d 818, 820 n.3 (9th Cir. 1974). And the statute criminalizes knowing transportations, rather than knowing violations of a statute, a critical linguistic difference discussed in Part IV.F.3, pp. 43-47 of our opening brief and Part VI.E of this reply. Finally, United States v. Johnson & Towers, Inc., 741 F.2d 662, 669 (3rd Cir. 1984), cert. denied, 469 U.S. 1208 (1985) reaches the exact opposite conclusion from Hayes, insisting on proof of knowledge that a permit is required, exactly the defense we sought.

United States v. Corbin Farm Service, 444 F. Supp. 510 (E.D. Cal. 1978) is likewise uninstructive. It too involves the word "knowingly" and an inherently dangerous item, pesticides. Either of these differences, standing alone, makes this case irrelevant to defining the term "willfully" in a statute which encompasses virtually any material known to man.

In its attempt to distinguish the authorities we cite, the government fails to mention 29 U.S.C. § 666(e), involving willful violations of occupational health and safety provisions. Contrary to the government's contention regarding public health and welfare laws, conviction under this statute indeed requires a mental element with regard to the fact of the law's requirements. United States v. Dye Construction Co., 510 F.2d 78, 82 (10th Cir. 1975).[14]

C. WILLFULNESS AS A PROTECTION FOR THE UNWARY

The government, in reliance on Fierros, 692 F.2d at 1294-95, asserts that only two categories of laws allow an "ignorance of the law" defense: crimes requiring knowledge of some legal status and crimes involving "truly complex regulatory schemes." Brief at 34 (the phrase "truly complex" is the government's, not Fierros'.) Since, as discussed in Golitschek, 808 F.2d at 202, and the Model Penal Code, the

---

[14] The non-"public welfare" cases the government cites for its definition of willfulness do not bolster its position. The defense rejected in United States v. Fierros, 692 F.2d 1291, 1294 (9th Cir. 1982), cert. denied, 462 U.S. 1120 (1983) is the defense which the Model Penal Code and cases such as Liparota and Golitschek have labored so mightily to distinguish from the defense we sought. The defendants in Fierros contended that 8 U.S.C. § 1324, in criminalizing alien harboring, required knowledge that their actions were criminal. Similarly, United States v. Gris, 247 F.2d 860 (1957), involves the contention that the defendant had to know his act was criminal, not just that it violated other provisions of the Telecommunications Act. The statute in question in Gris, 47 U.S.C. § 501, in fact does require knowledge that one is violating provisions of the Act. United States v. Simpson, 561 F.2d 53 (7th Cir. 1977). Finally, the securities act cases, United States v. Peltz, 433 F.2d 48 (2nd Cir. 1970), cert. denied, 401 U.S. 955 (1971), United States v. Charney, 537 F.2d 341 (9th Cir.), cert. denied, 429 U.S. 1000 (1976), and Tarvestad v. United States, 418 F.2d 1043 (8th Cir. 1969), cert. denied, 397 U.S. 935 (1970) are irrelevant for the reasons discussed at p. 31, infra. The statute they address has unique language making clear that willfulness in that statute does not require awareness of the regulation being violated.

term "ignorance of the law" is virtually meaningless, the government's entire argument seems misplaced. In any event, _Fierros_ is wrong if it was trying to set forth firm rules for when a particular element is required. The issue is one of Congressional intent (with possible amelioration from constitutional guarantees). _Fierros_ is correct that such situations have provided guidance to the courts in interpreting Congress's intent when it uses the term "willfully." As our opening brief demonstrates, other situations where courts have found similar guidance involve _any_ statute which might pose a trap for the unwary, regardless of whether it involves a complex regulatory schemes.

We of course disagree with the government as to whether the Clean Water Act can pose a trap for the unwary. In discussing this issue, the government states that the kind of business in which defendants were engaged would put them on notice of the likelihood of regulation [Brief at 24, 35, 42]. But the issue is not what "willfully" means for these particular defendants, the issue is what "willfully" means for all defendants prosecuted under the Clean Water Act. In resolving that issue, this Court must look to all behavior encompassed within the Act, not just what was prosecuted in this case. We cite to numerous authorities and discuss this point at length at pp. 49-50 of our Opening Brief, a discussion the government totally ignores. As the cases we cited show, statutes which define willfulness as we suggest usually do include some acts which would put one on notice of likely regulations; the protection for the unwary is necessary so long as any of the covered acts would include otherwise-innocent behavior. Congress has altered the usual intent requirements solely in those statutes which encompass only such dangerous items. The fact that the government might have been able to prove that defendants were aware of the regulation does not eliminate our right to a jury trial on this issue.

The same problem applies to the government's discussion of the cases we cite. Thus, for example, the specific facts involved in Simpson are irrelevant; the court decided the mens rea requirements of 47 U.S.C. § 401, which made it a crime to willfully do any act prohibited by the Federal Communications Act. The court was not deciding only the mens rea requirements for that particular defendant, or that particular licensing requirement.

In our Opening Brief, we cited numerous examples of the kinds of innocent behavior which the Clean Water Act encompasses, to show that the Act would indeed pose a trap for the unwary, and thus to shed light on the mens rea which Congress would have required before criminalizing such actions. The government's response fails to rebut our position at all. As to our point that a swimmer discharges heat into the water and thus violates the Act, the government simply says that this recreational use is what the Act seeks to protect. We agree. But the government does not deny our point that such swimming would still be a violation of the Act, unless the important mens rea protections inserted by Congress are retained. The government makes no response to our examples of brushing sand off one's body, another discharge of pollutants into the water, or of skipping rocks.[15]

---

[15] We agree that the deliberate tossing of a paper cup into the water is not a totally innocent behavior. Our example, however, was of a cup which accidentally blows away. That example is relevant to the level

We agree with the government, in its citation to <u>Liparota</u> [Brief at 36 n. 10], that the burden of proving knowledge of the regulation would not be heavy and could be done through circumstantial evidence. That the burden is relatively light is further evidence that it is not inconsistent with Congress's goals under the Clean Water Act. Interpreting "willfully" as we suggest protects the unwary, who could otherwise easily violate this incredibly broad statute, but readily allows conviction of those Congress intended to reach, such as industrial polluters. The critical point is that this burden, no matter how slight, was not imposed on the government in this case, as it should have been.

D. LEGISLATIVE HISTORY OF THE ACT

As we mentioned in our opening brief, the recent amendments to the Clean Water Act replaced the term "willfully" with "knowingly." The government states that Congress could not have intended by that change to lower the <u>mens rea</u> requirement, because the penalties were also increased. We fail to understand the government's logic. Since Congress has two ways it can make a statute harsher, either by increasing penalties or by easing the burden of proof, there is no reason why it would not apply both methods at once. Notably, the government gives no explanation for this change in language. Given the great regularity with which the courts have treated "knowingly" and "willfully" as having two distinct meanings, <u>Flores</u>, 753 F.2d at 1505,

---

of negligence Congress intended to apply before subjecting a picnicker to a year imprisonment and a $10,000 fine for inadequately securing his cup.

Sirhan, 504 F.2d at 820 n. 3, we assume that Congress acted with full knowledge of those differing interpretations in amending the statute.

The original legislative history of the criminal provisions of the Act is sparse. The government interprets the comments of Rep. Harsha to provide merely an example of willfulness rather than an explanation of the term. Legislative History, Vol. 1 at 530. What the government ignores is that it is its obligation to come forward with "clear and definite language" demonstrating that Congress intended a harsher meaning for the term "willfully." McNally, 107 S.Ct at 2881. Otherwise, the principle of lenity demands interpreting the term in defendants' favor.

E. THE TERM "WILLFULLY VIOLATES"

In Part IV.F.3 of our Brief, we pointed out that the language of the Clean Water Act does not criminalize willfully performing certain acts, but instead willfully violating certain provisions. This language supports our interpretation of willfulness as including knowledge that a provision is being violated. We cite nine different statutes in which comparable language has been held to require proof of such knowledge.

The government cites four cases as supposed counter-examples. None of them contradict our position. United States v. International Minerals & Chemical Corp., 402 U.S. 558 (1971), was interpreting 18 U.S.C. § 834(f). That provision involved "knowing" violations, not "willful" violations. The consistent law of this Circuit is that, when Congress uses the term "willfully" instead of "knowingly," it intends a higher level of intent. Flores, supra; Sirhan, supra.

APPENDIX B   B-189

Unitd States v. Hayes Intern. Corp., 786 F.2d 1499 (11th Cir. 1986) involves 42 U.S.C. § 6928(d)(1). That section does not prohibit the willful or knowing violation of other provisions; it deals with knowing transportation of hazardous waste. In fact, the court specifically distinguished the statute from those, such as the Clean Water Act, which word their prohibition in terms of violation of some provision. 786 F.2d at 1503. Similarly, 8 U.S.C. § 1324, the statute involved in Fierros, 692 F.2d 1291, does not use the sort of language at issue in this case. It prohibits knowing acts, not willful violations of laws.

Title 15 U.S.C. § 77x, discussed in United States v. Brown, 578 F.2d 1280 (9th Cir. 1978) is the only statute cited by the government which involves "willfully violates" language. That statute is radically distinguishable for two reasons. First, the opinion in Brown relies heavily on cases interpreting a related provision of the securities laws, Section 32(a): Peltz, 433 F.2d at 54 and United States v. Schwartz, 464 F.2d 499 (2nd Cir.), cert. denied, 409 U.S. 1009 (1972). These decisions are based on the unique language of Section 32(a), which provides penalties for willful violation of regulations but imposes lower penalties if the defendant had no knowledge of the regulation. It thus makes clear that, in that particular statute, willfulness does not entail such knowledge. In statutes which lack this language, such as the Clean Water Act, willfully has been defined as we suggest.

The other major factor which led to the result in Brown is that the crime in question, fraud, inherently involves willfulness. The

Published by The Bureau of National Affairs, Inc.

court found that the fact that the fraud involves securities is simply a jurisdictional fact and thus no _mens rea_ is required as to that fact. A crime involving fraud poses no trap for the innocent simply because the jurisdictional fact is unknown. In sum, the government has cited only one statute, and a totally non-comparable one, in rebuttal to the lengthy and wide-ranging list of statutes in which Congress has used the "willfully violates" language to require knowledge of the violated provision.

The government then undertakes a lengthy discussion of the cases we had cited in Part IV.F.3 (Government's Brief, 37-40). We did not cite these cases because they were necessarily analogous in all respects to the Clean Water Act, we cited them in support of our position that the term "willfully violates" has consistently been interpreted as we suggest. The fact that they are distinguishable in one way or another does not undercut this particular argument (which is only one of several independent points, each demonstrating that "willfully" requires awareness of the prohibiting statute).[16] Furthermore, the government omits any discussion of the case which is not at all distinguishable, because it deals directly with public health and welfare: _Dye Construction_, 510 F.2d at 82.

---

[16] Thus, we need not discuss at length some misimpressions created in the government's discussion of these cases. One point merits brief mention. The government makes much of the fact that the prosecutor in _Golitschek_ conceded that 22 U.S.C. § 2778(b)(2) requires "specific intent." But the _Golitschek_ court did not rely on this concession, it squarely held that "the District Court correctly recognized that the offenses charges required knowledge of a legal obligation." 808 F.2d at 203. And the Ninth Circuit has so held. _United States v. Lizarraga-Lizarraga_, 541 F.2d 826 (9th Cir. 1976) (interpreting version of statute prior to recodification).

APPENDIX B

In addition, the government's discussion falls into the same error we discuss in relation to Simpson, p. 27-28, supra. The courts in these cases were deciding what mens rea was required under the statute to commit the crime, not what mens rea these particular defendants alone would have to possess. For example, the decision in United States v. Frade, 709 F.2d 1387 (11th Cir. 1983), interpreting the requirements of 50 U.S.C. § App. 16 for all cases, was not grounded on the fact that the defendants were priests, that their actions might rescue people, or that their actions were previously authorized by regulation. It was based on the conclusion that the activities denoted unlawful "include items not generally known to be controlled by the government." 709 F.2d at 1392. In fact, Frade is quite instructive for this case, where defendants' conduct was criminal only because they did not obtain a permit.

> Where licensing and/or reporting requirements are involved, specific intent cannot be shown unless the defendants are apprised of both the necessity for obtaining, and the possibility of obtaining such license.

Id. In this case, defendants were denied their right to show the jury that they had been apprised of neither fact.

E. CONCLUSION

No matter how much the government may look to statutes which require no mens rea or which apply some different standard than willfulness, this statute is clear: Congress required proof of willfulness (until it recently lowered that requirement). Except for rare and quite distinguishable exceptions, that term has been defined as we proposed. The court's instruction was reversible error.

DATED August 17, 1987.

LAW OFFICES OF DAN R. DUBITZKY

By _____
    Alan Zarky

By _____
    Dan R. Dubitzky
Attorneys for Defendants

APPENDIX TO BRIEF

Published by The Bureau of National Affairs, Inc.

APPENDIX A

DECLARATION OF ALAN ZARKY

I, Alan Zarky, declare and state as follows:

1. I am one of the attorneys in this case.

2. I have spoken with Irwin H. Schwartz, trial counsel in <u>United States v. Hoflin</u>, CR 85-82 T, Western District of Washington. Mr. Schwartz informed me that in that case, the standard by which negligence must be proven under the Clean Water Act was not an issue in the trial and did not concern him. The evidence was of intentional discharges rather than negligent discharges. He did not brief to the Court the meaning of negligence under the Act. He submitted an instruction defining negligence simply because that was one of the alternate means of proving one element. That instruction was given by the Court as Instruction 21. His records of the jury instruction conference, which reflects the objections he made to the Court's instructions, do not reflect that he made any objection to the Court's other instruction on negligence, Instruction 22.

3. I have spoken with William J. Gallagher, trial counsel in <u>United States v. Frezzo Bros.</u> He stated that the trial transcript is not available to him so that he cannot state with utmost certainty what objections he made. He did inform me that the evidence related to intentional as opposed to negligent discharges. As a result, he was unconcerned with the definition of negligence. To the best of his knowledge, there was no issue raised at trial regarding the definition of negligence. He also has no notation of objecting to that portion of the court's charge. Mr. Gallagher further states that had he made an

APPENDIX B

objection to that instruction, he would have raised it in his post-trial motions. He did not raise any such issue in those motions.

4. I have also spoken with Eddie N. Christian, trial counsel in United States v. Jack E. White, et al. Because he does not have the trial transcript, he is also not able to state with 100% certainty that he did not object to the court's definition of negligence. He did inform me that the Clean Water Act charges were not challenged seriously. This was for two reasons. First of all, they were a few misdemeanor charges in an indictment charging far more serious charges, including 45 felonies, among them racketeering, mail fraud, wire fraud, interstate transportation of fraudulently obtained funds, adulterating food, and false statements to the government. Furthermore, Mr. Christian believed that the evidence established that pollutants had been intentionally discharged in violation of the Act, thus making the definition of negligence irrelevant.

I declare under penalty of perjury that the foregoing is true and correct.

DATED August 17, 1987.

Alan Zarky

UNITED STATES DISTRICT COURT
WESTERN DISTRICT OF WASHINGTON
AT SEATTLE

UNITED STATES OF AMERICA,)
)
    Plaintiff-Appellee,)
) CR 86-129D
    v.)
) ORDER
PAUL D. SCHWITTERS and)
SEA GLEANER MARINE, INC.,)
)
    Defendants-Appellants.)
_____)

    This matter is before the Court on appeal from a jury verdict on three of four counts charging violations of the Clean Water Act.[1] Procedure for the Trial of Misdemeanors Before United States Magistrates, Rule 7(b). Having considered briefs filed by counsel, reviewed the record and heard oral argument, the Court concludes that Jury Instruction No. 20 was erroneous, requiring reversal and retrial of all counts against defendant Paul D. Schwitters. The Court, however, concludes that the remaining jury instructions and the Magistrate's evidentiary

---

    [1]Federal Water Pollution Control Act as amended in 1972, 33 U.S.C. § 1251, et seq.

ruling were not in error, thus the verdict against the corporate defendant is upheld.

CHARGES

Paul Schwitters personally and Sea Gleaner Marine, Inc. were charged in an information with four separate counts of either "negligently" or "willfully and negligently" discharging pollutants from a point source into Lake Union, a navigable water of the United States, without first obtaining a permit pursuant to 33 U.S.C. § 1342, in violation of 33 U.S.C. §§ 1311 and 1319(c)(1). (A "point source" is defined as "any discernible, confined and discrete conveyance, including . . . vessel or other floating craft, from which pollutants are or may be discharged." 33 U.S.C. § 1362(14).) The four counts refer to separate instances in which boats were sandblasted, scraped, sanded and painted over the water. The particular counts follow:

> Count I: On or about May 30, 1984, . . .
> SCHWITTERS and SEA GLEANER MARINE, INC. did
> negligently discharge pollutants (that is, spent
> abrasive blasting grit and paint particles) from a
> point source into Lake Union . . . without having
> first obtained a permit for such discharge . . . .
>
> Count II: On or about October 19, 1984, . . .
> SCHWITTERS and SEA GLEANER MARINE, INC. did
> negligently discharge pollutants (that is, spent
> abrasive blasting grit and paint particles) from a
> point source into Lake Union . . . without having
> first obtained a permit for such discharge . . . .
>
> Count III: On or about March 2, 1985, . . .
> SCHWITTERS and SEA GLEANER MARINE, INC. did
> willfully and negligently discharge pollutants
> (that is, spent abrasive blasting grit and paint
> particles) from a point source into Lake Union

... without having first obtained a permit for such discharge . . . .

Count IV: On or about March 10, 1985, . . . SCHWITTERS and SEA GLEANER MARINE, INC. did willfully and negligently discharge pollutants (that is, spent abrasive blasting grit and paint particles) from a point source into Lake Union . . . without having first obtained a permit for such discharge . . . .

Schwitters and the corporation were found guilty of Counts II, III and IV.

At 33 U.S.C. § 1342, the Clean Water Act provides for issuance of permits for discharging pollutants; § 1311 makes "the discharge of any pollutant by any person" unlawful except under certain conditions; and § 1319(c) provides for criminal penalties:

(1) Any person who willfully or negligently violates § 1311, 1312, 1316, 1317, or 1318 of this Title, or any permit condition or limitation implementing any of such sections in a permit issued under § 1342 of this Title . . . shall be punished by a fine of not less than $2,500, nor more than $25,000 per day of violation, or by imprisonment for not more than one year, or by both . . . .

. . . .

(3) For the purposes of this subsection, the term "person" shall mean, in addition to the definition contained in § 1362(5) of this Title, any responsible corporate officer.

BACKGROUND

Sea Gleaner Marine, Inc. is a ship repair facility located on the north shore of Lake Union in Seattle, Washington. Defendant Paul D. Schwitters was the president and co-owner of

Sea Gleaner. He generally managed the business during the period for which the misdemeanors were charged and often participated in work on the vessels. The specific acts for which defendants were charged relate to the sandblasting, power grinding and scraping of vessels which resulted in the discharge of pellets, paint chips and paint into the waters of Lake Union.

Defendants admit that pollutants were discharged into the water and that they did not possess a permit. They, however, allege errors in several jury instructions and error in limiting evidence, arguing that defendants lacked the requisite mens rea to be held liable. They further contend that whatever discharges did occur were caused by individuals for whom defendants were not legally responsible.

ISSUES

The following issues were presented in defendants' first appellate brief:

    1. May a corporate officer be held strictly liable for violations of the Clean Water Act, even though the Act explicitly states that only willful and negligent discharges may be prosecuted?

    2. May a person be convicted of negligence under doctrines of tort negligence rather than the criminal requirement of a gross deviation from the standard of due care?

    3. May a person be convicted of negligence without the standard requirement of both criminal and tort negligence that the standard of care must be determined in light of the circumstances as known by him to exist?

    4. Where the Act criminalizes "willfully violating" provisions of the Act, may a person be

convicted when he has no awareness that his actions constituted violations of those provisions?

5. Where the Act criminalizes "negligently violating" provisions of the Act, may a person be convicted when he was not negligent as to the fact that his actions constituted violations of those provisions?

6. May a corporation be held criminally liable for the acts of individuals who are not employees or agents of the corporation?

7. May a person be convicted of willfully causing another to act, without any instruction to the jury on the mental elements required?

ANALYSIS

For purposes of analysis, the Court divides defendants' challenges as follows:

(1) the degree of culpability required to convict a person or corporation who "willfully or negligently violates § 1311" (discharging a pollutant) without a permit as provided under § 1342 (Instructions 8 and 9, and evidentiary ruling);

(2) the definition of negligence (Instruction 9);

(3) alleged error in Instruction 10;

(4) the definition of aiding and abetting (Instruction 21);

(5) vicarious liability of the corporation and failure to define "agents" (Instruction 18); and

(6) liability of a responsible corporate officer (Instruction 20).

In part, this analysis requires a determination of legislative intent.[2]

1. **Willfully/Negligently**

Defendants argue that the willful and negligent elements in the statute create a specific intent crime, and thus defendants' knowledge of the law or negligent lack of knowledge of the law are required to support a criminal conviction. In arguing that knowledge of the law is a prerequisite to a criminal violation of the act, defendants object to its exclusion from the definitions of negligent and willful (Instructions 8 and 9). Additionally, defendants assert error in a pretrial ruling by the Magistrate granting the Government's motion in limine to exclude any evidence of defendants' knowledge or lack of knowledge as to whether they were violating the Clean Water Act.[3]

In objecting to the incompleteness of the jury instructions, defendants cite to a number of criminal law cases in which knowledge of the law is a prerequisite to the willful violation of the law. See, e.g., United States v. Winston, 558 F.2d 105, 108 (2d Cir. 1977) (imposition of criminal penalties under the Railway Labor Act (45 U.S.C. § 152) for willfully

---

[2] The standard of review on interpretation of a statute is de novo. United States v. Launder, 743 F.2d 686, 688-689 (9th Cir. 1984).

[3] Defendants' offer of proof indicates that Schwitters did not know a permit was required for sandblasting or painting over water, and he had seen such activities at a number of other establishments. Furthermore, Government officials who had visited his facility had made no mention of permit requirements.

interfering with employee unionization requires an intentional violation of a known legal duty). See also United States v. Dye Construction Co., 510 F.2d 78, 82 (10th Cir. 1975) (defendant must intentionally disregard the standard or be plainly indifferent to its requirement, interpreting 29 U.S.C. § 666(e), Occupational Safety and Health Act, and the words "any employer who willfully violates any standard . . .").

Further, defendants argue that relatively innocuous behavior would fall under the harsh criminal penalties of § 1319(c) "punishable by $25,000 per day of violation, or by imprisonment of not more than one year, or both," and civil penalties are available under § 1319(d), permitting assessments not to exceed $10,000 per day of violation.[4]

This Court, however, disagrees with defendants' arguments that the statute requires specific intent to impose criminal penalties. Counsel for both sides concede the paucity of legislative history to guide the Court. Congress did, however, outline the goals of the Clean Water Act to include elimination of "the discharge of pollutants into the navigable waters . . . by 1985." 33 U.S.C. § 1251(a)(1).

In the few cases imposing criminal penalties under the Clean Water Act, specific intent has not been required. See, e.g., United States v. Frezzo Brothers, Inc., 546 F. Supp. 713

---

[4] See United States v. Anton, 683 F.2d 1011, 1015 (7th Cir. 1982) (non-penal alternative indicative of Congress' intent not to impose strict liability under statute governing reentry of deported alien).

(E.D. Pa. 1982), aff'd, 703 F.2d 62 (3rd Cir.), cert. denied, 464 U.S. 829 (1983); United States v. Hamel, 551 F.2d 107 (6th Cir. 1977).

> In clear language, the statute informs all that pollution into navigable waters is forbidden unless the polluter has obtained a permit from the government. By its terms, the statute does not require that a defendant intend a criminal act in order to be convicted of a statutory violation.

546 F. Supp. at 721.

In one of the cases cited by the Government, involving transport of hazardous material contrary to regulations promulgated under 18 U.S.C. § 834, the United States Supreme Court held that knowledge of the regulation was not required to support a criminal conviction. United States v. International Minerals and Chemical Corp., 402 U.S. 558 (1971). The statute at issue in International Minerals imposed criminal penalties on one who "knowingly violates" regulations of the Interstate Commerce Commission. The Court did not interpret the statute as excusing ignorance of the law, nor did it interpret the statute as imposing strict liability. Instead, the Court concludes that where there was knowledge of the fact of transporting sulphuric acid, criminal liability would lie despite a lack of knowledge of the regulation. Defendants distinguish the International Minerals case on the basis that sanding a boat over water is not the sort of activity which would put a person on notice of probable violation of a law. See also United States v. Fierros, 692 F.2d 1291, 1294-95 (9th Cir. 1982) (ignorance of the law may excuse defendants prosecuted "under complex regulatory schemes that have the potential of snaring unwitting violators.")

The Court is not persuaded by defendants' arguments. The statute is clear in its prohibition of discharges without a permit. The contamination of the water by quantities of sand pellets and paint debris was obvious and in some instances left a film on the water hours after the operation. The statute is hardly "a trap for the unwary."

2. **Negligence Instruction**

In addition to objecting to the exclusion of a knowledge element as discussed above, defendants contend that the definition of negligence should not have been the standard tort instruction (Instruction 9). Rather, defendants argue for an instruction of criminal negligence, drawing from the Model Penal Code. In Article 2, describing general principles of liability, the Model Penal Code describes "negligently" as follows:

> A person acts negligently with respect to a material element of an offense when he should be aware of a substantial and unjustifiable risk that the material element exists or will result from his conduct. The risk must be of such a nature and degree that the actor's failure to perceive it, considering the nature and purpose of his conduct and the circumstances known to him, involves a gross deviation from the standard of care that a reasonable person would observe in the actor's situation.

Model Penal Code § 2.02 (1985) (as adopted by the American Law Institute, May 24, 1962). Defendants also cite to 1 W. LaFave and A. Scott, <u>Substantive Criminal Law</u> (2nd Ed. 1986), § 3.7(b) at 329 to 333 and n.26. Defendants point out that in this analysis of state criminal legislation, the authors report at least 22 states which have recently defined negligence in line with defendants' approach and only one, South Dakota, which applies a standard comparable to normal tort negligence. The authors, however, also acknowledge the difficulty of finding an alternative definition for criminal negligence:

> Though the legislatures and the courts have often made it clear that criminal liability generally requires more fault than the ordinary negligence which will do for tort liability, they have not so often made it plain just what is required in addition to tort negligence--greater risk, subjective awareness of the risk, or both. Statutes are sometimes worded in terms of "gross negligence" or "culpable negligence" or "criminal negligence" without any further definition of these terms.

LaFave and Scott, § 3.7 at 329-330.

The Government counters that the "public welfare" goal of the Clean Water Act to eliminate all pollution and the strict liability standard imposed by a precursor to the Clean Water Act (Rivers and Harbors Act of 1899, 33 U.S.C. §§ 407 and 411) justifies a relaxed reading of "negligence." Moreover, in dialogue before the Committee debating amendments to the Clean Water Act, Congressman Harsha refers to prosecution for "simple negligence." A Legislative History of the Water Pollution Control Act Amendments of 1972, Congressional Research Service of the Library of Congress, Serial No. 95-1, Volume 1 at 530.[5]

---

[5] Although counsel invite the Court to draw inferences from amendments to the statute made by the Water Quality Act of 1987 (Pub. L. 100-4) which make the penalty for negligent violation a misdemeanor and the penalty for "knowing" violation a felony, the Court declines. Congress' action is inconclusive

This Court concludes that Congress meant what it said, and would have defined "negligently" or added a requirement of "gross deviation" if it intended something beyond the tort definition of unreasonable care. Thus there is no error in Instruction 9.

3. **Instruction 10**

Defendants object to Instruction 10 and its implication that defendants could be judged by circumstances unknown to them at the time:

> The conduct in question must be viewed in light of all the surrounding circumstances, as shown by the evidence in the case.

Instruction 10.[6] Defendants' proposed instruction on negligence would have required consideration of "the circumstances known to" defendants.

The Court finds no error in this instruction particularly in the context of this case when defendants had never argued that either Schwitters or the corporation was unaware of the activities in question.

4. **Vicarious Responsibility Instruction**

Defendants take exception to the Court's instruction on vicarious responsibility or aiding and abetting (Instruction

---

and could support either side's argument.

[6]The Government argues that defendants have not preserved this argument on appeal. The Court concludes, however, that defendants did reasonably object to the tort definition, and to the phrase at issue in Instruction 10. See transcript at 453 and 461.

21).[7] They first object to the failure to include the word "willfully" in naming acts which constitute aiding and abetting: "counsels, commands, induces or procures." Secondly, they object to the failure to define "willfully." ("Willfully" is defined in Instruction 8, but as described above, defendants disagree with this definition and the failure to require specific intent.)

This Court agrees that conviction under a theory of vicarious responsibility (aiding and abetting) requires specific intent to further some criminal activity. See, e.g., Manual of Model Jury Instructions for the Ninth Circuit § 5.03 (1985); United States v. Avila-Macias, 577 F.2d 1384, 1390 n.5 (9th Cir. 1978). Although Instruction 21 could be clearer as to the

---

[7] Instruction No. 21:
The term "vicarious responsibility" refers to a person's criminal liability for the acts of his associates. Under certain circumstances you may find a defendant guilty of an offense charged in an information without finding that he personally committed each of the acts constituting the offense or that he was personally present at the commission of the offenses.

Whoever commits an offense against the United States, or counsels, commands, induces, or procures its commission, or willfully causes an act to be done which if directly performed by him or another would be an offense against the United States is punishable as a principal. That is, he is as guilty of the offense as if he had personally committed each of the acts constituting the offense.

Mere physical presence by a defendant at the time and place of the commission of an offense is not by itself sufficient to establish his guilt. Some conduct by the defendant of an affirmative character in furtherance of a common criminal design or purpose is necessary.

necessary criminal intent, the Court concludes that in the context of this case, the instruction as a whole is not erroneous.

5. **Vicarious Responsibility of a Corporation**

Defendants argue that Instruction 18's failure to define the word "agents" in explaining corporate liability is reversible error.[8] Instruction 18 states in part:

> A corporation can act only through its agents, that is, its employees, officers or other authorized representatives. Therefore, it is responsible for the acts of its agents performed in the course of their employment.

Defendants object to the words "authorized representatives" without limitation or explanation.

The parties acknowledge that this is an unsettled area of the law. Defendants insist that at a minimum, the ability to control the manner of work is necessary to impose tort liability on the corporation for the acts of independent contractors. See, e.g., Logue v. United States, 412 U.S. 521, 527-28 (1973); United States v. Georgetown University, 331 F. Supp. 69 (D.C. Cir. 1971).

Again, the Court cannot say that this instruction constituted error under the facts of this case, in which all

---

[8] The Government again argues that defendants have not preserved their objection for appeal. Defendants offered a proposed instruction (defendants' No. 28) which defined agents along traditional tort principles. The Government disagreed with this definition; however, it is clear that defendants objected to the failure to limit corporate liability in Instruction 18. Transcript at 463.

APPENDIX B   B-209

activities involved use of Sea Gleaner's dock and material. It
should be noted that the Magistrate permitted Count I to go to
the jury even though an independent contractor had been employed
by the vessel owner for the sandblasting. The jury returned a
not guilty verdict as to Count I.

6.   **Liability of Responsible Corporate Officer**

Defendants argue that Instruction 20[9] creates strict
liability for Schwitters as a responsible corporate officer,
despite the fact that the underlying offense (water pollution) is
not a strict liability crime.[10] The Government counters that

---

[9]Instruction 20:

The Federal Clean Water Act specifically provides
that "responsible corporate officers" can be held
responsible criminally for the acts of their
corporation. Not every corporate officer is a
"responsible" officer or one in a "position of
authority" upon whom Congress has placed the burden
of vigilance and foresight. A "responsible
corporate officer," or one in a "position of
authority" for criminal purposes, has been defined
as one who has a responsible share in the
furtherance of the transaction or occurrence which
the statute forbids. Another way of defining this
is as follows: if a corporate officer has the
responsibility, and powers equal to that
responsibility, to devise whatever measures are
necessary to ensure compliance with the Clean Water
Act, then he is a responsible corporate officer.

If you find that SEA GLEANER, INC., is guilty of
the crime charged in any of these counts, and if
you find beyond a reasonable doubt that defendant
PAUL D. SCHWITTERS had, by virtue of his position
in the corporation, the power to prevent or correct
such a violation, and if you find that he failed to
exercise that power to prevent or correct the
wrongdoing, then you may find him guilty.

[10]Again, the Government contends that defendants have not
preserved this issue on appeal. Again, the Court disagrees with

Published by The Bureau of National Affairs, Inc.

the instructions taken as a whole require a finding of willfulness or negligence on Schwitters' part before he could be held responsible for a corporation's offense (relating Instruction 20 back to the criminal elements delineated in Instruction 5 and the specific charges).[11] The Court agrees with defendants, however, that a reasonable juror could understand the instruction to impose liability on Schwitters if the corporation violated the Clean Water Act and he had the power to stop or prevent the violation. It would thus be possible to find Schwitters guilty without finding that he negligently or willfully violated the statute.

Under the criminal penalty section of 33 U.S.C. § 1319(c)(3), "persons" are also defined to include "any responsible corporate officer." This "responsible corporate officer" language is not defined in that statute. It is, however, a term used in a number of cases imposing strict liability on corporate officials for their corporation's violations of the federal Food, Drug, & Cosmetic Act, 21 U.S.C. § 331(k). See, e.g., United States v. Park, 421 U.S. 658 (1975); United States v. Dotterweich, 320 U.S. 277 (1943). Neither side

---

the Government. Defendants specifically objected to instruction 20 and its language: "They can be held responsible for the acts of their corporation." Transcript at 457. Defendants did not specifically object on the basis of instruction 20 relating back to instruction 5, but there is no evidence that that was the Government's position at the time final jury instructions were promulgated.

[11] Jury instructions are to be read as a whole. United States v. Park, 421 U.S. 658, 674 (1975).

APPENDIX B

in this case, however, contends that the underlying offense of polluting water is a strict liability crime.

The Government finds support for its argument in <u>United States v. Cattle King Packing Co., Inc.</u>, 793 F.2d 232 (10th Cir. 1986). In that case, the Tenth Circuit Court of Appeals upheld use of a jury instruction on liability of a responsible corporate officer, following <u>United States v. Parks</u>, <u>supra</u>. Defendants in <u>Cattle King</u> had been found guilty of violations of the Federal Meat Inspection Act, 21 U.S.C. §§ 601-604, 661-680. The apparent issue before the <u>Cattle King</u> court was application of the felony provisions of the laws invoked in <u>Park</u> and in <u>Cattle King</u> upon a showing of "intent to defraud." 793 F.2d at 240. The full text of the instruction in question is not printed in the <u>Cattle King</u> opinion, thus providing little guidance for this Court.

The parties apparently agree that the only case directly addressing the Clean Water Act and liability of a responsible corporate officer is <u>United States v. Frezzo Brothers, Inc.</u>, 602 F.2d 1123 (3rd Cir. 1979), <u>cert. denied</u> 444 U.S. 1074 (1980). In a footnote in <u>Frezzo Brothers</u>, the court made the following statement:

> The Government argued the case on the "responsible corporate officer doctrine" recognized by the United States Supreme Court in <u>United States v. Park</u>, 421 U.S. 658 (1975), and <u>United States v. Dotterweich</u>, 320 U.S. 277 (1943). We have examined the judge's charge and we perceive no error in the instruction to the jury on this theory.

Id. at 1130 n.11 (parallel citations omitted).

There is, however, considerable argument between the parties as to the applicability of this case. The parties have stipulated to submission of the transcript of the charge to the jury in the original trial. Additionally, defendants have produced as a supplement to the record the brief filed by appellants in the Third Circuit case. That brief indicates that the issue on appeal to the Third Circuit was whether "defendants could be liable outside their capacity as alleged co-owners and responsible officers of the corporation" when the indictment charged only vicarious liability as co-owners and responsible officers. Thus this Court's reading of the *Frezzo* opinion, the jury instructions in the original *Frezzo* trial, and appellant's brief filed before the Third Circuit indicates that the issue of "strict liability" or the necessary mens rea of the corporate officer was not argued to the Third Circuit.

This Court concludes that Schwitters could have been convicted under an improper theory of liability. That is, a jury could have found him guilty of the three separate counts on the basis of strict liability. This is contrary to the provisions of the Clean Water Act, requiring a finding that he "willfully or negligently" violated the Act.

THEREFORE, conviction of the corporate defendant Sea Gleaner Marine, Inc. is affirmed. Conviction of Paul D. Schwitters is reversed. The parties must inform the Court within

30 days of issuance of this Order if they continue in their consent to trial before the Magistrate.

The Clerk of the Court shall direct copies of this Order to all counsel of record and to Magistrate Philip K. Sweigert.

DATED this 23 day of October, 1987.

CAROLYN R. DIMMICK
United States District Judge

WITHDRAWN